Indian Insurance Industry: Transition and Prospects

About the book...

Insurance services account for a major component of the tertiary sector of an economy. Hence, a vibrant insurance industry can substantially contribute in accelerating the growth rate of the economy. The present book is designed to examine and assess the interrelationship between insurance services and economic development, the rationale and variants of regulations exercised by the government on insurers, the present stage of development of insurance industry in India and its future prospects in the context of fast changing business environment. The various aspects of insurance industry such as marketing strategies, product designing and pricing, reinsurance, risk management, use of information technology have been analysed and evaluated in the light of the experience of other countries, particularly the developing countries. All these issues have been examined keeping in view the emerging competitive environment.

The book will prove valuable to insurers, researchers, analysts, policy makers and all those who are interested in the future of insurance industry in India.

About the editors...

D.C. Srivastava holds postgraduate degree in Economics from Lucknow University and Ph.D. degree in Economics from Sardar Patel University. He taught economics at S.P. University before joining the civil services. He had held important assignments in Government of India including tenures in the Ministry of Industry and in the Insurance Division of the Ministry of Finance. He also served on the faculty of LBS National Academy of Administration, Mussorie. He was a visiting fellow at the Institute of Development Studies at the University of Sussex, UK. He has participated in various international seminars and workshops and contributed to economic literature on diverse subjects.

Shashank Srivastava is a graduate of Shri Ram College of Commerce and the Manchester Business School. He has extensive global experience in financial services industry, working internationally with firms such as Swiss Re, Prudential and Dresdner RCM. Having worked and studied across three continents, Shashank was one of the founding directors of Projection, a specialised financial services consulting firm. Presently, he works with the consulting major Arthur Andersen as part of their strategy, finance and economics team.

Indian Insurance Industry
Transition and Prospects

Edited by

D.C. Srivastava and Shashank Srivastava

NEW CENTURY PUBLICATIONS
Delhi-110 033

NEW CENTURY PUBLICATIONS
34, Gujranwala Town, Part-2,
Delhi-110 033 INDIA

Tel.: 27138192, 27247805
Fax: +91-11-27464774
E-mail : indiatax@del2.vsnl.net.in

Copyright © 2001 by D.C. Srivastava and Shashank Srivastava

All rights reserved. No part of this book may be reproduced, stored in a retrieval system, or transmitted in any form or by any means, mechanical, photocopying, recording, or otherwise without the prior written permission of the publisher.

First Published April 2001
Reprinted August 2001
Reprinted January 2002
Reprinted September 2003

ISBN: 81-7708-006-7

Published by New Century Publications and printed at Singhal Print Media Pvt. Ltd., DELHI – 110 007

PRINTED IN INDIA

Contributors

D.C. Srivastava: Formerly Director, Ministry of Finance, Government of India, New Delhi.

Shashank Srivastava: Working with the Strategy, Finance and Economics team at Arthur Andersen.

S.K. Kanwar: Consultant, Reliance General Insurance Co. Ltd. and formerly Chairman-cum-Managing Director, The New India Assurance Co. Ltd., Mumbai.

A.N. Poddar: Formerly Chairman-cum-Managing Director, National Insurance Co. Ltd., Kolkata.

H. Ansari: Member, Insurance Regulatory and Development Authority, New Delhi.

B.D. Banerjee: Chairman-cum-Managing Director, The Oriental Insurance Co. Ltd., New Delhi.

R.D. Samarth: Advisor, Mitsui Marine and Fire Insurance Co. Ltd., Japan.

A.P. Pradhan: General Manager, The New India Assurance Co. Ltd., Mumbai.

Dileep Mavalankar: Assistant Professor, Indian Institute of Management, Ahmedabad.

Ramesh Bhat: Assistant Professor, Indian Institute of Management, Ahmedabad.

Gaurav Garg: Vice-President, Tata AIG General Insurance Co. Ltd., Mumbai.

R. Beri: Secretary, Tariff Advisory Committee, Mumbai.

E.K. Dastur: Director, K.M. Dastur Reinsurance Brokers Pvt. Ltd., Mumbai.

S.S. Shekhar: Risk Engineer, Zurich Risk Management Services (India) Pvt. Ltd., Mumbai.

Devesh Srivastava: General Insurance Corporation of India, New Delhi.

K.R. Makhania: Deputy General Manager, K.M.Dastur Reinsurance Brokers Pvt. Ltd., Mumbai.

S.D. Totade: Professor and Chief Information Officer, National Insurance Academy, Pune.

Prince Azariah: Consultant, Times of India, Mumbai.

Contents

Foreword   xi
Preface   xiii

Part I

1. **Economic Development and Insurance: Global Experience with Special Reference to India**   1-35
   D.C. Srivastava and Shashank Srivastava

2. **Role of State in Growth and Regulation of Insurance Industry: Global Experience and Lessons for India**   36-63
   D.C. Srivastava and Shashank Srivastava

3. **Growth of General Insurance Industry in India**   64-92
   D.C. Srivastava and Shashank Srivastava

Part II

4. **Future of Marketing in Non-life Insurance**   93-105
   S.K. Kanwar

5. **Marketing Strategies for Insurance Products in the Emerging Scenario**   106-115
   A. N. Poddar

6. **Product Design In an Emerging Market**   116-127
   H. Ansari

7. **Some Issues in Product Development**   128-140
   B.D. Banerjee

8. Pricing of Insurance Products in Liberalised
   Economies: Lessons for India   141-155
   R.D. Samarth

9. Capital Investment of General Insurance Industry:
   Issues and Challenges   156-176
   D.C. Srivastava and Shashank Srivastava

10. Investment Management of Non-life Insurance
    Companies   177-181
    A.P. Pradhan

11. Health Insurance in India: Opportunities,
    Challenges and Concerns   182-203
    Dileep Mavalankar and Ramesh Bhat

12. Agriculture Insurance: Status, Concerns and
    Challenges   204-237
    D.C. Srivastava and Shashank Srivastava

13. Role of Insurance Intermediaries in the
    Emerging Market   238-254
    Gaurav Garg

Part III

14. Tariff Advisory Committee: Redefined Role
    in the Liberalised Scenario   255-266
    R. Beri

15. Reinsurance in Indian Perspective   267-281
    E.K. Dastur

16. Risk Management and Financial Planning 282-289
    S.S. Shekhar

17. **Risk Management and Insurance Industry** Devesh Srivastava	290-304
18. **Alternate Risk Transfer Techniques via Finite Risk Insurance** E.K. Dastur and K.R. Makhania	305-311
19. **Information Technology and Insurance** S.D. Totade	312-327
20. **Information Technology in General Insurance** Prince Azariah	328-336
Annexures	337-346
Select Bibliography	347-350
Index	351-352

Foreword

Development plans of different countries aim at increasing the welfare of masses and placing them at higher levels of satisfaction on sustained basis. Enhancing consumers' satisfaction is the ultimate goal that all the countries in the world cherish to achieve. Despite consistent efforts made by developing countries to accelerate the development process, about 515 million people constituting 43% of the total population still live below the poverty line in South Asia. For reducing the level of poverty, there has to be continuous increase in productivity in all sectors of the economy, which will translate itself in generating income and productive employment to different sections of the society on a self-sustained basis. Although different sectors of the economy do not develop in unison and contribute to each other's development, yet the development experience in both developed and developing economies reveals that as the economy progresses, the service sector assumes a predominant role and its share in the national income rises.

The financial sector constitutes one of the major components of the services sector, and within that sector, insurance services assume a paramount importance. The growth of insurance services in the world began about 300 years ago with Lloyds of London. In India, the growth of general insurance may be traced back to 1850 when the first general insurance company was set up at Calcutta. From 1973 onwards, the general insurance industry grew as a state monopoly under a sheltered environment, as was the case with most of the manufacturing and service sectors of the economy. The new economic policy pursued from mid-1980 onwards focused attention on increasing productivity and efficiency of the economy through the instruments of competition and interplay of market forces. As a sequel to the above policy, financial sector reforms were initiated in 1991 and insurance reforms in 1999.

During the pre-reform period, although there was a significant growth of the insurance industry, yet the deepening and widening of insurance services were not in tune with other developing economies of the world. The share of general insurance premium was as low as 0.23% of the world general insurance premium in 1997. The quality of the consumer services was also poor. The new environment ushering in competition will generate immense benefits both to the consumer as well as to the economy taking care of the prevailing shortcomings in the insurance industry.

The present book highlights the role of the insurance industry in stimulating economic development, the present stage of growth of the industry in India in the context of its development in other developing economies of the world and opportunities and challenges which will be encountered by the insurance firms in a liberalised scenario. Various aspects of insurance industry warranting modification in the changing environment have been critically evaluated. The book provides a pleasant blend of theory with the actual pattern of growth of insurance services at the field level. The articles have been contributed by noted academicians and insurance professionals of long standing. I am sure the book will be immensely helpful to researchers, policy makers and regulators, insurers and to the general public interested in understanding the dynamics of insurance services. The book will supply the long felt gap in the insurance literature. I congratulate the editors on this venture.

N. Rangachary
Chairman
Insurance Regulatory and Development Authority
New Delhi

Preface

The growth of insurance industry is associated with the general growth of industry, trade and commerce. The origin of insurance services may be traced back to 14th century in Italy when ships carrying goods were covered under different perils. The systematic and orderly beginning of the insurance industry took place in UK at Lloyds coffee house in Tower Street in London. In developing countries, insurance sector has assumed special significance as it has the potential to speed up the rate of growth of the economy.

Insurance industry assists the development process of an economy in several ways. Primarily, it acts as mobiliser of savings, financial intermediary, promoter of investment activity, stabiliser of financial market, risk manager, and an agent to allocate capital resources efficiently. Although the insurance industry has grown rapidly in the industrialised countries, its growth in developing countries has neither been satisfactory nor in tandem with the growth of other sectors of the economy. The 12 most industrialised countries in the world still account for 88% of global premium volume. The share of developing countries is extremely low. The slow growth of insurance services in developing countries calls for an in-depth analysis of the nature and pattern of the evolution of these services. Policies pursued to develop the insurance industry and constraints thereof also need close examination.

Regrettably, the Indian insurance industry has lagged behind even amongst the developing countries of the world. Although general insurance services started in India about 150 years ago, their growth has been dilatory, as reflected by low insurance penetration and density. Several factors are responsible for this state of affairs, the chief being the monopoly status of the industry till recently. The life insurance business was nationalised in 1956 and the general insurance industry in 1973. The lack of competition has impeded the development of insurance industry in India, resulting in low productivity and poor quality of customer services.

The process of liberalisation and globalisation of the Indian economy started in right earnest in mid-1980s. The market mechanism was the motivating factor underlying the new economic policy. In consonance with the new economic policy, insurance sector was opened up for the private sector in 1999. The new competitive environment is expected to benefit the consumers, industry and the economy at large. The consumers will have a greater choice in terms of number and quality of products, low premium rates, efficient after sales service while the economy will benefit in terms of larger flow of savings, increased availability of investible funds for long-term projects, enhanced productivity and growth of multiple debt instruments.

The present book traces the growth of insurance industry in India, examines its present structure and explores its potential in the backdrop of liberalised scenario.

The book is divided into three parts.

Part I, consisting of three chapters, examines the interrelationship between insurance services and economic development, the role of the state in regulating insurance activities, the present stage of development and future prospects of insurance industry in India. While analysing these issues, the experience of other countries, particularly of developing countries, has been taken into account.

Part II deals with various aspects of insurance industry such as marketing strategies, product designing, product pricing, health insurance, agriculture insurance etc.

Part III addresses itself to areas relating to tariff structure and management, reinsurance, risk management, alternate risk transfer and information technology. All the areas covered in the book have been discussed with reference to emerging environment in the insurance sector. The book extensively clarifies the theoretical concepts associated with the insurance industry as their understanding helps better appreciation of the dynamics of insurance services. We hope the book will prove valuable to all those who are concerned with the future of insurance industry in India. The book should be of special interest to academicians, researchers, policy makers and insurers. The present book strives to cover the general side of the insurance industry. The life side of insurance industry in India would be released through a separate volume.

Both at the stage of planning and completion of the book, we received immense co-operation and constructive observations from friends, colleagues and family members. First and foremost, we express our gratitude to all the authors who have contributed articles for the book. In particular, thanks are due to S.K. Kanwar and R.D. Samarth who, besides contributing articles for the book, were helpful at every stage of the progress of the work. N. Rangachary, Chairman, Insurance Regulatory and Development Authority, was a continuous source of encouragement right from the idea of attempting this work was conceived. His valuable suggestions contributed significantly to improve the quality of the book. We are extremely grateful to him.

Thanks are also due to all the family members who in one way or the other assisted us in completing the book, notably R.C. Sinha who provided the moral support for this venture. Special thanks are due to Sandeep Sury, Chief Executive, New Century Publications, for his personal interest and painstaking efforts to bring the book in its present shape.

New Delhi
March 22, 2001

D.C. Srivastava
Shashank Srivastava

Part I

Editorial Note

Part I consists of three chapters. These chapters examine the role of insurance industry in accelerating the growth of national income; the rationale and variants of regulations exercised by the government or regulating body on the activities of insurers and their effects on the growth of insurance industry; and the growth of general insurance business in India and potentialities for its future growth in a liberalised economic environment.

Chapter 1 thoroughly evaluates the inter-relationship between insurance services and economic development. Chapter 2 attempts to examine the role of state in controlling and regulating the activities of insurers. These control measures could be divided into two categories: macro management and micro management techniques. It has been argued in the paper that the basic objective of protecting the interest of policyholders could well be achieved through macro-management policies without resorting to regulating day to day activities of insurance firms at micro level.

Chapter 3 attempts to review the growth of general insurance in India in historical perspective, critically evaluates its performance, reviews claim experience and projects the growth potential over a period of time. The paper also examines the pre-requisite conditions for conducting insurance business and its distinguishing features as compared to life business.

1

Economic Development and Insurance: Global Experience with Special Reference to India

D.C. Srivastava and Shashank Srivastava

The role of insurance services in contributing to the process of economic development has not been properly appreciated and examined in economic literature. While a large number of studies and research material are available on the role played by other services such as banking, transport, communication, public administration, defence etc. in accelerating the national income of an economy, there is a dearth of material on interlinkages between economic development on the one hand and insurance services on the other. One of the most lucid and exhaustive literature on the subject is by Harold D. Skipper, Jr. who has comprehensively evaluated the contribution of insurance services to the growth process. The present paper attempts to examine the relationship between the two on a theoretical plane as well as on empirical platform.

In order to have clear perception of interlinkage between the two, it would be worth clarifying the concept of economic development as defined and understood in economic literature, since concept has undergone revolutionary changes over a period of time. As far as the concept of insurance is concerned, there is universally accepted definition of the same without any ambiguity and difference of opinion. Insurance may be defined as a contract between insurer and insured under which insurer indemnifies the loss of the insured against the identified perils for which mutually agreed upon premium has been paid by the insured. The contract lays down the time framework within which the losses will be met by the insurer.

Part I

In the present section, an attempt has been made to broadly clarify the meaning of the concept of economic development based upon the vast literature that has proliferated on the subject. Tracing the history of economic thought over a period of time right from classical economists, one discovers that the central theme and concern of these economists had been to identify the factors which contribute towards increasing the wealth, prosperity and welfare of the masses. The most authentic, lucid and comprehensive literature in Economics by Adam Smith was itself titled as "Inquiry into the Nature and Causes of the 'Wealth of Nation' (1776). He observed that 'capital is the main determinant of the number of useful and productive labourers' who can be set to work. He said that labour is put to motion by capital.

In most of earlier economic literature, the prosperity of the nation was measured through the yardstick of the increase in the national income of the economy. The national income could be measured through its different variants such as gross domestic product (GDP) or net domestic product (NDP) at current or constant prices. Economic development was perceived as sustained increase in the gross domestic product (GDP) or per capita GDP over a period of time. Normally, in order to assess the real pace of development, the growth in GDP at constant prices was taken into account. These writings did not consider the qualitative changes such as structural and institutional transformation of the productive system within the ambit of the concept of economic development. The issues such as alleviation of poverty, reduction in inequalities of income and unemployment were assumed to be taken care of by the mere growth of GDP as it was conceived that the growth will automatically trickle down to the masses and to the grassroot levels on a self-sustained basis.

Later writings on the subject questioned the concept of economic development solely based upon the quantitative changes in the GDP/per capita GDP as it fails to reflect upon the qualitative changes in the life of an individual and the nation. These qualitative changes were measured through indices such as changes in the composition of production, technological and institutional organisation of production, distributive pattern of income, reduction in absolute poverty, unemployment, inequalities of income etc. In relation to an individual and at the micro level, the indices comprised of raising the level of education, health, nutrition etc.

Economic development has thus been defined as to incorporate both sustained increase in the GDP/GDP per capita as well as improvement in the basic indicators affecting the quality of life of the people. These economists distinguished the concept of growth from that of development. The concept of growth was defined as sustained increase in GDP/GDP per capita while development meant both the rise in the national income as well as qualitative changes in the economic institutions and organisations of the country.

However, there was no unanimity of opinion amongst these economists regarding the indices to be taken into account for measuring qualitative changes and also the weightage to be assigned to them. One of the most popular approach in this field had been that of Morris David. Morris used the indicators of infant mortality, life expectancy and basic literacy to construct a simple composite index (PQLI).

In this paper while examining the relationship between development and insurance, development has been taken up in the sense of growth implying sustained increase in the GDP/per capita GDP of the country. The qualitative concepts have by and large not been taken into consideration except in those areas where it is possible to quantify.

The growth of GDP is a function of host of factors, both economic and non-economic in nature, which directly or indirectly subscribe to it. From an economic angle, these factors could be grouped into the following four categories (Samuelson-Economics):
- Human resources (labour, education, discipline, motivation etc.).
- Natural resources (land, minerals, fuels, climate etc.).
- Capital formation (machines, factories, roads etc.).
- Technology (science, engineering, management, enterprise).

One of the most important factor contributing to the process of economic development particularly in developing or underdeveloped economies is the capital formation. The relationship between capital formation and insurance services in both developed and developing economies of the world has been quite pronounced and significant.

Part II

In this section, the role of insurance services in raising the rate of capital formation has been examined and analysed.

Capital Formation and Insurance

Capital formation may be defined as an increase in the capital stock of a country consisting of plant, equipments, machinery, tools, factory, buildings, raw material, semi-finished products, means of transport, communication etc. Capital itself may be defined as a means of production which has already been produced. In economic literature, capital has always been regarded as a means to increasing specialisation, roundabout of production, productivity in the economy and thereby contributing to the future stream of income to the economy as a whole. Capital performs the function of increasing both the total output as well as the output per worker in the society. For sustained growth of the economy, what is required is that the capital stock should grow not only at the rate adequate to replace the depreciated stock but should also contribute to the net addition to the same.

The process of capital formation envisages three essential steps. These are:

1. Real savings.
2. Mobilisation and channelising of savings through financial and non-financial intermediaries for being placed at the disposal of investors.
3. The act of investment.

The contribution of insurance in the process of capital formation is through all these stages. Insurance services act as a tool to mobilise savings, function as financial intermediary and at times, though rarely, also indulge in direct investment. Its role under these specific areas has been examined.

Savings and Insurance

The act of saving involves refraining from the present consumption and thereby placing a proportion of income for being consumed at a later date. The act of investment can only take place, when there are savings in the economy. As a result, historically it has been established that economies with high rate of savings had also the high rate of growth of GNP. This trend is explicitly visible in the development process of majority of the countries as has been depicted in Figure 1. IMF study has revealed that out of the 20 fastest growing economies over the preceding ten years, 14 had saving rates greater than 25 per cent of GDP and none had saving rates less than 18 per cent. As against above, out of 20 slowest growing countries, 14 had saving rates less than 15 per cent (As quoted by Harold D. Skipper, Jr.). The relationship between saving/investment and the growth of GDP is quite simple and can be explained as follows:

$$g = \frac{s}{k}$$

where g = rate of growth of GDP
 s = saving ratio, and
 k = capital-output ratio

Capital-output ratio is defined as the number of units of capital required for producing one unit of output. For instance, if capital-output ratio is 4:1, it implies that 4 units of capital are required to produce 1 unit of output. Thus with saving ratio of 20 per cent and capital output ratio of 4:1, the resulting growth rate of GNP will be 5 per cent.

$$g = \frac{20}{4:1}$$

It establishes direct positive correlation between rate of saving on the one hand and the rate of growth of GNP on the other. Of course, at a constant rate of saving the rate of growth can also be increased by lowering capital-output ratio which may be possible through new technologies or other methods resulting into increased productivity. At any given point of time, saving ratio has to be identical to the rate of investment in the economy.

The sources of generation of savings could be both internal and external. The sources of internal savings could be voluntarily cut in consumption, involuntarily cut in consumption through taxation, forced lending to the government, inflation etc. The internal savings

Figure 1: Savings and GDP Growth

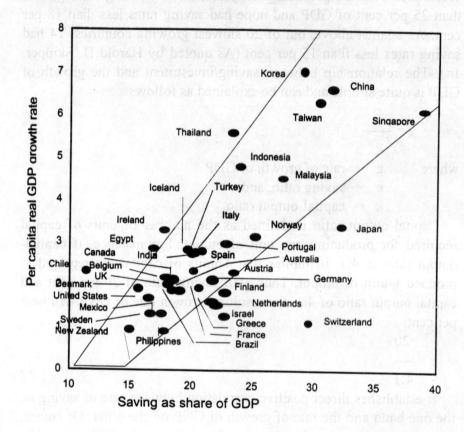

flow from the following three sectors:
1. Household sector.
2. Private corporate sector.
3. Public sector.

The savings from the household sector constitute the major proportion of the total savings in the country. The household savings comprise of two components: physical and financial. The savings could be used to purchase physical assets such as land, buildings, gold, jewellery etc. or these could be in the form of financial assets such as bank deposits, bonds, shares, mutual funds, small savings certificates, debentures, provident and pension funds and life insurance policies. As the economy progresses and attains maturity, progressively larger proportion of savings are invested in financial assets.

The life insurance premium takes the shape of contractual savings. The premium has basically two components, one going for risk coverage and the other going towards savings. Life insurance funds constitute one of the important components in the financial savings of an economy. The non-life funds could not strictly be termed as savings as the premium paid is not returned back to the insured and it only covers the losses suffered by him. Of course, in the general insurance and industry also, there could be savings-linked policies as has been the case in Japanese economy. These savings linked policies could become an important source of financial savings in an economy similar to life insurance funds.

Table 1 depicts the growth of domestic savings and contribution made by the above three sectors over a period of time. The rate of savings have fluctuated between 21 per cent in 1980-81 to 25 per cent in 1995-96. The contribution of household sector has throughout been maximum contributing more than 75 per cent of the total saving during all these years. In 1999-2000, out of the total savings of 22.3 per cent, household sector contributed 19.8 per cent of the gross domestic product (GDP). It accounted for 88.8 per cent of the total gross domestic savings (GDS). The private corporate sector's saving amounted to only 3.7 per cent of GDP and 16.5 per cent of GDS. For the last two years, public sector's contribution to the saving rates was negative being -1.2 per cent of GDP and -5.3 per cent of GDS.

Table 1: Composition of Gross Domestic Savings

Year	Household Sector	Private Corporate Sector	Public Sector	TOTAL
(1)	(2)	(3)	(4)	(5)
				Old Series (Base: 1980-81)
1980-81	16.1 (75.9)	1.7 (8.0)	3.4 (16.1)	21.2
1990-91	20.5 (84.3)	2.8 (11.5)	1.0 (4.2)	24.3
1991-92	17.7 (77.3)	3.2 (13.9)	1.9 (8.8)	22.9
1992-93	17.7 (80.4)	2.8 (12.7)	1.5 (6.9)	22.0
1993-94*	18.4 (81.7)	3.5 (15.5)	0.6 (2.8)	22.5
1994-95	19.8 (79.2)	3.5 (14.0)	1.7 (6.8)	25.0
1995-96	18.5 (72.5)	5.0 (19.6)	2.0 (7.9)	25.5
1996-97	17.1 (73.4)	4.5 (19.3)	1.7 (7.3)	23.3
1997-98	17.8 (75.7)	4.2 (17.9)	1.5 (6.4)	23.5
1998-99 (P)	19.1 (86.8)	3.7 (16.8)	-0.8 (-3.6)	22.0
1999-2000 (Q)	19.8 (88.8)	3.7 (16.5)	-1.2 (-5.3)	22.3

* As per New Series
P= Provisional
Q= Quick Estimates
Figures in brackets indicate percentage to the gross domestic savings
Source: Economic Survey (*Various years*), Government of India; Report on Currency and Finance (*Various years*), Reserve Bank of India.

What is of relevance is that the bulk of domestic savings are generated from the household sector and within this category of saving, insurance funds are one of the major constituents. Although in Indian economy, the percentage of insurance funds in domestic savings is relatively at a low level, in developed economies it happens to be quite large and substantial.

Table 2 depicts the share of life insurance premium in the gross domestic savings (GDS) of different countries of the world. In South Africa, life funds as percentage of GDP were as high as 80 per cent. It was also quite high in UK (55.4 per cent), Switzerland (28.2 per cent), France (27.5 per cent), Japan (27.1 per cent), Australia (27.1 per cent), South Korea (25.9 per cent), USA (25.4 per cent), Ireland (24.9 per cent), Netherlands (18.3 per cent). These trends have also been exhibited in Figure 2.

In so far as Indian economy is concerned, the percentage share of financial savings in household savings has slowly increased from 39.4 per cent in 1980-81 to 53 per cent in 1999 - 2000. The savings in the form of physical assets have declined from 60.6 per cent of household savings in 1980-81 to 47 per cent in 1999-2000. Life insurance funds comprised 3.9 per cent of the household savings in 1980-81 and increased to 7.1 per cent in 1999-2000. However, these funds remained by and large constant at 6 per cent from 1990-91 onwards. The trend after 1990-91 indicates that as percentage of household savings, these funds have remained static. Table 3 brings out these trends between 1980-81 to 1999-2000.

Table 4 indicates the share of life insurance funds in the gross domestic product (GDP) of the country. Household sector's savings as a percentage of GDP fluctuated between 17 to 20 per cent during 1990-91 to 1999-2000. Financial savings as percentage of GDP were between 8 to 11 per cent between 1993-94 to 1999-2000. Life insurance funds as percentage of GDP have also remained stationary and have oscillated around one per cent. These funds remained unchanged at 1.1 per cent between 1993-94 to 1996-97, but have gradually increased from 1.2 per cent in 1997-98 to 1.4 per cent in 1999-2000. Further life insurance funds as percentage of financial assets varied between 9 to 11 per cent between the above years. This is depicted in Figure 3.

These trends are indicative of the fact that there is a vast scope and potential for insurance funds to be increased as these are quite low as

Table 2: Life Premium as Percentage of Gross Domestic Savings

Country	Life Fund as % of Gross Domestic Savings
USA	25.40
Canada	15.70
Brazil	2.20
Argentina	3.20
Mexico	0.57
Columbia	3.20
Venezuela	0.12
Germany	4.05
UK	55.40
France	27.50
Italy	8.50
Spain	11.20
Netherlands	18.30
Switzerland	28.20
Sweden	10.80
Russia	1.30
Ireland	24.90
Poland	4.10
Greece	7.50
Japan	27.10
South Korea	25.90
China	1.70
Israel	24.50
Malaysia	9.20
India	**6.20**
Hongkong	8.20
Thailand	2.60
Indonesia	1.80
Singapore	7.10
Philippines	4.10
Pakistan	1.90
South Africa	80.90
Kenya	2.00
Australia	27.10
Newzealand	8.00

Source: Calculated from the World Development Report-1998-99, 1999-2000 and *World Insurance in 1997: Booming Life Insurance but Stagnating Non-Life Insurance Business*, Sigma-Swiss, No. 3/1999.

Economic Development and Insurance 13

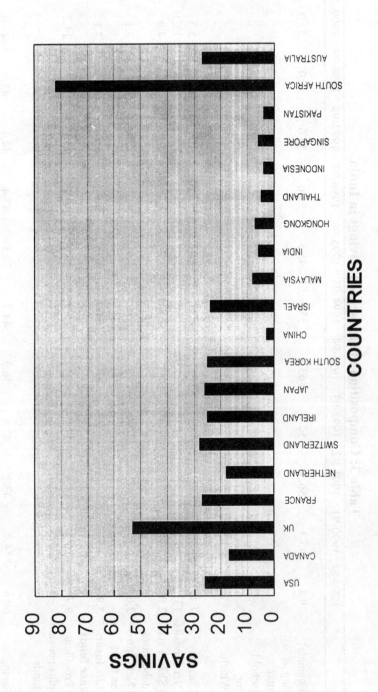

Figure 2: Life Premium as Percentage of Gross Domestic Savings

Table 3: Composition of Household Savings in India

	1980-81	1990-91	1991-92	1992-93	1993-94	1994-95	1995-96	1996-97	1997-98	1998-99	1999-2000
A. Financial Saving as % of total household saving	39.4	45.3	56.9	52.4	63.1	55.6	45.5	52.6	55.6	57.0	53.0
Of Which											
(i) Currency	7.4	5.7	7.5	5.3	8.9	8.1	7.9	5.2	4.9	6.2	5.5
(ii) Net deposits	13.7	10.2	13.3	15.9	21.9	16.5	12.5	23.1	22.0	19.9	15.1
(iii) Shares and debentures	2.0	7.7	14.5	11.1	9.9	7.9	3.8	3.7	2.1	2.0	4.0
(iv) Net claims on Govt.	2.6	6.7	4.1	2.8	4.1	6.6	4.4	4.5	7.9	8.4	7.1
(v) Life insurance funds	3.9	4.9	6.1	5.4	6.1	5.6	6.3	6.0	6.8	6.8	7.1
(vi) Provident plus pension funds	9.7	10.2	11.4	11.9	12.2	10.9	10.6	10.1	11.9	13.7	14.2
B. Saving in physical assets	60.6	54.7	43.2	47.6	36.9	44.3	54.5	47.4	44.4	43.0	47.0

Source: Economic Survey (various years), Government of India; Report on Currency and Finance (various years), Reserve Bank of India; National Accounts Statistics, EPW Research Foundation (1998).

Table 4: Composition of Savings in India (As percentage of GDP at current market prices)

	1980-81	1990-91	1991-92	1992-93	1993-94	1994-95	1995-96	1996-97	1997-98	1998-99	1999-2000
1. Household Sector	-	20.5	17.7	17.7	18.4	19.7	18.1	17.0	17.8	19.1	19.8
I. Financial saving	-	-	-	-	11.0	11.9	8.9	10.3	9.9	10.9	10.5
(a) Currency	1.2	1.2	1.3	0.9	1.6	1.6	1.4	1.0	0.8	1.2	1.1
(b) Net deposits	-	-	-	-	3.8	4.2	2.9	4.4	3.9	3.8	3.0
(c) Shares and debentures	0.3	0.9	1.1	1.2	1.7	1.7	0.8	0.8	0.3	0.4	0.8
(d) Net claims on Govt.	0.5	1.5	0.8	0.6	0.7	1.3	0.8	0.8	1.4	1.6	1.4
(e) Life insurance funds	0.7	1.0	1.1	1.0	1.1	1.1	1.1	1.1	1.2	1.3	1.4
(f) Provident + pension funds	-	1.6	2.1	2.0	2.1	2.1	1.9	2.2	2.1	2.6	2.8
II. Saving in physical assets	-	-	-	-	7.4	7.8	7.3	6.7	8.0	8.2	9.2
2. Private Corporate sector	-	-	-	-	3.5	3.5	4.9	4.5	4.2	3.7	3.7
3. Public Sector	-	-	-	-	0.6	1.7	2.0	1.7	1.5	-0.8	-1.2
4. Gross Domestic Savings	21.2	24.3	22.9	22.0	22.5	24.8	25.8	23.2	23.5	22.0	22.3
5. % of Life insurance funds in financial assets	9.9	10.7	10.6	10.3	9.7	10.1	13.9	11.4	10.9	11.0	-

Source: As for Table 3.

Economic Development and Insurance

16 Indian Insurance Industry: Transition and Prospects

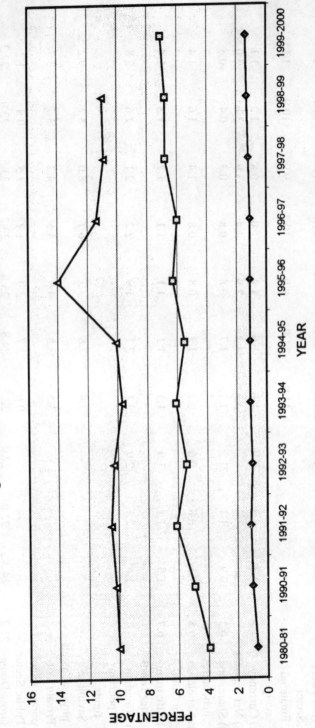

Figure 3 : Life Fund as % of GDP, GDS, FA

percentage to gross domestic savings, financial assets and gross domestic product and are capable of significantly contributing to the process of capital formation and economic development of the country.

Insurers as Financial Intermediaries

As mentioned earlier, in the process of capital formation, one of the important steps involved is the mobilisation of savings and placing them at the disposal of investors. The above function is carried out by the financial intermediaries. In a market oriented economy, while the act of savings is performed by a large number of units scattered across the country, the investment functions are carried out by different entities which are also scattered widely. Financial intermediaries perform a very useful function of channelising savings into domestic investment. These financial intermediaries with their specialised knowledge place the savings of these units into most productive investment channels. These intermediaries facilitate the efficient allocation of capital resources which in turn improves productivity and economic efficiency of the economy. It largely contributes in reducing the capital-output ratio in the economy. Insurance companies, both life and non-life, in their role as financial intermediaries perform extremely useful functions in the economy.

Harold D. Skipper has pointed out that insurers promote financial system efficiency in the following three ways:

1. Reduction in Transaction Costs

Insurers, particularly life insurers, collect the premium from a very large number of policyholders and thereby command a huge funds at their disposal. These insurers invest these funds in variety of projects scattered over different regions of the country. But for these companies, the policyholders would have been required to indulge in direct lending and investing which is both specialised job and is also time consuming. Thus insurers help in reducing the transport costs in the economy.

2. Creating Liquidity

The funds at the disposal of insurers are being used for long term projects and loans. The funds collected are out of the premium paid by the policyholders against the losses to be met by the insurance companies. In case of occurrence of loss, insurers immediately compensate for the losses and pay the claim amount to the policyholders. Thus, the funds of policyholders are extremely liquid as there is no time lag between occurrence of loss on the one hand and receiving the claim on the other. Besides, the borrowers of the funds are not required to repay the loans immediately. If the policy holders start direct lending of their funds, they may land up locking their funds in long-term illiquid assets. As pointed out by Skipper, "Insurers, thereby reduce illiquidity inherent in direct lending".

3. Facilitating Economies of Scale in Investment

Insurers in their role as financial intermediaries are in a position to invest in large projects requiring heavy investment. Insurance companies command huge funds at their discretion collected from large number of policyholders, which they can invest in huge projects requiring large investment such as national road projects, railways, ports, power projects etc. These large projects create economies of scale, facilitate technological innovations and specialisations and thereby promote economic efficiency and productivity in the economy. With these funds the large investment projects become feasible.

Role in Developing Economies

In fact, the role of financial intermediaries arises because of imperfection in the economic system. There exists an information gap between the suppliers of funds on the one hand and the investors on the other. They do not possess information about each other's location, volume of funds, nature of investment projects etc. It necessitates the growth of financial intermediaries to perform these above functions. It has, therefore, been contended that in a developed economy where the financial market is relatively more perfect, the role of intermediaries will diminish and their functions will increasingly be taken over by the financial market itself. However, in developing economies financial intermediaries play relatively larger role in supplying the funds and amongst these intermediaries insurers play an important role.

Insurers vs. Other Financial Intermediaries

In the economy, the functions of financial intermediaries are performed by several institutions, viz. insurers, co-operative banks, mutual fund and asset management companies etc. The advantage with insurance companies is that they are capable of deploying their funds in long term projects compared to banks and other intermediaries who invest their funds mostly in short duration projects.

In addition to acting as mobiliser of savings and as financial intermediary, insurer also contributes to the third stage of capital formation, i.e. the act of actual investment. Broadly, as pointed out by Skipper, insurers stimulate investment activities in the following manner:

1. Efficient Management of Risks

An investor while undertaking investment projects is subjected to several risks of varying intensity. These risks have been classified into different categories such as commercial risks, operational risks, supply and market risks, political risks etc. Insurers play vital role in identifying, evaluating and pricing these risks. It promotes healthy and congenial investment environment. In particular, insurers facilitate the investment activities through risk coverage in the following ways:

Risk Pricing: Insurers identify the risks to which the investment projects may be exposed to and depending upon the severity of the risk, the price (premium) is fixed up. They may also refuse to cover certain risks, if they find them as extremely hazardous, even at extremely high price. The information gained by the insurers which is transparent and is transferred to investors enables them to take preventive and precautionary measures to meet risk challenges. The above information also helps the investor to rationally calculate the rate of return on their projects. Further, insurer thoroughly examines the credit-worthiness of the firm to whom it advances the loan and the knowledge so gained assists the potential investors and other interested parties to take appropriate decision on feasibility of the project.

Risk Transformation: Insurance companies enable the entrepreneurs and the individuals to transform their risks to insurers at a price (premium) and thereby stimulate investment in the economy. The policyholders are in a position to convert their savings into insurance products which are both safe and liquid.

2. Risk Pooling and Reduction

The insurance is primarily based upon the principle of risk pooling implying therein that the insurers transfer to themselves the risks of large number of units, whether individual or business enterprises, and this aggregation helps them in several ways. Larger the number of the risk aggregation, greater the precision in the prediction of losses that may occur in future. It reduces the fluctuations in the expected losses to the insurers. That enables insurers to charge lower premiums and these premiums are also stable over a long period of time.

Further, risk pooling places large number of funds at the discretion of the insurers enabling them to diversify their investment portfolios. The diversified nature of their investment helps them to compensate for the losses sustained from unsound borrowers through the profits generated from the sound borrowers. The experience gained therein, which is made possible through risk pooling, enables the insurers to charge lower rate of interest for their loans, which in turn induces investment in the economy.

As was mentioned earlier, the process of economic development involves sustained increase in the GDP and in this process besides the role played by capital formation, there are host of variables which facilitate the growth in GDP in one or the other way. Insurance services positively affect these variables, which in turn promote increase in GDP. Insurance services having positive impact on these variables have been examined below:

Loss Prevention Measures: Right from the construction stage of the investment project to the final stage of production of final goods and services, the project is exposed to several risks and perils which are insured by the insurance companies. Over a period of time, based upon the long underwriting experience, insurers built of expertise knowledge and skill to prevent or minimise these losses. Even at the time of insuring a product, insurers insist for installation of preventive devices to prevent and minimise these losses as a pre-condition to extend the cover. They also transfer their skill to insured in loss prevention techniques. In India, even Loss Prevention Association has been set up by the insurance companies which is continuously engaged in innovating loss prevention techniques and passing it to insureds through publicity, advertisement, awareness camps etc. Insurance companies also continuously monitor the measures taken by the insureds to minimise the occurrence of losses. Insurers, thus play an important role in the prevention of losses to the business enterprises and individuals which is a tangible benefit to the economy and society.

3. Promoting Trade and Commerce

The increase in GDP is positively correlated to the growth of trade and commerce in the economy. Majority of products and services are produced only if liability insurance is available to them. For carrying out both domestic and international trade, insurance of traded products happens to be a pre-condition. Even the venture capitalists also insist for the comprehensive insurance cover for the products and services proposed to be produced through the borrowed capital. Financial specialisation and flexibility in the economic system play important contributory role in the healthy and smooth growth of trade and commerce. Insurance covers promote such specialisation and flexibility in the system.

Further, normally banks while advancing collateral or individual loans for purchase of assets demand insurance cover of the assets before advancing the loans and the insurance premium constitutes a part of loan repayment schedule. For instance in India, Integrated Rural Development Programme (IRDP), cattle insurance and other rural asset building programmes have in-built mechanism for coverage of assets through insurance. In this way also insurers promote trade and commerce in the society.

4. Facilitates Efficient Capital Allocation

Insurers insure large number of firms, enterprises and businesses and also deploy their funds in number of investment projects. The experience so gained builds up the vast pool of knowledge and expertise amongst the insurers so as to distinguish between productive and high return projects on the one hand and unproductive and inefficient projects on the other. The knowledge so gained helps the small savers and investors to invest in most productive projects. On their own it would have not been possible for these savers and investors to evaluate these projects on merit owing to lack of time and resources at their disposal. The insurers continuously monitor the projects financed by them and act as their watchdog and ensure that the management of these companies do not indulge in such activities which may lead to increase in the risk profile of these companies. In this process, management of these companies functions in the best of interests of customers, creditors, employees, stockholders etc. Insurers, therefore, promote efficient and productive allocation of capital resources which in turn leads to improved productivity and efficiency in the system. It helps in reducing capital-output ratio in the economy.

5. Encouraging Financial Stability and Reducing Anxiety

Insurers promote financial stability in the economy. They insure the risks and losses of individuals, firms, organisations etc. and in case of occurrence of loss, the insureds are immediately compensated and their losses are indemnified. In the absence of these covers, insureds would have been required to resort to borrowing from friends, relatives, private lenders, etc. and thus create financial instability in the market. In case of uninsured large losses, the firms may not be in a position to bear them, may become insolvent, and may even be forced to close down the business, which in turn may result into unemployment, loss to the firms supplying the raw materials and other inputs, loss to the customers in being deprived of these products and even loss of the revenue (excise duty sales tax, corporation tax) etc. to the Government.

The individuals and business enterprises get mentally worried when they suffer losses to their life, property and assets. The mental tension so caused often leads to delay or completely halting decision making process in the firm. In so far as the insurable losses are concerned, the firms do not get panicky as these losses are transferred to the insurance companies. Insurers, therefore, help in reducing worries and anxieties of the individuals and firms.

6. Reducing the Burden on Government Exchequer

Insurance companies particularly life insurers provide a variety of insurance products covering the needs of children, women, aged etc. These products serve as a social security network for a large segment of population and thereby reduces the burden on Government in providing these services. To the extent, Government saves expenditure on these items, the same can be utilised for development activities in other sectors thereby accelerating growth of GDP in the economy. The role of insurers in this respect has been explicitly pointed out in a study by OECD. It states: "The fact that so many life insurance policies are purchased undoubtedly releases pressure on the social welfare systems in many states. To that extent, life insurance is an advantage in the context of public finance, and, as a result, is generally viewed with favour by governments. A number of governments knowledge this is tangible form by granting tax relief to policy-holders. At this point, tax incentives for life insurance contributions are widespread among OECD member countries." (Quoted by Skipper).

Further, one of the studies conducted by Swiss Reinsurance Company (1987) has established that in 10 OECD countries there was a negative correlation between the spread of life insurance on the one hand and the social security programmes funded by the government on the other.

In the preceding sections, the role played by insurers in economic development has been examined and analysed. The studies have also established that economic development itself promotes the insurance services in an economy. Insurance services from this angle become an effect of growth of GNP in the country. The effect of economic development on insurance spread has been examined below.

Composition of GDP and Insurance Penetration

The data from industrialised countries indicate that larger the share of service sector in the composition of the GDP, higher the insurance penetration in these countries. In these countries, insurance penetration is inversely correlated to the share of agriculture and industry in the composition of GDP. This trend is clearly visible in Table 5 and Figures 4, 5 and 6.

In so far as the developing economies are concerned, it has been established that the higher the percentage of agriculture in GDP lower insurance penetration in these economies. Further, in these economies the visible trend is that larger the share of industry in the GDP, higher the insurance penetration. This is depicted in Table 6 and Figures 7, 8 and 9.

Economic Development and Insurance Density

The insurance density has been defined as per capita expenditure on insurance premium. The insurance density has a direct correlation to per capita GDP income of the country. The low per capita GDP translates itself into low insurance density in the country. The per capita of GDP is as high as US $ 17,246, on an average, for all industrial countries as against an average of US$ 5,793 for all developing countries (even this reduces by a third to US$ 3,755, if we ignore Singapore and Hongkong, which are developing in name only). The per capita GDP in India is US$ 375 as against average of US$ 5,793 for all developing countries. From the above data, it can be inferred that the higher per capita income translates, itself into high insurance density and conversely the countries with low per capita GDP have low insurance density. Tables 7 and 8 portray the above trend.

Conclusion

The above analysis reveals that insurance sector plays a very vital role in the process of economic development of the country. The process of capital formation is stimulated by the insurance services. The sector acts as mobiliser of savings, as financial intermediary, as promoter of investment activities, as stabiliser of financial market, and as risk manager. Insurance services lead to efficient and

Economic Development and Insurance 25

Table 5: Non-Life Insurance Penetration in Industrialised Countries

	Non-Life Premium 1998 (US $ Billions)	GDP 1998 (US $ Billions)	GDP Breakup			As % of GDP			Services Breakup % of GDP		(As Insurance
			Agriculture	Industry	Services	Agriculture	Industry	Services	Other Services	Insurance	
USA	359.414	7746	154.92	1,781.58	5,809.50	2	23	75	70.36	4.64	
Netherlands	14.832	360	10.80	97.20	252.00	3	27	70	65.88	4.12	
Australia	14.037	391	15.64	109.48	265.88	4	28	68	64.41	3.59	
UK	42.485	1272	25.44	356.16	890.40	2	28	70	66.66	3.34	
France	40.653	1397	27.94	363.22	1,005.84	2	26	72	69.09	2.91	
Croatia	0.494	19	2.28	4.75	11.97	12	25	63	60.40	2.60	
Japan	102.949	4202	84.04	1,596.76	2,521.20	2	38	60	57.55	2.45	
Denmark	3.912	161	6.44	49.91	104.65	4	31	65	62.57	2.43	
Norway	3.534	153	3.06	45.90	104.04	2	30	68	65.69	2.31	
Sweden	5.221	228	4.56	72.96	150.48	2	32	66	63.71	2.29	
Italy	26.106	1145	34.35	332.05	778.60	3	29	68	65.72	2.28	
Czech Rep.	1.166	55	3.85	34.65	16.50	7	63	30	27.88	2.12	
Poland	2.679	136	8.16	53.04	74.80	6	39	55	53.03	1.97	
Finland	2.204	116	6.96	46.40	62.64	6	40	54	52.10	1.90	
Slovakia	0.374	20	1.00	6.20	12.80	5	31	64	62.13	1.87	
Hungary	0.702	45	3.15	14.40	27.45	7	32	61	59.44	1.56	
Bulgaria	0.132	9	0.90	2.97	5.13	10	33	57	55.53	1.47	
Russia	4.851	441	30.87	171.99	238.14	7	39	54	52.90	1.10	
Greece	1.035	119	19.04	33.32	66.64	16	28	56	55.13	0.87	
Romania	0.182	35	7.35	14.00	13.65	21	40	39	38.48	0.52	
Ukraine	0.132	44	5.72	17.16	21.12	13	39	48	47.70	0.30	
Canada	25.929	603	0.00	0.00	0.00	0	0	0	0.00	4.30	
Germany	80.010	2100	0.00	0.00	0.00	0	0	0	0.00	3.81	
Switzerland	10.577	293	0.00	0.00	0.00	0	0	0	0.00	3.61	
Ireland	2.189	72	0.00	0.00	0.00	0	0	0	0.00	3.04	
Spain	15.134	531	0.00	0.00	0.00	0	0	0	0.00	2.85	

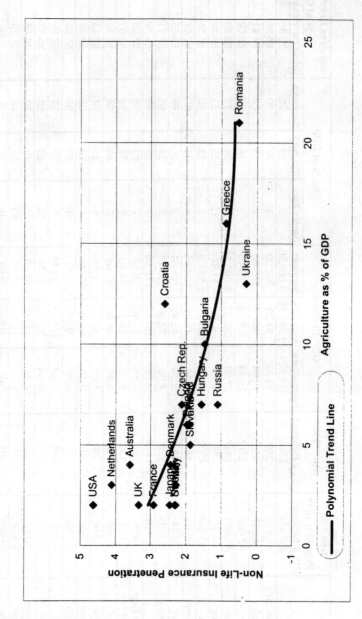

Figure 4: Non-Life Insurance Penetration Vs Agriculture as % of GDP in Industrialised Countries

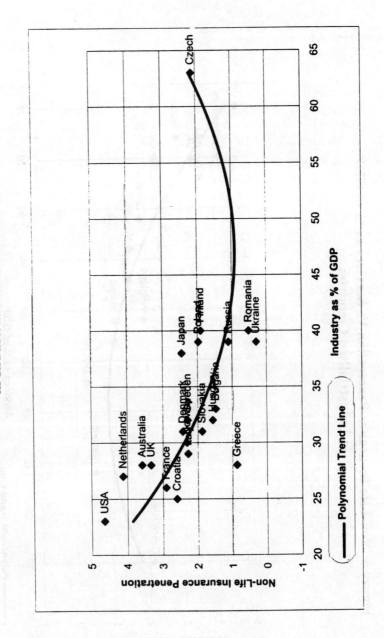

Figure 5: Non-Life Insurance Penetration Vs Industry as % of GDP in Industrialised Countries

28 Indian Insurance Industry: Transition and Prospects

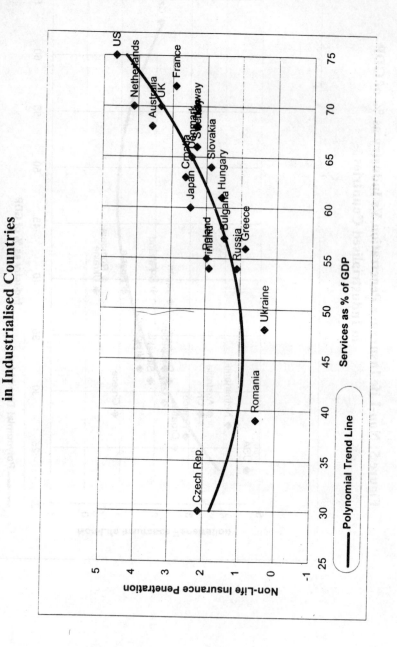

Figure 6: Non-Life Insurance Penetration Vs Services as % of GDP in Industrialised Countries

Table 6: Non-Life Insurance Penetration in Developing Countries

	Non-Life Premium 1998 (US $ Billions)	GDP 1998 (US $ Billions)	GDP Breakup			As % of GDP			Services Breakup (As % of GDP)	
			Agriculture	Industry	Services	Agriculture	Industry	Services	Other Services	Insurance
South Korea	16.790	443	26.58	190.49	225.93	6	43	51	47.21	3.79
South Africa	4.489	129	6.45	50.31	72.24	5	39	56	52.52	3.48
Kenya	0.257	10	2.90	1.70	5.40	29	17	54	51.43	2.57
Malaysia	2.146	98	12.74	45.08	40.18	13	46	41	38.81	2.19
Zimbabwe	0.189	9	2.52	2.88	3.60	28	32	40	37.90	2.10
Morocco	0.617	33	6.60	10.23	16.17	20	31	49	47.13	1.87
Colombia	1.530	85	13.60	17.00	54.40	16	20	64	62.20	1.80
Brazil	13.676	786	110.04	282.96	393.00	14	36	50	48.26	1.74
Venezuela	1.072	67	2.68	31.49	32.83	4	47	49	47.40	1.60
Singapore	1.258	96	0.00	34.56	61.44	0	36	64	62.69	1.31
Thailand	1.915	157	17.27	62.80	76.93	11	40	49	47.78	1.22
Argentina	3.896	322	19.32	99.82	202.86	6	31	63	61.79	1.21
Ecuador	0.219	19	2.28	7.03	9.69	12	37	51	49.85	1.15
Hong Kong	1.915	171	0.00	25.65	145.35	0	15	85	83.88	1.12
Philippines	0.664	83	16.60	26.56	39.84	20	32	48	47.20	0.80
Mexico	2.647	335	16.75	87.10	231.15	5	26	69	68.21	0.79
Nigeria	0.281	37	16.65	8.88	11.47	45	24	31	30.24	0.76
Peru	0.409	62	4.34	22.94	34.72	7	37	56	55.34	0.66
Indonesia	1.398	215	34.40	90.30	90.30	16	42	42	41.35	0.65
China	5.280	825	165.00	420.75	239.25	20	51	29	28.36	0.64
Kuwait	0.203	35	0.00	14.70	20.30	0	42	58	57.42	0.58
India	2.016	360	97.20	108.00	154.80	27	30	43	42.44	0.56
Egypt	0.390	75	12.00	23.25	39.75	16	31	53	52.48	0.52
Pakistan	0.269	64	16.64	16.00	31.36	26	25	49	48.58	0.42

30 Indian Insurance Industry: Transition and Prospects

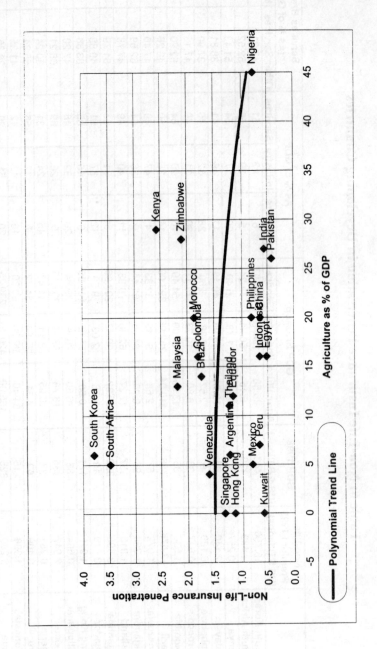

Figure 7: Non-Life Insurance Penetration Vs Agriculture as % of GDP in Developing Countries

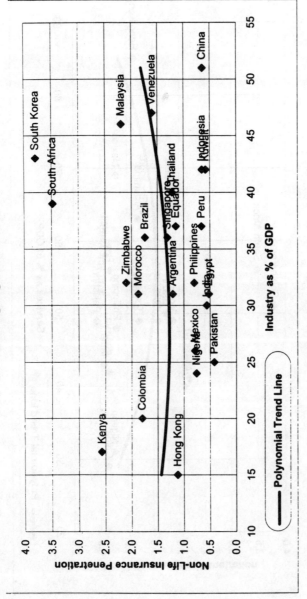

Figure 8: Non-Life Insurance Penetration Vs Industry as % of GDP in Developing Countries

Figure 9: Non-Life Insurance Penetration Vs Services as % of GDP in Developing Countries

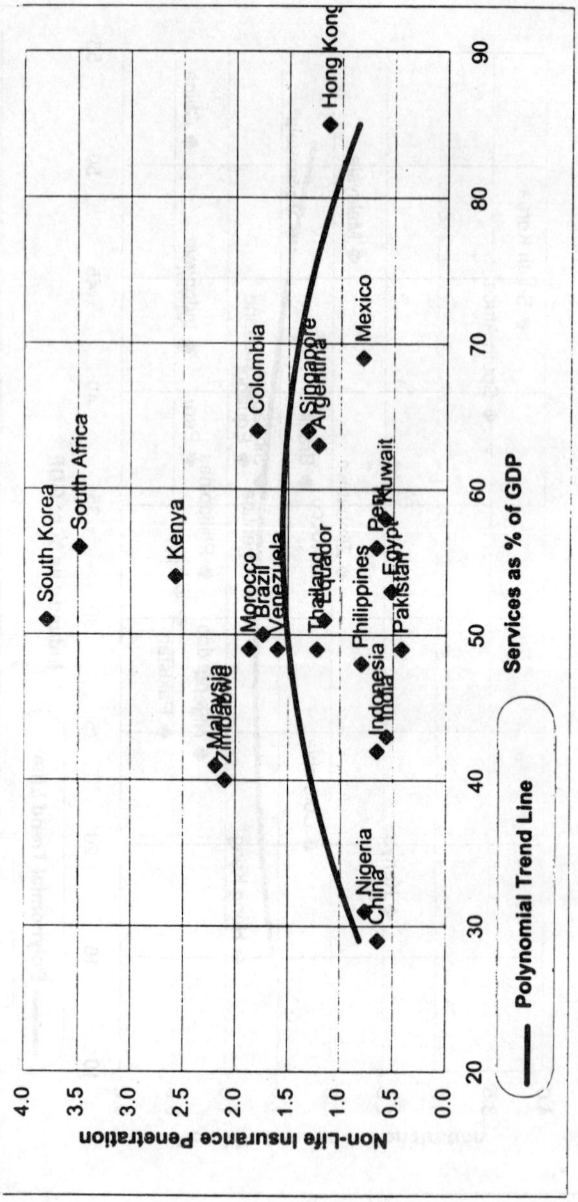

Table 7: Insurance Density and Per Capita GDP -1998 in US $ (Developing Countries)

	Per Capita GDP	Per Capita Premium
Singapore	32,000	1,645
Hong Kong	24,429	867
Kuwait	17,500	117
Zimbabwe	11,534	788
South Korea	9,630	1,485
Argentina	8,944	158
Brazil	4,793	102
Malaysia	4,667	204
Mexico	3,526	45
South Africa	3,395	589
Venezuela	2,913	48
Thailand	2,574	63
Peru	2,480	21
Colombia	2,237	51
Ecuador	1,583	20
Egypt	1,250	8
Morocco	1,179	29
Philippines	1,137	17
Indonesia	1,075	13
China	672	10
Pakistan	467	3
India	375	7
Kenya	357	11
Nigeria	314	3
Average	5,793	263

Table 8: Insurance Density and Per Capita GDP -1998 in US $
(Industrialised Countries)

	Per Capita GDP	Per Capita Premium
Switzerland	41,857	4,998
Norway	38,250	1,744
Japan	33,349	3,959
Denmark	32,200	2,003
USA	28,903	2,454
Germany	25,610	1,672
Sweden	25,333	1,196
France	23,678	2,190
Finland	23,200	1,800
Netherlands	22,500	2,117
UK	21,559	2,419
Australia	20,579	1,877
Canada	20,100	1,481
Italy	20,088	838
Ireland	18,000	1,507
Spain	13,615	733
Greece	10,818	188
Czech Rep.	5,500	159
Croatia	4,750	140
Hungary	4,500	105
Slovakia	4,000	104
Poland	3,487	96
Russia	3,000	42
Romania	1,522	8
Bulgaria	1,125	18
Ukraine	880	4
Average	17,246	1,302

productive allocation of capital resources, prevent the losses to the firms by encouraging loss preventive measures, facilitate growth of trade and commerce, substitute for government's social security programmes and assist the individuals and firms in efficient management of risks. In turn economic development also facilitates spread of insurance both in terms of its penetration and intensity. The larger share of services in the composition of GDP has resulted into higher insurance penetration in industrialised countries. However, in these countries there was an inverse correlation between share of industries in GDP and insurance penetration. In developing economies, the share of agriculture in GDP has been found to be negatively correlated with the insurance penetration. In so far insurance density is concerned, countries with higher per capita GDP/income have higher insurance density and those with low GDP/income have lower insurance density.

2

Role of State in Growth and Regulation of Insurance Industry: Global Experience and Lessons for India

D.C. Srivastava and Shashank Srivastava

Insurance constitutes one of the major segments of the financial market. Insurance services play predominant role in the process of capital formation of the country as mobiliser of savings and also as financial intermediary. The insurance industry commands large funds through sale of insurance products to a large number of individuals and organisations located in different parts of the country. During the process of conducting insurance business, insurers also create liabilities and commit themselves to compensate for the losses occurring to the policyholders at a future date. The funds at the disposal of insurance companies belong to policy holders and are public money. It is, therefore, essential that insurance companies conduct their operations in a healthy and sound manner based upon prudent business practices and do not indulge in unethical practices.

In view of the large sum of public funds commanded by them, in most of the countries insurance industry was kept as a state monopoly without permitting entry of private sector for a long time and even after opening the industry for the private players, many governments have imposed several controls on their activities. The present paper is an attempt to examine the different forms of controls exercised over the insurance sector in different parts of the world, their effect on growth and lessons for India which has recently opened the sector for private companies.

The paper has been divided into three parts. Part I deals with rationale and variants of regulations imposed on insurance industry in general, Part II concerns itself with the experience of few developing economies in privatising and controlling the insurance sector and Part III evaluates the nature and pattern of regulations as exercised on

Indian insurance industry.

Part I

The forms of controls and regulations exercised over insurance industry have differed from country to country. The nature and pattern of controls in a country are shaped by its political and economic philosophy, economic and social compulsions, pressure from interested groups, past experience etc. Based upon these factors different countries have evolved their own regulatory mechanism being applicable on insurance industry. Some of the countries have also imposed controls over the activities of insurers to promote free and healthy competition amongst them, while others have encouraged self control mechanism through greater role being assigned to actuaries, auditors, professionals etc. For instance in UK, insurance services grew as early as in 16th century, the sector was practically without government control and intervention till 1870, when Life Insurance Act was passed. The Act as such did not impose any restriction on the sector but simply made it obligatory on these companies to disclose their financial and other details to the public and get their finances evaluated by an actuary. The companies were required to be transparent in their dealings and make their accounts and valuation report available to the Board of Trade. It may be pertinent to mention that no powers were delegated to the board to initiate any action against any company. Basically it reflected the political philosophy of UK, which believed in the policy of *laissez-faire*. In contrast, the controls exercised in USA, Continental Europe and Japan were more severe and widespread in nature.

However, most of the countries do exercise some control on the activities of insurance companies, although the nature and content of these controls may differ from country to country. These controls are exercised either directly by the government or through the regulatory/supervisory body especially constituted for the purpose. The rationale behind such controls has since been examined.

Rationale

Insurance companies while conducting their business collect

premium money and build up huge reserve of funds over a period of time. These funds belong to policyholders. However, simultaneously insurers have also created liabilities on themselves as they are bound by the contract to pay the claim amount to the policyholders as and when they arise. In order to meet these liabilities immediately without default, it is imperative that insurance companies carry out their business operations on sound lines, maintain adequate reserves, invest in assets of economically strong and sound companies and follow healthy business practices. There may be temptation on the part of few insurance companies to indulge in unethical and unscrupulous practices so as to earn quick and fast income and may invest funds in bad debt instruments. They may default on their liabilities. Since it is public money, which needs to be protected against misuse, governments have imposed several restrictions on these companies so as to ensure their healthy and efficient functioning. Thus, the basic objective behind regulations is to protect the interests of the policyholders.

In addition to ensuring solvency of the companies as a tool to protect the interests of the consumers, other methods such as regulating the prices of insurance products, approving the quality and wordings of products, facilitating expeditious settlement of claims, determining the division of profit to be shared between policyholders and shareholders, ensuring the quality of intermediaries etc. have also been used to protect the interests of consumers. The consumer's interest are also protected through promoting free and healthy competition amongst the insurance firms and providing larger choice to the consumers in terms of insurance products and insurance providers. It is quite likely that at times, there may be a conflict in simultaneously pursuing these objectives. For instance, the objective of lower premium rates may conflict with the objective of maintaining a high degree of solvency. Lower premium rates result into decreased financial strength of insurance companies. The regulator has to strike a balance between these conflicting objectives. In some of the countries, the role played by the government had been that of sponsoring the insurance companies and the role may, at times, conflict with the objective of protecting the interests of policyholders.

There has been difference of opinion on the extent to which controls should be exercised for protecting policyholder's interests. There are extreme views on the subject. On the one hand, a view is held that the policyholders should have access to all the information they need from the insurance companies to enable them to take a decision on their own for the purchase of the product and the company from which they want to have dealings. That necessitates framing requisite rules on the part of regulator so as to make it obligatory on the part of insurer to disclose and make public all the relevant information and data. It could be relating to the manner in which funds have been deployed, amount of reserves, net worth, claim ratio in different class of business, investment income and yield on investment, underwriting results etc. According to this view, there should not be any physical control on the activities of insurance companies. The consumers will be furnished with necessary data and information that they require to enable them to take a decision on the purchase of insurance products. At another end, the view held is that the controls should be extensive covering the areas such as determining the premium rates, drafting the policy wordings, directing deployment of funds, supervising the management of companies etc.

The nature of regulations and the extent to which they are applied in a country will go to determine the basic structure of insurance industry in that country, the degree of competition amongst insurance firms as well as the range of choice of products and firms to the consumers. It is quite likely that at times the regulatory policies which are quite different in nature and content may produce identical results in terms of safety of funds and value of money. On the other hand, the policies which are apparently similar may produce quite contradictory results and may have significantly different impact on insurance industry.

However, it may be pertinent to point out that to ensure complete foolproof solvency and financial stability of insurance companies at all the times and under all the circumstances may not be possible, whatever, may be the nature and intensity of the regulations. The aim, is to beep the risk of insolvency at the minimum level through the regulations. Of course, these regulations involve a cost both directly in terms of supervision cost and indirectly in terms of the structure of insurance industry that emerges out of these controls, the extent of competition amongst insurance firms and range of choice available to the consumers.

A view is also being held that insolvency of insurance company may not be that bad for the economy as it helps keeping the weak firms out of the industry and thereby helps in promoting healthy insurance environment. However, it has not been possible to quantify the tolerable level of risk of insolvency and the objective has been to keep the risk of insolvency as low as possible.

Instruments of Control

As mentioned above, different countries have evolved different forms of regulations to control the activities of the insurers. Broadly, the instruments used by the regulators may be classified as under:

1. Licensing: One of the basic and foremost element of regulation has been that no company is allowed to carry on insurance business without proper licensing or authorisation by the government or regulatory authority. The need to have license to enter insurance business is basically meant to ensure that only those companies enter in the industry which are financially sound and strong and have adequate managerial skill and expertise to conduct insurance business. While in some of the countries, the main eligibility factor for license may be minimum capital requirement while in others it could be availability of expertise to conduct insurance business or it could be both financial strength as well as managerial expertise. The details called in the licensing forms may include types of business company proposes to write, the nature of products, policy wordings, basis on which premium rates will be fixed up, the channels through which products will be sold, the quality of intermediaries it proposes to engage etc. It may also require the business plan and projections for coming three to five years, the staffing pattern, the management expenses, the extent of reinsurance, if required, the basis for establishing technical reserves. Basically, through licensing the government ensures that the firms proposing to enter insurance industry have required financial strength, possess required managerial expertise, are genuinely interested in insurance business, have clear conception about the products to be marketed, premium to be charged, marketing channels to be used etc. It ensures smooth and orderly growth of the industry.

2. Nature of Products: The regulations may extend to taking prior approval of the government before launching new products in the market. The argument advanced in favour of the above control is that the nature of product is one of the major factors protecting the interests of policyholders. The policy wordings, the perils covered under policy documents, the products already marketed by other companies for the identical perils etc. are quite crucial affecting the interests of the policyholders. However, there is difference of opinion as to whether the companies should have freedom to launch their products based upon their own judgements and calculations or these products should have prior approval of the regulator. Those who are against the above control argue that it goes against the principle of competition and liberalised economic environment. At times, it may prove to be counter-productive. However, a mid-way between these two extreme views may be worked out. The prior approval may be required only in respect of certain class of business such as in the case of general insurance it could be in respect of third party motor liability. The other way out could be to make it obligatory on the part of insurance companies to furnish detailed information about the product to the policyholders, intermediaries, media, consumer organisations, etc., before they are introduced in the market. Regulators may also restrict the requirement of prior approval only in respect of new companies or existing companies with poor track record.

3. Premium Rates: Another method of control used by regulators in some countries is the prior approval of the price of the product (premium rate) to be introduced in the market by the insurance companies. Similar to the controversy regarding prior approval of the regulator on the nature of the product, there are contradictory opinions regarding the desirability of controlling the premium rates by the regulator. The protagonist of this type of control argue that the premium rates charged by the insurer is a primary factor in determining their financial strength and solvency in future, which is crucial in protecting the interests of the policyholders. They argue that these companies, owing to fierce competition, may have a tendency to charge low premium rates which may not be able to cover their liabilities in future. They may tend to default paying the claim amount to the policyholders. On the other hand, there is also a possibility that few insurance companies may form their cartel and may start charging higher premium rates by assuming monopolistic or oligopolistic position in the market. It may warrant intervention by the regulator. Those opposed to above control have argued that it restricts the level of competition in the market and thereby adversely affects the interests of the consumers. The market forces of supply and demand should be allowed to operate to determine the price of the products which will be in the interest of both the insurer as well as the consumer. These decisions may be left to the dictate of the market. In respect of premium rates also several alternatives purported to achieve the same objective may be worked out. These could be making it obligatory on the part of insurance companies, through disclosure provisions, to divulge all the information concerning premium rates to the policyholders, consumer groups, media etc. The companies may also be required to produce certificate from qualified actuary that the proposed premium rates are based upon scientific and rational calculations. A via media could be approval of rates in respect of few selected class of business. Similarly, insurer may be required to inform in advance the price of product to the regulator before launching the product without requirement of taking prior approval and regulator may raise objections if price is found to be unreasonable.

4. Matching of Assets with Liabilities: One of the most important functions of the government is to ensure that insurance companies have adequate assets to meet their liabilities at any point of time at a short notice without any time lag. Insurance is a contract between an insurer and insured which binds the insurer to meet the losses of the insured's in future in consideration of the premium received by it. During the course of conducting insurance business, insurance companies accumulate large funds which they invest in market in different types of securities and build up their assets. These companies are supposed to invest their funds in those assets which are both safe and liquid. Within these two constraints, they are supposed to maximise their returns. Since the funds invested by the insurance companies belong to the policyholders, and the insurers are committed to meet the liabilities at extremely short notice, it is essential that at any point of time, assets held by these companies should match the liabilities. Assets should be such which could be converted into cash at short notice and the flow of investment income and maturity proceeds should be able to meet the cash outflow on a continuos basis. Although it may not be necessary to realise the value of all the assets immediately in one go, except in case the company is being wound up, but it is necessary that the nature and term of assets should be appropriate to the nature and term of liabilities. Insurers should avoid investing in undue risky assets and the value placed on assets should be fair and justifiable. In some countries, insurers are required to invest a proportion of their investible funds in government securities which are both safe and also enables the government to utilise the funds on projects of national importance.

For valuing the assets, different methods have been used. Broadly, these could be in terms of historical cost, written-down historical cost, amortised value, market value and market value with limitations. Each of these approaches to the valuation of assets has its own advantages and shortcomings and is being used depending upon the past practice followed in a country.

Normally, the method applied to value the assets has an important bearing on the way the liabilities of the companies are assessed. In case assets are valued in terms of passive approaches (historical cost) the methods applied to value the liabilities are also passive. It has also been found that as and when the assets are valued on market valuation basis, the liabilities are assessed on active approach basis.

Even if a specific approach to valuing the assets is followed, there is a wide scope for differences in the value of liabilities of an insurance company. While in some countries, regulatory authorities have specifically prescribed the method through which the liabilities should be valued, in others the decision have been left to the discretion of actuary or the directors of the company. The regulatory authorities may simply require that the valuation methodology to be adopted by these companies may be communicated in advance and may also be made public. This could be accomplished through disclosure norms.

One of the major parameters to assess the financial position of an insurance company is the provision made for all the outstanding liabilities. In case of general insurance companies, it would mean a reserve for unexpired risks, a reserve for unexpired risks including claims incurred but not reported (IBNR) and a reserve for the future expenses on settling claims and running of the current book of business.

In some of the countries, regulatory authorities may also require maintenance of equalisation reserves, which is a reserve to meet the possible losses that may occur in future while running the business.

For general insurance the calculation of reserves had been problematic. Since the claims under some class of business may be settled after a very long period of time, the regulatory bodies have left it to the wisdom of insurance companies to maintain the technical reserves based upon the past experience without any need to have certification from an actuary.

5. Solvency Margin: The maintenance of minimum level of solvency margin has, by and large, prescribed by regulatory authorities in all countries of the world. Although it has also been argued that when regulatory authorities lay down the methods of valuation of assets and liabilities and monitor matching of assets with liabilities, there may not be any need to prescribe the solvency margin to be maintained by insurance companies. However, solvency margin is one of the important tools at the disposal of regulatory authorities to ensure that the insurance companies do not turn out to be insolvent. In its simplest form, the solvency margin requirement may mean maintaining a particular level of capital which could be in the form of aggregate money terms. But now in most of the countries, the solvency margin requirement is in terms of the total free assets of the company as related to its liabilities created during the course of business operations. For instance in most of Western European countries, the solvency margin requirement is related to the size of the business operations and is not correlated to the specific risk to which the company is exposed to. In contrast in USA and Canada, the requirement is on the basis of risk-based capital which requires the companies to maintain the capital commensurate with the types of risks they are subjected to during its business operations.

In addition to serving the objective of reducing the risk of insolvency, the tool of solvency margin also helps the regulator to intervene in the affairs of the companies who are tending to become insolvent and sick. In case of deteriorating financial strength of a company as reflected by the fall in the level of solvency margin, regulatory authorities may direct the company to formulate a plan for restoration of its financial strength and rehabilitation.

6. Audit and Account: For efficient functioning of an insurance company, it is essential that its accounts and records are audited properly and in a fair manner and are well maintained. The value of assets and liabilities should also be assessed as per the sound accounting practices. Regulatory authorities may require insurance companies to get their accounts audited by the independent qualified auditor and to be certified by the directors of the company. In some countries, it has been made mandatory for a company to have a certificate from an actuary regarding adequacy of provisions and reserves. However, certification by actuary regarding adequacy of reserves and provisions is mainly in respect of life insurance companies rather than for general insurance companies. In case of general insurance companies, the decision of management is considered to be adequate. In some cases, regulator may also require a certificate from actuary regarding the value of liabilities of a company or it may need a complete certificate stating therein that the assets owned by a company are adequate to meet the liabilities of the company.

7. Appointment of Actuary: The appointment of actuary by a company may be made obligatory by the regulator.

The primary function of an actuary is to monitor the financial position of the company on a sustained basis. He or she is supposed to continuously investigate the matters such as adequacy of reserves to meet the liabilities, the level to which solvency margin requirements are met, the investment policy of the company, the new products being introduced and their price etc. Based upon these investigations, the actuary is supposed to keep informed the management and directors of the company and also to the regulator on a continuous basis. In some of the countries, the actuary may even directly report to the regulator. The management of the company is supposed to take corrective measures as recommended by the actuary, if so required.

8. Marketing Channels: The regulator may also supervise the marketing channels through which the companies sell their products. It may involve prescribing minimum qualifications and professional skill for intermediaries associated with these companies. Even the brokers may be required to obtain a licence before commencing their business. The commission for the brokers and other marketing agencies may be fixed up. However, it is subject to debate as to whether the companies should be left on their own to determine the commission and the marketing channels or they should be subjected to the directives of the regulator.

9. Professional Reporting: Although the companies may be required to produce certificates from auditor and the actuary, still the regulator may insist for a full professional report on the evaluation of technical reserves. The report may cover the aspects such as critical evaluation and analysis of data, examination of methodology for evaluating technical reserves, description of checks applied, assumptions made, results obtained, sensitivity analysis etc. In case of life insurance companies, the professional report may be prepared by the actuary while in case of general insurance it may be prepared by professionally competent individual. He or she may have to be professionally accountable for such report.

The professional report may be confined to reporting on technical reserves or it could be extended to reporting both the assets and liabilities of the company and commenting upon the adequacy of the assets to meet the liabilities. It may also be required to report upon the adequacy of capital and reserves for efficient running of the business.

10. Review of Balance Sheet by the Regulator: The regulator has to play an important role in analysing the balance sheet of the company and determine as to whether the technical reserves are adequate or not. The balance sheet is presented on an annual basis and normally it is made available after a sufficient time-lag after the end of the financial year. It takes time for the auditor to audit the accounts and prepare and certify the balance sheet of the company.

Regulator may require the report on a quarterly basis so as to get apprised about the financial position of the company. Of course, the quarterly report may be a statement of facts about the financial position of the company without being certified by the auditors. For assessment of financial position of the general insurance company, the regulator may require the detailed information regarding the pending claims class-wise and on time analysis basis. The information helps the regulator in estimating the liabilities which may arise in future for settling the pending claims. The regulator may hold discussions with the companies on the nature of business written and may advise them to take corrective measures to reduce the number of pending claims. The regulator may also require the companies to plan out reinsurance programme for meeting catastrophic losses arising from natural calamities such as earthquake, cyclones, windstorm etc. The regulator may also evaluate the likely future financial position of the companies and direct the companies accordingly. The evaluation may be based upon the study of the type of business being written by the company, the overhead expenses, the staffing pattern, management expenses etc.

11. Other Miscellaneous Controls: In addition to the approaches to the controls and regulations exercised by the regulator as mentioned above, the other methods of regulating insurance companies may be determination of division of surplus between policyholders and shareholders, regulating the merger of insurance companies, granting licence to the surveyors etc. The regulator may also have to intervene in case an insurance company is being wind up. The regulator will insure that the liabilities of the policyholders are met before the company closes down. The regulator may work out the formula for compensating the policyholders in case the company suffers losses due to reasons such as fraud, mismanagement, insolvency etc.

Part II

In this section an analysis has been made on the present status of insurance industry and role played by the Government in the growth of the sector in few developing and developed economies of Asia.

China

Chinese insurance industry offers more than 300 classes of insurance in almost all lines of business. The People's Insurance Company of China was established in 1949. Subsequently, two other nation-wide companies were set up in 1988 and 1991. The industry was opened up for the private sector in 1988 when first of non-state insurance company was set up. Accordingly, a number of foreign funded companies have obtained licences to start operations in the country. The new insurance law was adopted on 1st October, 1995, which prescribes guidelines for all insurance activities, both domestic and foreign. The People's Bank of China (PBOC), acting as China's Central Bank, is the state's supervisory authority. Presently all the insurance activities in China are controlled by the PBOC. Specific legislation is contained in the new insurance law for governing the insurance industry. The life business has completely been separated from the non-life business. The maximum registered and paid up capital for setting up an insurance industry is Yn 200 m per licence either life or non-life. All the insurance companies, whether national or of foreign origin are governed by the same law and regulations. After the establishment of an insurance company, 20 per cent of its registered capital has to be allocated to a guaranteed fund and deposited in a bank. The only compulsory insurance in China applies to all vehicles or public roads.

The solvency regulations require that the capital must amount to 25 per cent of premiums and individual cover may not exceed 10 per cent of capital and collateral. For a foreign company to acquire a license, it is necessary that it must have set up the representative office at least three years in advance. They are also given licence to conduct business operations in designated regions. The premium per capita (insurance density) was US $ 10.9 while it was US $ 4.7 for non-life business and US $ 6.2 for life business. The share of gross domestic product (insurance penetration) was 1.46 for the total business and it was 0.64 per cent and 0.82 per cent for non-life and life business respectively. The real growth rate of insurance industry amounted to 35.4 per cent in 1996-97. It was 0.7 per cent in non-life and 84.6 per cent in life side during the above year. It commanded 0.63 per cent of the total world market.

Indonesia

Indonesian economy is one of the largest amongst the developing countries and faces more or less the same problems which are being faced by Indian economy. The deregulation process in Indonesia started in 1970s and insurance sector was deregulated in 1983. The insurance market has been growing at the rate of about 25 per cent per annum. The real growth rate of insurance industry in 1996-97 amounted to 12.2 per cent and it was 6.1 per cent and 19.8 per cent for non-life and life business respectively. The share of total premium to the world premium was 0.12 per cent. The insurance penetration was 1.23 per cent of GDP, while it was 0.65 per cent for non-life business and 0.58 per cent for life business. Insurance penetration has tripled during the last 10 years. The insurance density was US $ 13.1 for the total insurance business and was US $ 6.9 and US $ 6.2 for non-life and life business respectively in 1997 (Swiss Recommendations. Sigma No. 311999).

The insurance commissioner is responsible for the registration, control and regulation of all insurance business. For non-life business, the minimum capital requirement is IDR 3 billion while for life side it is IDR 2 billion. The minimum paid up capital for foreign joint venture company is IDR 15 billion for non-life company and IDR 4.5 billion for life company. For joint venture company the paid up capital of foreign company could be up to 80 per cent. Minimum of 20 per cent of paid up capital must be held by a local company. The law requires that 20 per cent of the paid up capital should be placed in guarantee fund. The solvency margin requirements are that capital must amount to 10 per cent of net premiums in non-life business. There are about 98 non-life and 56 life companies in the insurance industry. The only compulsory insurance required by the Government is that of worker's combination with the national body. Even after 14 years of opening the sector, the local companies still hold about 83 per cent of the market share.

Malaysia

The average growth rate of premium in Malaysia had been about 18 per cent per annum during the last decade. The real growth rate of total insurance business was 7.9 per cent during 1996-97; for non-life business it was 4.4 per cent; and for life business it was 11.7 per cent. It commands 0.2 per cent of the world market. The insurance density was US $ 198.9 for the total insurance business while it was US $ 99.8 and US $ 99 for non-life and life business respectively in 1997. The insurance penetration was 4.37 per cent for the total business while for non-life and life it was 2.10 per cent and 2.18 per cent respectively during the above year. A total of about 18 companies are in insurance business covering about 25 per cent of the total population. The insurance industry is governed by insurance Act, 1963. The entire industry is governed by the Central Bank of Malaysia and the governor of the Central Bank acts as Director General of Insurance (DGI). The minimum capital requirement for obtaining licence is MYR 5 million or MYR 10 million for composite companies. The solvency margin requires a surplus of assets over liabilities of not less than M$ 5 million or 20 per cent of its net premium whichever is greater and M$ 10 million for composite insurers. Motor insurance and workers under the Workmen's Compensation Act 1952 are the compulsory insurances.

Philippines

The insurance industry of Philippines is relatively small and underdeveloped. About 15 per cent of the total population has been covered by insurance industry. The insurance density amounted to US$ 17.1 with density in non-life and life business being US$ 9.1 and US$ 8.0 in 1997 respectively. The insurance penetration was 1.5 per cent with non-life business accounting for 0.8 per cent and life business 0.71 per cent during the above year. The real growth rate for the entire insurance industry was 7.9 per cent during 1996-97. In non-life business it was 5.5 per cent, while for life business it was 10.5 per cent during the above year. The share of entire insurance industry in the world market was 0.06 per cent. The joint venture with foreign equity participation up to 100 per cent was permitted in 1994. Earlier foreign equity participation was limited to 40 per cent. There are a total of about 31 insurance companies, out of which 21 are domestic, 8 foreign companies and 2 are joint ventures. The insurance industry is governed by Insurance Code of 1978 and the insurance companies are governed and controlled by the office of the Insurance

Commissioner established under the Department of Finance of the Government. For obtaining licence to conduct insurance business, the company should have a minimum of PHP 50 m. if established before 1992 and PHP 100m if being set up after 1992, of which PHP 75 should be paid up capital. The solvency margin in respect of non-life insurance companies requires that the capital must at least be 10 per cent of net premiums and 50 per cent of capital must be invested in government bonds. Motor liability for bodily injury is the compulsory insurance under the law.

Japan

Japan has one of the most developed insurance sector in the world. The insurance density was as high as US$ 3896 for the total business and US$ 804 and US$ 3092 for non-life and life business respectively. The insurance penetration was as high as 11.87 per cent for the total business and 2.45 per cent for non-life and 9.42 per cent for the life business. The real growth rate of entire industry was 0.8 per cent in 1996-97, while in non-life and life business it was -4.0 and 2.1 per cent respectively. The share of the total insurance premium to the world premium was as high as 23.05 per cent; it was 11.29 per cent in non-life business and 31.61 per cent in life business. The entire insurance business is regulated under Insurance Business law, 1995. The insurance business is supervised by the Insurance Division of the Ministry of Finance. For obtaining a licence to conduct insurance business, the minimum capital requirement is JPY 30m. Under the new business Act, both foreign insurers and domestic companies receive the same treatment.

South Korea

The South Korean insurance industry has grown along with the growth of the economy in general and is one of the largest in the world. The premium per capita was US$ 1232.3, being US$ 303 for non-life and US$ 929.3 for life business. The premium as percentage of gross domestic product was as high as 15.42 for the total business and 2.45 per cent and 9.42 per cent for non-life business respectively. The insurance sector is regulated by the Ministry of Finance and Insurance Supervisory Board (ISB). The administration of insurance laws and issue of licence are under the direct control of Ministry of Finance. For obtaining a licence the minimum capital required is KRW 30 billion, and out of that 30 per cent is to be deposited with the Ministry of Finance. The real growth rate of insurance premium was 19.9 per cent in 1996-97; while it was 14.7 per cent and 21.6 per cent in non-life and life business respectively. The share of total premium of the country to the world business was 2.66 per cent.

Singapore

The open door policy towards foreign trade and investment has been responsible for spectacular growth of the economy including growth of insurance sector. The real growth rate of insurance premium during 1996-97 was 19.9 per cent and for non-life and life business it was 1.2 per cent and 28.1 per cent respectively. The share of country's premium to the total world premium amounted to 0.20 per cent. The insurance industry is regulated by the Insurance Commissioner's Department under the supervision of the Monetary Authority of Singapore (MAS), the de facto central bank of the country. The industry is guided by the Insurance Act, 1967. The minimum capital required for starting insurance company is S$ 1 million for a captive insurer, S$ 10 million for a reinsurer and S$ 5 million for other companies. The solvency margin of a non-life company should be highest of S$ 5 million or 50 per cent of net premium income or 50 per cent of the loss reserves of the fund. The solvency margin for a life company are at a lower level amounting to capital of S$ 1 million or 20 per cent of net premiums or 20 per cent of loss reserves. The motor business and workers covered under worker's compensation have to insure compulsorily under the law. The insurance industry is highly international in character and about three-quarters of direct insurers are foreign owned.

Thailand

The insurance industry in the country has been growing rapidly. The growth rate of non-life premium had been between 18 to 42 per cent on an annual basis. Between the year 1989 to 1994, the average growth rate of non-life premium amounted to about 29 per cent. The share of total (non-life and life) premium to the total world premium was 0.15 per cent in 1997. It was 0.18 per cent for non-life and 0.13 per cent for the life business. The insurance industry is controlled and supervised by the Department of Insurance under the Ministry of Commerce. For establishing an insurance company the minimum capital is THB 300 million for non-life and THB 500 million for life business. Further, for the existing non-life and life companies, the minimum capital is THB 30 million and THB 50 million respectively. The foreign companies are allowed to hold up to a maximum of 25 per cent of the equity capital. The solvency margin requires that capital should be at least 100 per cent of net premiums or at least THB 30 million.

Taiwan

Taiwan is one of the fastest growing countries amongst the developing economies. Along with the growth of the national income, there has also been rapid growth of insurance industry in the country. Despite being a small country, the premium of total insurance industry as percentage of world premium was 0.81 per cent. It was 0.53 per cent for non-life business and 1.01 per cent for life business. The insurance penetration in the country was 6.09 per cent, for non-life business it was 6.09 per cent and for life business 4.4 per cent. Per capita premium (insurance density) was as high as US$ 800 per capita premium in non-life business and life business was US$ 222 and US$ 578 respectively. The sector was opened to foreign insurers in 1986. An insurance company can be either domestic or foreign origin, but must be in the form of joint stock company, not a mutual company. The minimum capital required for starting an insurance company is TWD 2 billion, while for existing companies it is TWD 100 million. The entire control including issue of licence is exercised by the Department of Insurance of the Ministry of Finance. The solvency regulations require contribution of 0.1 per cent of gross premiums to guarantee fund.

Hong Kong

The economy of Hong Kong has grown very rapidly and so the insurance industry. Per capita premium for the industry as a whole was as high as US$ 945.1, while for non-life and life business it amounted to US$ 299.2 and US$ 646.3 respectively. The insurance premium as share of gross domestic product was 3.55 per cent and it was 1.12 and 2.43 per cent in non-life and life business respectively. The financial requirements for starting a new company amounts to HK$ 5 million. For companies writing composite or statutory business it is HK$ 16 million. The solvency margin as specified are 20 per cent of the first HK$ 100 million written, and 10 per cent of any excess premium. The supervision and control on the industry is exercised by the Insurance Authority established under the Insurance Companies Ordinance, 1983.

Competition and Growth Rate of Insurance Industry

The analysis of the growth experience of insurance industry in the above countries indicate that the deepening and widening of the insurance services are positively correlated to the degree of competition and the number of firms in the market. This is reflected through the parameters of insurance density and insurance penetration. In a closed and restricted market environment, the growth of insurance services slows down. The comparison of the growth rate of the insurance premium before and after the sector was opened up both for domestic and foreign companies clearly brings out the fact that there was substantial increase in growth rate after opening up the sector. The countries which have followed the open and liberalised policy right from the beginning have experienced quantum jump in the insurance services. The experience of Hong Kong, Singapore, Taiwan, Malaysia, Japan and South Korea indicates above trend. In small countries like Hong Kong, Singapore and Taiwan there are about 230, 150 and 29 companies respectively engaged in insurance business. The growth experience of these countries further reveals that the growth rate got accelerated after the sector was opened up to the foreign companies. These foreign companies with long experience brought with them innovative products, management expertise, better marketing channels, fund management techniques etc. The customers were ultimate beneficiaries in terms of wide range of products and competitive prices and choice to select the best amongst the large number of firms.

The average annual growth rate of insurance premium of the countries which liberalised the insurance sector and promoted competition through deregulation is given in Table 1.

Table 1: Average Annual Growth of Real Premium Volumes 1988-95 (per cent)

Country	Non-life	Life
China	8	20
Indonesia	11	23
Thailand	23	18
Malaysia	15	18
Taiwan	11	14
Singapore	10	25
South Korea	20	12

Source: Sigma/Swiss Re, 1996.

The identical trend emerges in Latin American economies which opened their sector to both domestic and foreign companies. There was phenomenal growth of insurance premium and its percentage in Gross Domestic Product (GDP) increased rapidly as is evident from Table 2.

Table 2: Insurance Density (Premium as % of GDP)

Country	1980	1990	1995
Argentina	1.7	1.8	1.7
Brazil	0.8	1.5	2.0
Chile	0.7	2.7	3.2
Mexico	0.7	1.2	1.5
Colombia	1.2	1.8	2.3

Source: Sigma/Swiss Re, 1995.

Another trend distinctly visible from the growth experience of these countries is that the growth was by and large higher in those countries where relatively less controls were imposed on insurance industry compared to those countries where there were large network of controls over the sector. Regulations and controls if pursued and imposed beyond a point may prove to be inhibitive and counter-productive.

Part III

In this section, the controls and regulations as exercised by the government and regulatory authority on Indian insurance industry have been examined.

The Indian insurance industry is governed by Insurance Act, 1938, General Insurance Business (Nationalisation) Act, 1972, Life Insurance Corporation Act, 1956 and Insurance Regulatory and Development Authority Act, 1999 (IRDA, 1999).

General Insurance industry is guided by all the above acts except the Life Insurance Corporation Act, 1956 which is specifically meant for life business. Indian insurance industry has recently been opened up for private companies, both domestic and foreign. The opening of the sector has been facilitated through IRDA which under its third schedule amended section 24 of the General Insurance Business (Nationalisation) Act, 1972. The above section had given exclusive privilege to the Government companies to carry out general insurance business.

In the state of monopoly environment, there was one holding company known as General Insurance Corporation of India and its four subsidiaries known as National Insurance Co., New India Assurance Co., Oriental Insurance Co., and United India Insurance Co.

As per section 7(a) of Insurance Act, 1938 the general insurance business may be carried out only by an Indian Insurance Company which is formed and registered under the Companies Act, 1956 and in which the aggregate holdings of equity shares by a foreign company either by itself or through its subsidiary companies or its nominees, domestic not exceed 26 per cent paid up equity capital of such Indian insurance company.

The capital requirement for starting a general or life insurance company is equity paid-up capital of Rs. 100 crore and for starting reinsurance company it is Rs. 200 crore. The solvency margin requirement have been laid down in Section 64VA of the Act. It has been stated that the required solvency margin shall be the highest of the following : (a) Rs. 50 crore (Rs. 100 crore in case of reinsurer); or (b) a sum equivalent to 25 per cent of the premium income; or (c) a sum equivalent to 30 per cent of net incurred claims.

The supervisory control or insurance companies is exercised by Insurance Development and Regulatory Authority (IRDA) and these powers flow from Insurance Act, 1938 as well as from IRDA Act, 1999. IRDA Act 1999 states:

"Subject to the provisions of this Act and any other law for the time being in force, the Authority shall have the duty to regulate, promote and ensure orderly growth of insurance business and reinsurance business." Regulatory and supervisory powers of the authority are wide and pervasive. Basically these could be summarised as under:

1. Registration/Licensing

Any company proposing to enter in the insurance business has to apply to the authority for registration certificate. The authority has the powers to issue the licence subject to its satisfaction that the proposed company is financially sound and has the managerial expertise to run the business. The authority has also got the powers to renew it, modify it or even suspend and cancel such registration.

2. Product and its Pricing

The authority shall be satisfied about the nature of the product and its pricing before it is placed for marketing amongst the consumers. The powers to control the price of the product is in addition to the premium rates which are fixed by the Tariff Advisory Committee (TAC) constituted under section 64U of Insurance Act, 1938. Chairman of the authority is also ex-officio Chairman of TAC. The authority should also be satisfied with the terms and conditions mentioned in the policy documents.

3. Investment of Funds

The investment policy of the insurance companies is governed by the broad guidelines framed by the authority. It may direct the insurer to invest certain proportion of their funds in specified securities. For instance, the present directives are that general insurance companies have to invest minimum of 30 per cent of their funds in government securities and 15 per cent in housing projects including purchase of fire fighting equipments by state governments. Only 55 per cent of the funds may be invested in market securities and amongst market securities only in approved securities.

4. Solvency Margin

The authority has to ensure that insurers maintain the solvency margin as laid down in the Act. In case companies fail to comply to solvency margin requirements, authority can initiate disciplinary action against the defaulting companies.

5. Appointment of Actuary

As per the directives of the authority, it is mandatory for insurer to appoint an actuary. The qualifications of actuary have been laid down. The functions and duties of actuary have been prescribed by the authority.

6. Appointment to Chief Executive/Managing Director

It is obligatory on the part of insurance companies to take prior approval of the authority before appointing chief executive, managing director or whole time director in the company. The authority has also been vested with the power to remove any managerial person and also appoint any additional director in the company, if so desired.

7. Power of Investigation and Inspection

The authority can institute any inquiry against the insurer to investigate the affairs of the company and for this purpose can appoint any person as investigator. Based upon the report, authority can take disciplinary action against the insurer including suspension of its registration.

8. Accounts, Balance Sheets

The insurers are required to prepare a balance sheet, a profit and loss account, a separate account of receipts and payments and a revenue account in respect of each class of business. These are to be audited by a qualified auditor.

9. Intermediaries

The authority shall also monitor the activities of intermediaries who are being engaged by the insurers to market their products. The licence to the agents will be issued by the authority. As and when brokers are allowed to operate, they will also have to obtain the licence from the authority.

10. Surveyors and Loss Assessors

The qualifications for surveyors to be eligible to obtain a licence are prescribed by the authority. Their licences are also being issued by the authority.

11. Reinsurance

Reinsurance programmes of insurance companies are being monitored by the authority on a continuous basis. As per the directives of the authority, insurance companies are required to cede a part of their premium income to designated Indian reinsurer. Insurers are supposed to keep authority apprised about their insurance programme, both outward and inward, and seek authority's approval.

Conclusion

The nature of insurance industry is slightly different compared to other manufacturing and service industries. The stages in operations of insurance services involve conceiving and designing a product, determining its price, publishing it amongst consumers, launching it in the market through network of intermediaries, collecting the premium and building up reserve of funds, creating liabilities to meet the losses of consumers and investing the funds in the market. The fundamental difference between insurance products and other product is that while in the insurance products consumer's interests are actively involved even after the sale of the products since their liabilities have to be met by the insurer, no such consumer's interests are involved in other products. The activities carried out by insurance companies even after sale of products are of crucial importance from consumer's point of view as these companies are contractually bound to compensate for the potential losses to the consumers that may arise in future. The funds at the disposal of insurers are essentially policyholders' (consumers) funds. The misuse and mismanagement of these funds may result into failure on the part of insurers to fulfil their liabilities and consequent loss to the consumers. In other products, once the products have been sold the only commitment on the part of seller may be to ensure efficient and expeditious after-sales services. From this angle, the insurance products are placed on a different platform. It warrants some control in one or other form on the activities of the insurers so that consumer's interests are properly protected and are not sacrificed.

However, opinions differ on extent and intensity of control that should be exercised by the government or its representative. In most of the countries, plethora of controls and regulations have been imposed on insurance sector. These range from issuing of licence to approving the nature and pricing of products, location of business activities, appointment to the top managerial positions, regulating activities of intermediaries and loss assessors, supervising investment of funds, inspecting balance sheet and books of accounts, monitoring solvency margin requirements, framing policies on reinsurance operations etc.

Is it necessary to have such wide network of regulations and constraint the insurers with these laws and rules so as to prevent them from taking independent decisions based upon market forces? Will these regulations not prove to be counter productive and harm the interests of the very consumers whose interests are supposed to be protected through these regulations? Is it not possible to achieve the objective of protecting the interests of consumers through macro level management and policies without interfering in the micro level management of insurance companies and leaving to the dictates of market forces?

An objective analysis of these issues reveals that in most of the countries, insurance industry has not been allowed to operate in a free and competitive environment and is saddled with avoidable restrictions. Take for instance, the regulation relating to the nature of products and its pricing. In a market-oriented economy, it is left to the producers to produce and supply the products as per their own wisdom, which in turn is based upon the consumer's tastes and preferences and feed back from the market. Products which do not match consumer's tastes and demand will not be able to last longer in the market and will vanish automatically. Similarly, prices of products should be allowed to be determined by the market forces and through the interplay of supply and demand. The supply function takes care of cost of production. As such in most of the countries, insurance companies are required to compulsorily engage the services of actuaries to carry out the costing of the products. Insurers charging higher or lower than the market determined prices will not be able to survive long in the industry. In case of fixing higher prices for the products, insurer would loose the market and in case of putting lower prices, the incurring underwriting losses will force the firm to close down its operations.

Thus, the market forces are the best judge to determine as to which are the best products in the interests of consumers and what should be their optimum price. The government or the regulatory authority may not be the best judge to evaluate the quality of products and their price structure. It may also be short of expertise to evaluate the quality of hundreds of products and their prices which might be offered by the insurance companies in the market.

Take another area of investment of funds by insurance companies. Here again, there appears to be no need to prescribe investment norms and direct the insurers to invest their funds in specified securities. Let the market forces be allowed to operate and determine the flow of funds in those securities which are high yielding as well as liquid and safe. The companies as per their business requirements may be allowed to carry out their financial planning and build up their equity portfolio based upon sophisticated mathematical models. Of course, the assets should be valued as per the prescribed norms and methodology to be certified by an auditor. The firms mismanaging their funds and investing them in unsafe and unsound assets will find it difficult to maintain solvency margin which is being monitored by the government and may warrant punitive action.

Another area meriting attention is the prior approval of the government for appointment to the top executive posts in the company. The promoters of the company blocking their huge funds are the best judge to constitute the team of management personnel to efficiently run the affairs of the company. In case the management team is inefficient and fails to deliver the goods, it would adversely affect the turnover and profitability of the company warranting its replacement. The ultimate signal is given by the market.

In case of marketing of products, the insurers may be given the freedom to deploy whatever marketing channels and force they desire in the best interests of the company. It is obvious that the forces of competition will induce these companies to make use of best of marketing personnel and agencies, otherwise their survival in the industry will be in danger. Even the requirement of licensing of brokers appears to be unwarranted in a matured economy. In so far as the loss assessors are concerned, prescribing essential qualifications to act as a surveyor may be reasonable requirement and their associations may be promoted to issue the required certificate. The responsibility to upgrade their skill and observing certain code of conduct may be entrusted to these associations. In respect of reinsurance, government may make it obligatory on the part of these companies to cede certain proportion of their premium income to national reinsurer. It may also be made mandatory that not more than certain proportion of total premium income be reinsured in foreign markets. There may not be any requirement to get the approval of the government for the reinsurers with whom business is proposed to be placed.

The primary objective behind these regulations is to ensure financial strength of these companies so that the interests of policyholders are protected. The objective could efficiently be achieved through macro level policies and management. These companies may also be encouraged to observe self-discipline and code of conduct. For instance, strict compliance to maintain solvency margin will itself ensure healthy financial strength of these companies. The method of disclosure norms may extensively be used and enforced with legislative backing. It may be made obligatory on the part of these companies to disclose and make public information relating to nature of products proposed to be launched, the methodology used to arrive at their prices, the likely claim ratio, their equity portfolio, management expenses, investment income and yield, underwriting results etc. to the consumers and to the media so that based upon the above information, consumers may take a decision regarding the products to be purchased and company with whom they want to have the dealings. That would infuse element of transparency in insurance business. For investment, macro management may include making it obligatory on the part of insurers to invest in the assets of only those companies which have secured high rating from reputed credit rating agencies. Government may frame strict regulations to prevent formation of cartels by these companies and indulging in restrictive trade practices. The objective of protecting the interests of consumers may well be achieved through these macro management policies without any need to resort to regulating micro level activities of these companies. It has been general experience of most of the countries including India that controls lead to corruption and delays resulting into inefficiency and increased cost of production. By and large, the decision as to what products should be produced, how they should be produced, when to be produced, where to be produced and for whom to be produced may be left to the dictates of marketing forces.

3
Growth of General Insurance Industry in India

D.C. Srivastava and Shashank Srivastava

The present paper attempts to review the growth of general insurance in India over a period of time, examine its distinguishing features, trace its growth in different class of business, review claim experience and analyse its potential over a period of time, in a competitive environment.

The paper has been divided into four parts. Part I traces its growth in historical background, Part II deals with its main characteristics, Part III brings out its growth in terms of sectoral development, classwise division of business and their respective claim ratio, underwriting experience, profitability etc. and Part IV sets out the areas of future growth as well challenges in a liberalised economic environment.

Part I

The concept of general insurance is linked with the human urge to protect and secure ones goods and property in different forms against known perils. With the growth of industry, trade and commerce the insurance also grew over a period of time and gained maturity. Historically the growth of general insurance in its crudest form may be traced back to 14th century in Italy when ships carrying goods were covered against different known perils. From there it gradually entered UK when ships and goods transacted through it used to be covered against frequent perils. Thus, the first known form of general insurance was in marine portfolio. It scientifically developed in UK at Lloyd's coffee-house in Tower Street, London. Edward Lloyd was the owner of the coffee-house. The coffee-house used to be meeting place for merchants, bankers, captains and seafarers. During these coffee sessions they used to discuss various problems and risks involved in marine transaction of goods and services. Individual merchants gradually started adopting marine risks, which culminated into present form of insurance. Subsequently Lloyd's Act was formed facilitating other forms of insurance business.

Presently, Lloyd's is the largest underwriter in the world. Lloyd's Registrar of shipping is still most reliable and dependable source of information. It is one of the largest source of shipping and reinsurance information in the world.

In the context of the growth of general insurance over a period of time, it may be defined as a contract between the insurer and insured whereby insurer covers insured perils in lieu of mutually agreed upon premium paid by the insured. It is primarily based upon the principle of sharing of losses of few by many. From this angle, a large base of insured population is always beneficial in terms of competitive premium rates.

In India, general insurance was brought by Britishers. Their operation was through agencies. The Triton Insurance Company Ltd. was the first general insurance company established in India in 1858 at Kolkata. It was totally British owned company and its share were held by them. The first general insurance company to be set up by Indian was Indian Mercantile Insurance Company Ltd. in Mumbai in 1907. It was to transact all types of general insurance business. Thereafter, a large number of both Indian and foreign insurance companies were set up in the country. However, till independence as much as 40% of the insurance business was held by foreigners mainly Britishers.

With the setting up a large number of insurance companies, it was felt that there should be a code of conduct to be followed by these companies in order to ensure fair and sound business and prevent unethical practices. As a result Insurance Association of India through its General Insurance Council framed a code of conduct, which was to be administered by the Controller of Insurance. Its head office was located at Delhi with branch offices at Mumbai, Kolkata and Chennai. Further, the need was also felt to retain maximum business in India. To achieve the above objective, Indian Reinsurance Corporation was established in 1956. All the insurance companies voluntarily decided to cede 10% of their gross direct premium to the above Corporation. In 1961 the Govt. constituted Indian Guarantee and General Insurance Company Ltd. as a Govt. owned reinsurance Company, which coexisted along with Indian Reinsurance Corporation. The insurance companies were required to cede 10% of their premium to each of these two companies. In addition, insurers established two other organisations namely Fire Insurance Pool and the Marine Insurance Pool and a percentage of companies fire and hull insurance business was ceded to these pools respectively. The business ceded to these pools was retroceded to the ceding companies thereby ensuring the spread of risks amongst the members of pools.

In 1968, the insurance Act, 1938 was amended which empowered the controller of Insurance to regulate deployment of assets, provide for maximum solvency margin, issue licenses to surveyors, investigate, search and seize their books of accounts etc. The amendment also facilitated setting up of Tariff Advisory Committee to be chaired by the Controller of Insurance. Its functions comprised of controlling and regulating rates, terms and advantages of General Insurance business in India.

After independence, under the planned development of the company, the Govt. came to the conclusion that a strong public sector under its direct control will be able to meet national objectives of growth, equity, resource mobilisation, employment generation etc. The financial sector was construed as one of the strategic sector capable of mobilising resources and placing it at the disposal of the Govt. for being invested as per the planned priorities. In pursuance to the above objective, life insurance was nationalised in 1956, and banking sector in 1969.

The General Insurance business was nationalized with effect from January 1, 1973, through the General Insurance business (Nationalization) Act 1972. However, as a prelude to the above act, the Govt. took over the management of all the operating companies in 1971, through General Insurance (Emergency provision) Act 1971. The emergency act provided for the appointment of custodians who were empowered to exercise controls over these companies subject to the directions of the Central Govt. At the time of nationalization of these companies, there were a total of 107 companies underwriting general insurance business in India. All these companies were amalgamated and grouped into four namely the National Insurance Company Limited, the New India Assurance Company Limited, the Oriental Insurance Company Limited, and the United India Insurance Company Limited with head offices at Kolkata, Mumbai, Delhi and Chennai respectively. The General Insurance Company (GIC) was formed as a holding company in November 1972. The GIC was constituted for the purpose of superintending, controlling and carrying out the business of general insurance. The entire capital of GIC was subscribed by the Government and that of four companies by the GIC on behalf of the Government of India.

The main objectives of nationalisation were to ensure the development of the general insurance business in sympathy with the best of interest and advantage to the community. Further, these companies were required to promote competition in the economy and to prevent the concentration of wealth and growth of monopoly. They were supposed to widely spread their activities over geographical area, innovate new products as per the requirements of different segments of population and also meet social objectives through formulating polices for weaker sections of society. The functions of GIC as laid down in the act were:

1. Carrying on of any part of general insurance business, if it thinks desirable to do so;

2. Aiding, assisting and advising the acquiring companies in the matter of setting up of standards of conduct and sound practice in general insurance business and in the matter of rendering efficient service to holders of policies of general insurance;

3. Advising the general insurance companies in the matter of controlling their expenses including the payment of commission and other expenses;

4. Advising the acquiring companies in the matter of investment of their funds;

5. Issuing direction to acquiring companies in relation to the conduct of the general insurance business.

Part II

In this section of the article, the pre-requisite conditions for conducting general insurance business, and its distinguishing features have been discussed:

The general insurance business is based upon certain pre-conditions [1] which need to be present for its healthy and sound growth. These are:

1. Insurance Interest.
2. Indemnity.
3. Utmost good faith.
4. Proximate cause.

A brief about these conditions is given as under:

Insurance Interest

For conduct of general insurance, the insured should have insurable interest in the property that he proposes to ensure. It would basically mean that first, there has to be property capable of being insured, second the proposed property should be subject matter of insurance, and third the insured should have legal relation with the property to be insured, which may be through different ways such as ownership, mortgage, trustee, lessee etc.

Indemnity

The indemnity objective is basically based upon the principle that the insured does not make any profit originating from insurance operations. He is supposed to be placed in the identical financial position as he was before the occurrence of insurance peril. However, in case of marine insurance the indemnity is determined by the mutual agreement between insurers and insured as provided in the Marine Insurance Act, 1963. Further, in case of personal accidents, it is not possible to place a value on life. The indemnification is normally facilitated through following four methods. These are:

1. Cash payment.
2. Repair.
3. Replacement.
4. Reinstatement.

It may also be mentioned that all contracts of indemnity are based upon the principles of subrogation and contribution. The principle of subrogation entitles the insurer to all the powers to recover the loss from the third party after the loss has been paid for. The principle of contribution implies that the payment to the insured by the insurer is limited to the extent it was insured with a particular insurer. It prevents emergence of profit by insured in insurance operations.

Utmost Good Faith

The general insurance is based upon the fact that the insured discloses all the relevant facts about the property/object to be insured in good faith without any concealment. Based upon the above information the insurer decides as to whether it is worth ensuring as well as the premium rates, terms and conditions of the policy.

Proximate Cause

The contact between insurer and insured is in respect of covering specific perils, which are laid down in the policy documents. The insurer is liable to pay only against such specified perils and not against, those not covered in policy documents.

Unique Features

The general insurance is characterized by certain unique features, which distinguishes it from other forms of financial services. Mukherjee [2] has very clearly spelled out the following four conditions of general insurance, which places it in different category as compared to other financial services.

Firstly, the general insurance is a contingency oriented activity and unlike other financial services, there is no guaranteed return from the general insurance operation. The insured is paid only when the insured peril has occurred during the period of insurance policy.

Secondly, there are limits to insurability meaning thereby that the capacity of insurer is positively correlated to the units of insured exposed to similar contingency/peril. The larger, the number, the spread of risk is wider with favorable impact on a premium rates.

Thirdly, the cost price of the product i.e. premium cannot be determined before the sale of the insurance product. Since the claims arise only after the sale of the product, the optimum price of insurance products can only be determined after a time lag based upon the past experience.

Fourthly, since the actual claim cost is uncertain and cannot be pre-conceived, there is always the possibility that the amount to be paid as claim may exceed the provisions made for the same. It may cause financial strain on these companies. It, therefore, necessitates sound financial position and solvency of insurance companies on a sustained basis.

Part III

Growth of General Insurance

The growth of general insurance over a period of time could be evaluated in terms of parameters such as growth of gross and net premium, geographical spread of the business, class wise distribution of business, underwriting results, reinsurance operations, investment income, free and technical reserves, net worth, overall profitability etc. The overall claim ratio expenses on management may also be examined. In this section, growth of the general insurance has been examined in the context of the above parameters. Based upon the data as given in Table 1 the following picture emerges.

1. The gross domestic premium income in India (GDPI), which was Rs.184 crore in 1973, has increased to Rs. 9522 crore in 1999-2000, recording an average growth rate of about 16.90%. The premium income originating outside India went up over the level of Rs. 24 crore in 1973 to Rs. 460 crore in 1999-2000, registering annual growth rate of about 11.95%. The total gross premium income, which was Rs. 208 crore in 1973, stood at Rs. 9,982 crore in 1999-2000, recording average annual growth rate of about 16.50%. The total net premium income increased to Rs. 9364 crore from the level of Rs. 222 crore in 1973. It recorded average annual growth rate of about 15.75%. The net premium income as percentage to total premium income was 93.8% in 1999-2000, indicating that only about 7% of GDPI went outside the country through reinsurance. As

Growth of General Insurance Industry in India

Table 1 : Performance of the General Insurance Industry in India (Rs. crore)

	1973	1989-90	1990-91	1991-92	1992-93	1993-94	1994-95	1995-96	1996-97	1997-98	1998-99	1999-2000
Paid up Capital	37	168	268	268	268	375	375	375	375	375	375	375
Gross premium written direct in India	184	2175	2796	3287	3792	4449	4959	6047	7021	7736	8759	9522
Gross Premium Outside India	24	104	117	216	278	317	312	330	327	350	399	460
Total Gross Premium	208	2279	2913	3503	4070	4766	5271	6377	7348	8086	9158	9982
(% increase)	--	21.3%	27.8%	20.3%	16.2%	17.1%	10.6%	21.0%	15.2%	10.0%	13.3%	9.01%
Net Premium in India	--	1909	2419	2945	3284	3681	4102	5087	6041	6725	7732	8648
Net Premium Outside India	--	277	323	505	584	746	777	869	693	632	670	716
Total Net Premium	222	2186	2742	3450	3868	4427	4879	5956	6734	7357	8402	9364
Underwriting Profit	18	-119	-118	-77	-119	81	-705	-646	-628	-384	-687	-1215
Profit Before Tax	38	371	482	669	779	1082	503	831	1084	1623	1467	1152
Income Tax paid	21	114	148	241	276	411	126	280	365	368	390	278
Net Profit	14	258	334	428	503	670	377	551	721	1255	1077	874
Investment Income	21	449	566	752	859	957	1150	1475	1697	1978	2220	2392

Source: Annual Reports of GIC.

compared to 1973, the GDPI in India has grown by about 47 times. This is depicted in Figure 1.

2. The net claim payable were at Rs. 7,586 crore in 1999-2000 as against Rs.1,123 crore in 1973, accounting for 81% to net premium.

3. The expenses including management expenses, commission and other outgo which were Rs. 68 crore in 1973 increased to Rs. 2,510 crore in 1999-2000. It constituted 31% and 27% of net premium income in 1973 and 1999-2000 respectively.

4. The expenses of the management increased from Rs. 43 crore in 1973 to Rs. 2,264 crore in 1999-2000. It amounted to 22.7% of gross premium income and 24.1% of net premium.

5. The total investment increased from Rs. 355 crore in 1973 to Rs.16,659 crore in 1999-2000. It grew by about 47 times. The compound annual growth in investible funds was about 17%. The investment income increased from Rs. 21 crore in 1973 to Rs. 2,392 crore in 1999-2000. The average annual gross yield on mean funds amounted to about 13%.

6. The paid up capital and free reserves increased from Rs. 34 crore and 62 crore in 1973 to Rs. 375 and Rs. 7,745 crore in 1999-2000 respectively. The increase in reserve for unexpired risk which was Rs. 23 crore in 1973 increased to Rs. 485 crore in 1999-2000.

7. In so for the class wise distribution of business is concerned, the fire, miscellaneous and marine accounted for 24%, 66%, and 10% in 1999-2000 respectively. The net incurred claim ratios were 41%, 99% and 70% in fire, miscellaneous and marine business in 1999-2000 respectively. In miscellaneous portfolio, motor business, which is a loss making business has steadily grown over a period of time and accounted for about 32% of the total business of the industry. However, this is in consonance with the world wide trend since in most of the countries of the world motor business was more than 30% of the total business. For instance, it was about 63, 56 and 54 percent in Thailand, Malaysia and Taiwan respectively (Figures 2 and 3).

8. The geographical spread of the premium written in India indicates that the maximum, i.e. about 40% was generated from western region and minimum i.e. about 9% from the eastern region. The northern and southern region contributed about 26% and 24% of gross premium in 1999-2000 respectively.

Growth of General Insurance Industry in India 73

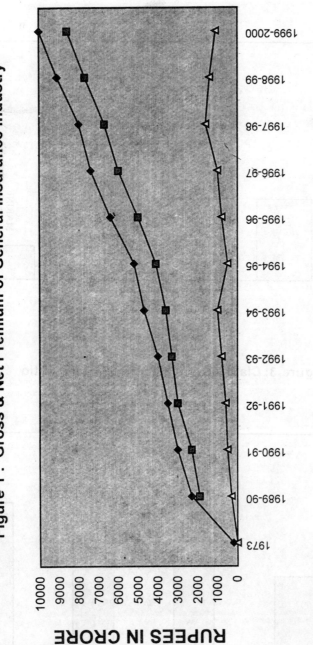

Figure 1 : Gross & Net Premium of General Insurance Industry

74 Indian Insurance Industry: Transition and Prospects

Figure 2: Classwise Distribution of General Insurance Business

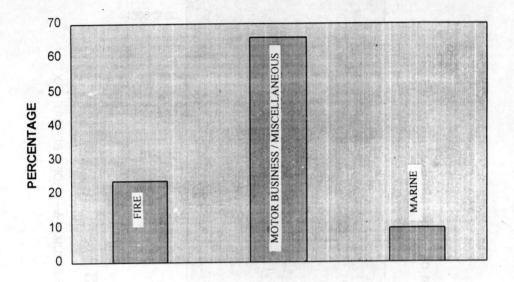

Figure 3: Classwise Net Incurred Claim Ratio

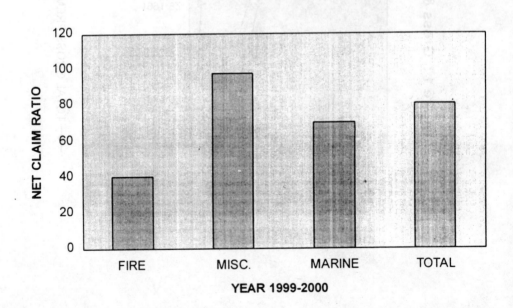

9. The underwriting profit of the industry was Rs.18 crore (8.2% of the net premium) in 1973. However, over a period of time underwriting operations have resulted into losses and these losses amounted to Rs. 1,215 crore in 1999-2000, accounting for 13% of net premium income.

10. The investment income amounting to Rs. 2,392 crore was in excess of underwriting losses and produced profit for the industry. The level of profit was Rs. 1,153 crore before tax payment and Rs. 874 crore after tax payment. In 1973 the profit before tax and after tax were Rs. 38 crore and Rs.14 crore respectively (Reference Figure 1).

11. Although the total number of insurance products in the general insurance industry are around 175, only a few i.e. 40 to 50 products have dominated the market controlling about 75 to 80% of the total market. Rest of the products have not been popular as they lack mass base, may be due to poor publicity and marketing, lack of awareness, higher premium rates, and might have been introduced without adequate database.

12. The rural and non-traditional business, which was practically nil in 1973, has gradually increased over a period of time. The premium collected through this business was only about Rs. 425 crore in 1999-2000, constituting only 4% of the total gross premium income. It calls for innovating new products for the rural population suiting to different income groups and marketing them aggressively. However, if the total policies issued by office in rural areas are taken into account, the premium from rural areas will account for about 30%.

13. The reinsurance operation of the industry indicate that the total reinsurance premium was Rs. 1,011 crore in 1997-98, accounting for about 13% of the gross premium. It indicates that about 87% of the premium was retained in the country. The operations between 1990-91 to 1997-98 reveal that the retention was about 85.5% of the gross premium. Further break up of reinsurance premium indicates that about 45% is required for placement of large projects and specialised risk on facultative basis and another 45% is for the surplus treaties, which is necessary to create capacity. The cost of reinsurance reveals that in 1997-98 while the commission earned was Rs. 271 crore

(3.5% of GDP), the claim recoveries were Rs. 557 crore (7.2% of GDP), accounting for a total of Rs. 828 crore. It amounted to 10.7% of GDP against the reinsurance premium of Rs. 1011 crore. Thus, the net outflow of premium works out to be Rs. 183 crore which may be termed as net cost of reinsurance, accounting for 2.4% of GDP. For the years between 1990-91 to 1998-99, the average total reinsurance cost, commission earned, claim recovery and net cost of reinsurance as percentage of GDP works out to be 14.5%, 3.5%, 7.9% and 3.1% respectively (Table 2).

In so far as the inward reinsurance business is concerned, in 1996-97, the total premium earned was Rs. 374 crore (5.3% of GDP), the commission paid was Rs. 124 crore (1.7% of GDP) and the balance resulted into net outflow of Rs. 81 crore (1.1% of GDP).

14. The general insurance industry has operations in 30 countries. Out of these in 16 countries it is operating directly and in 14 countries through subsidiary and associated companies. During 1999-2000, the total gross and net premium income from business operations in these countries were Rs. 488.76 crore and Rs. 440.36 crore respectively. The net claim during the year amounted to Rs. 288.19 crore amounting to 65.7% of the net premium.

Despite the fact that the industry has grown after nationalisation in terms of premium income, introduction of new products, wide coverage of individuals and organisations, innovating new covers for weaker sections of society, investment in social sectors, creating infrastructure at grassroots level etc., several weaknesses have also come to surface during these years of operation. These are :
1. Low level of insurance penetration.
2. Low level of insurance density.
3. Poor quality of insurance services.
4. Lack of qualitative and quantitative insurance products.
5. Low productivity.
6. Inadequate application of information technology.

Each of these issue has been covered in the following section.

Insurance Penetration

Despite the growth of gross domestic premium by 47 times between 1973 to 1999-2000, the insurance penetration defined as

Table 2
(a) General Insurance Industry: Reinsurance Business

(Rs. crore)

Year	Gross premium (GDP)	Reinsurance cost	% to GDP	Commission as % of GDP	Claim recovery as % of GDP	Net cost as % of GDP
(1)	(2)	(3)	(4)	(5)	(6)	(7)
1990-91	2796	376	13.5	3.0	12.9	2.4
1991-92	3287	342	10.4	2.8	10.0	
1992-93	3792	508	13.4	3.7	4.7	5.0
1993-94	4449	768	17.3	4.0	12.7	0.6
1994-95	4959	857	17.3	4.2	6.5	6.6
1995-96	6047	961	15.9	3.5	8.4	4.0
1996-97	7021	981	14.0	3.1	5.1	5.8
1997-98	7736	1011	13.1	3.5	7.2	2.4
Total	**40087**	**5804**	**14.5**	**3.5**	**7.9**	**3.1**

Contd...

(b) Inward Insurance Programme

(Rs. crore)

Year	Premium	Commission	Claims	Balance
(1)	(2)	(3)	(4)	(5)
1994-95	506	145	571	-210
1995-96	586	174	390	22
1996-97	374	124	331	- 81

+ = Balance due from reinsurance
- = Balance due to reinsurance

Source : Compiled from various documents.

insurance premium as share of gross domestic product, was as low as 0.56% in non-life business in 1997. The life side accounted for 1.39% and the total penetration being 1.95%. It was as high as 4.64% and 4.53% for non-life side in USA and Newzealand respectively. The average for Asia was 1.90% while for the world it was 3.06%. Even amongst the developing economies and other East Asian Countries, the Indian insurance industry lagged far behind in this area. For instance it was 3.79% for South Korea, 2.45% for Japan, 1.69% for Taiwan, 2.19% for Malaysia, 1.31% for Singapore, and 1.22% for Thailand. Low insurance penetration is pointer to the fact that spread of insurance business has relatively been poorer in the country and large section of insurable population is still isolated from the insurance coverage (Figure 4/Table 3).

Insurance Density

Another parameter to measure the spread of insurance is the insurance density defined as premium per capita. The available data indicate that in 1997 for non-life side, it was US dollar 2.2. The total being US dollar 7.6, the life side accounting for US dollar 5.4, It was as high as US dollar 1403.7 in USA and US dollar 1296.6 in Switzerland. It was US dollar 176.8 for the world as a whole and 46.4 for Asia. Insurance density in the country was low even as compared to several developing countries. It was US dollar 338.3 in Singapore, US dollar 303 in South Korea, US dollar 299.2 in Hong Kong, US dollar 222.1 in Taiwan, US dollar 99.8 in Malaysia, US dollar 26.3 in Thailand, and US dollar 6.91 in Indonesia. It was as high as US dollar 804 in Japan. Most of the African countries were also ahead of India in this respect. Although insurance density is positively correlated to the per capita income which is quite low in India, but what surprises is that the insurance density is lower even compared to several developing countries whose per capita income is even lower than India. The low insurance density and penetration are also partly due to lack of awareness on the part of general masses regarding the benefits flowing from the insurance in improving their standard of living and welfare (Figure 5/Table 4).

80 Indian Insurance Industry: Transition and Prospects

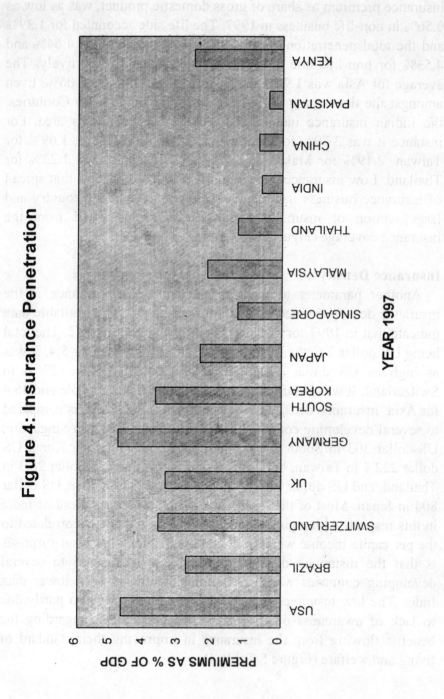

Table 3: Insurance Penetration (Premiums as Percentage of Gross Domestic Product) 1997

Country	Total business	Non-life	Life
North America			
USA	8.49	4.64	3.85
Canada	7.37	4.30	3.07
Latin America			
Argentina	1.77	1.21	0.56
Brazil	2.12	1.74	0.39
Mexico	1.29	0.79	0.50
Europe			
Switzerland	11.94	3.61	8.33
United Kingdom	11.22	3.34	7.87
France	9.25	2.91	6.34
Germany	6.53	3.81	2.72
Italy	4.17	2.28	1.89
Spain	5.38	2.85	2.53
Poland	2.74	1.97	0.77
Yugoslavia	2.75	2.73	0.02
Russia	1.41	1.10	0.31
Romania	0.55	0.52	0.03
Asia			
South Korea	15.42	3.79	11.63
Japan	11.87	2.45	9.42
Taiwan	6.09	1.69	4.40
Israel	5.89	3.02	2.86
Singapore	5.14	1.31	3.83
Malaysia	4.37	2.19	2.18
Hong Kong	3.55	1.12	2.43
Thailand	2.44	1.22	1.22
India	1.95	0.56	1.39

Country	Total business	Non-life	Life
United Arab Emirates	1.44	1.17	0.27
Philippines	1.51	0.80	0.71
China	1.46	0.64	0.82
Indonesia	1.23	0.65	0.58
Pakistan	0.72	0.42	0.30
Kuwait	0.67	0.58	0.09
Saudi Arabia	0.53	0.52	0.02
Africa			
South Africa	17.34	3.48	13.86
Mauritius	4.26	2.15	2.10
Zimbabwe	4.03	2.10	1.93
Kenya	3.19	2.57	0.62
Egypt	0.67	0.52	0.15
Oceanic			
Australia	9.12	3.58	5.53
New Zealand	6.26	4.53	1.73
America	7.21	4.02	3.19
North America	8.41	4.61	3.80
Latin America	1.86	1.37	0.49
Europe	6.78	2.93	3.85
Western Europe	7.41	3.14	4.28
Eastern Europe	1.69	1.29	0.39
Asia	8.80	1.90	6.27
Africa	5.72	1.59	4.13
Oceanic	8.71	3.72	4.99
World	7.32	3.06	4.26

Source: World Insurance in 1997: Booming Life Insurance but Stagnating Non-life Insurance Business, *Sigma-Swiss Re*, No.3/ 1999.

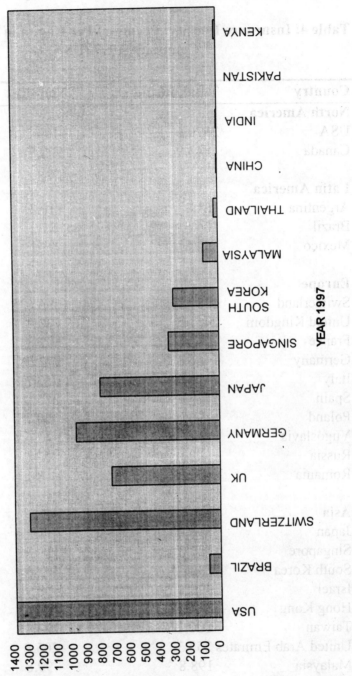

Figure 5: Insurance Density

Table 4: Insurance Density: Premium Per Capita in Selected Countries, 1997 (US $)

Country	Total business	Non-life	Life
North America			
USA	2570.6	1403.7	1167.0
Canada	1543.9	900.5	643.4
Latin America			
Argentina	161.1	110.3	50.8
Brazil	106.5	87.2	19.3
Mexico	53.8	33.1	20.7
Europe			
Switzerland	4289.7	1296.6	2993.1
United Kingdom	2451.5	730.9	1720.7
France	2203.6	692.8	1510.9
Germany	1666.1	972.6	693.5
Italy	829.9	453.5	376.4
Spain	726.3	385.0	341.3
Poland	96.0	69.1	27.0
Yugoslavia	47.9	47.6	0.4
Russia	43.0	33.5	9.5
Romania	8.6	8.1	0.5
Asia			
Japan	3896.0	804.0	3092.0
Singapore	1327.3	338.3	989.0
South Korea	1232.3	303.3	929.3
Israel	990.1	508.9	481.3
Hong Kong	945.5	299.2	646.3
Taiwan	800.1	222.1	578.1
United Arab Emirates	253.3	205.8	47.5
Malaysia	198.8	99.8	99.0
Kuwait	112.0	96.9	15.1
Thailand	52.5	26.3	26.2
Saudi Arabia	39.9	38.5	1.3

Country	Total business	Non-life	Life
Philippines	17.1	9.1	8.0
Indonesia	13.1	6.9	6.2
China	10.9	4.7	6.1
India	**7.6**	**2.2**	**5.4**
Pakistan	3.2	1.8	1.3
Africa			
South Africa	520.5	104.6	415.9
Mauritius	154.7	78.3	76.4
Zimbabwe	23.0	12.0	11.0
Kenya	11.1	9.0	2.1
Egypt	8.2	6.3	1.9
Australia	**1926.3**	**756.9**	**1169.5**
New Zealand	**1083.7**	**784.8**	**299.9**
America	**1043.4**	**581.5**	**461.9**
North America	2467.4	1353.1	1114.3
Latin America	82.6	60.9	21.7
Europe	**850.3**	**367.8**	**482.5**
Western Europe	1636.1	692.2	943.9
Eastern Europe	47.1	36.1	10.9
Asia	**199.4**	**46.4**	**153.0**
Africa	**72.9**	**20.3**	**52.7**
Oceanic	**1784.2**	**761.6**	**1022.6**
World	**423.3**	**176.8**	**246.4**

Source: World Insurance in 1997: Booming Life Insurance but Stagnating Non-life Insurance Business, *Sigma-Swiss Re*, No. 3/1999.

Share in the World Market

The total insurance business in India comprising both non-life and life business constituted only 0.42 % of the total world insurance market in 1997. The relative figures for Japan, South Korea, UK and USA were 31.61 %, 3.47 %, 8.24 % and 25.37 %. The share of entire Asian insurance business in the total insurance business was 38.53 %.

Quality of Insurance Services

In general the quality of insurance services has been at a low key. The quality of insurance services may primarily be evaluated in terms of expeditious settlement of claims, delivery of policy documents and after sales services. At the end of March 2000, a total number of 10,09,542 claims were outstanding, of which about 55% were suit claims. Of the total suit claims, motor suit claims accounted for about 75%. Time wise analysis of pending claims indicate that about 45% claims were pending for more than one year and out of these about 23% were pending for more than three years. Although a total number of documents issued during 1999-2000 were quite large amounting to 3,39,70,855, yet as many as 10,12,908 documents were still outstanding as on March 2000. The delivery of these documents also takes a long time. Although the cost of the insurance services measured in terms of the price of insurance products for the non-tariff products has been by and large, fair and competitive but there is still ample scope for lowering the rates with proper control on management expenses, optimal utilization of investible resources and through wider coverage of insurable population.

Availability of Insurance Products

Although the general insurance side, there are a total of about 175 products covering most of the common insurance products in their portfolio, yet hardly 30 to 35 products are actively traded in the market. Today customers desire to purchase package products instead of purchasing several multiple policies. There are very limited number of such package policies (such as Industrial All Risks Policy and Office Umbrella Policy). The policies catering to special needs of the public such as Advance Loss of Profit, Director's and Officer's Liability etc. are quite limited in number. The products catering to rural sector where disposable income is increasing are limited in number and existing products have not been properly marketed. The policies in segments of Health covers, Household Risk covers, have not been properly marketed and publicised. For instance, health insurance products roughly cover only 25 lakh population with premium income of about Rs. 20 crore. The entire thrust on health insurance has been on the products after the occurrence of illness while the preventive aspects have been ignored. The health care aspect in health insurance has yet to gain in importance. The products covering environmental and financial risks are non-existent. Another area, which has remained untapped, is the development of saving linked non-life policies in the country. The countries like Japan has innovated several saving linked non life policies and the premium from these covers was as much as 40% of the total non life business premium in 1986.

Productivity

There could be several parameters to measure the productivity in the insurance sector. These could be in terms of collection of premium per development officer, issuance of documents per employee, claim settlement per employee, underwriting results, yield on investment income etc. However, measuring productivity in terms of collection of premium per development officer, issuance of policy documentation and claim settlement by class III employees indicate that it was quite on a low scale and needs to be enhanced. For instance collection of premium per development officer is about Rs. 30 lakh, issuance of documentation per class III employee is about 600 and the claim settlement per class III employee is 50 on an annual basis.

Internet and Information Technology

The spread of information technology in the industry has not been to the desired extent. The upgradation of technology does not necessarily restrict itself to the process of computerization, which is already taking place in the industry, but through it a wide database has to be built up for being utilized by the insurance companies, agents and consumers. There is a need to create technology infrastructure such as electronic fund transfer, internet, automatic teller machines, interactive voice response, electronic data inter change, local network services etc. The use of internet and e-commerce for selling the insurance products has yet not commenced in the industry. Presently about 0.2% of premium in USA and 0.02% in Europe is generated through internet. However, the increasing importance of internet in marketing of insurance products is revealed by the fact that out of the total customers with internet access, 45% in USA and 7% in Europe used internet for on-line search even though the policies were sold through conventional methods. Further, as per the estimates of the Swiss Re Economic Research and Consultancy by 2005 out of the total of personal lives business, the on-line sale will rise by 8% in USA and 4% in Europe.

Part IV

Future Potential and Challenges

The opening of the insurance sector offers ample opportunities to both existing as well as new players to penetrate into untapped areas; sectors and sub-sectors and unexploited segments of population as presently both insurance density and penetration are at a low level. As mentioned earlier, insurance penetration broadly measures the significance of insurance industry in relation to a country's entire economic productivity. It indicates importance of insurance industry in the national economy as a whole. On the other hand, insurance density reflects upon the country's insurance purchasing power. Both indices being at very low level in the country even compared to the countries with the same level of economic development and per capita income, are indicative of the vast potential of the growth of this sector in future. Besides, as the economy grows at the rate of 6% in future, the scope for increasing insurance network in the country further grows up.

Primarily, the scope of for higher premium growth in the country is due to the following factors:
1. Low level of insurance penetration.
2. Low level of insurance density.
3. Growth of national income at the rate of 6% and above.

4. Increasing level of awareness amongst the masses about the benefit of insurance and availability of insurance products owing to increased publicity and advertisement.

5. The introduction of new tailored made products, based upon extensive market research and database catering to the needs of different segments of the population, and organisations. These new products will mainly be in areas of financial sector such as credit guarantee, performance guarantee, product liability sector, political risk sector, rural sector, information technology sector, health care etc. The scope for saving linked long-term personal products is also maximum in this country. The growth of such saving linked products in Japan is a case in point. The package policies, which are limited in number offer extensive scope for development in competitive environment.

6. The supply of products at fair and competitive prices and with increased coverage of perils and losses.

7. The market potential will also increase due to efficient delivery system of insurance services and professional selling of products through brokers, banks, sales through internet, telesales, counter sales through departmental stores, direct marketing etc.

The world-wide experience in different countries where insurance sector has been opened up indicates that after liberalisation of the insurance industry, there has been substantial growth of insurance market on a sustained basis. For instance, in Indonesia, which started insurance deregulation in 1983, the insurance market has been growing at the rate of about 25% p.a. and during the last 10 years insurance penetration has tripled in that country. Similar trends have been observed in the economies of Philippines, South Korea, Thailand, Malaysia, Hong Kong etc.

The general insurance business in India has grown at the rate ranging between 10 to 20 percent over a period of time. The average growth rate of gross domestic premium in India amounts to about 16% p.a. As mentioned above, there is scope for accelerated growth rate of premium in the country, which will be in tune with the world trend where insurance sector has been opened up both for domestic and foreign players. It may safely be assumed that the market may start growing at the rate ranging between 16% to 20% p.a. from the year 2001 onwards.

The projected growth of premium is shown in Table 5.

Table 5: Projected Premium Growth Rate

(Rs. crore)

	16% GDPT	17% GDPT	18% GDPT	19% GDPT	20% GDPT
1999-00	9982	9982	9982	9982	9982
2000-01	11579.12	11678.94	11778.76	11878.58	11978.4
2001-02	13431.78	13664.36	13898.94	14135.51	14374.08
2002-03	15580.86	15987.3	16400.75	16821.26	17248.9
2003-04	18073.8	18705.14	19352.88	20017.3	20698.68
2004-05	20965.61	21885.02	22836.4	23820.58	24838.41

In case the market grows at an average rate of 16% p.a. the total gross direct premium in India will be around Rs. 20,965 crore by 2004-5. In case the market grows at the rate of 20% p.a., the total gross direct premium income in India will be around Rs. 24,838 crore by 2004-5.

It is expected that the premium will grow in between these two limits but with the large number of firms operating in the market, it is likely to pickup starting from around 16% in 2001 and may touch 20% by 2004-5. Even the growth at that rate will be less as to touch the level of insurance penetration in the country to 1%. The total gross premium income was Rs. 9982 crore in 1999-2000. During the next five years, the scope for additional premium is in the range of Rs. 11,000 to Rs. 14,000 crore (Figure 6).

The shift from monopoly to competitive market besides being an opportunity, also poses challenge to both existing as well as to new firms. The challenge will be in terms of increasing sensitivity of the consumers to the quality of services offered by the firms, in terms of policy conditions, time consumed in the delivery of policy documents, pricing of products, expeditions settlement of claims,

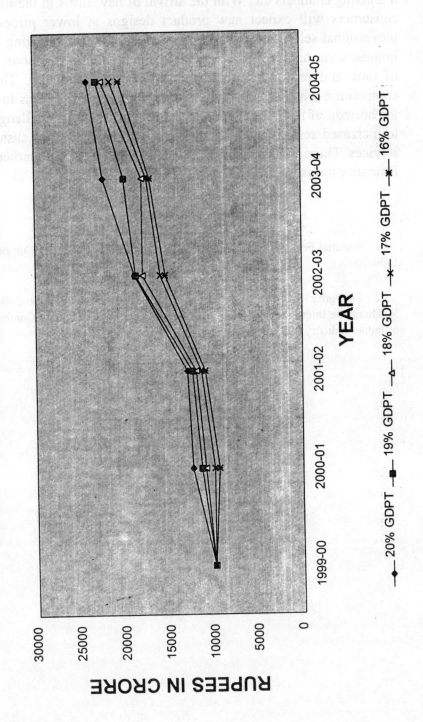

Figure 6 : Projected Premium Growth Rate

marketing channels etc. With the arrival of new firms in the industry, consumers will expect new product designs at lower prices, their professional selling, responsive services and the firms lagging behind in these areas are likely to loose share of market in a very short period of time and may even be forced to leave the industry. Thus the competition while offering ample opportunities to the firms to widen the horizon of the market are also subjected to serious challenges due to increased sensitiveness of consumers to the quality of customer's services. There will be change from sellers to the buyers market in the insurance industry.

Notes

1. Essential Features of General Insurance in General Insurance Compendium, 1999-2000.

2. *Emerging Realities of General Insurance in India: Vision 2000*, A.C. Mukherjee in International Conference of Insurance: Vision 2000 by Confederation of Indian Industry (CII).

Part II

Editorial Note

The issues which have been discussed in Part II relate to marketing of insurance products, product design and product development, pricing of insurance products, investment operations, health insurance, agriculture insurance, and role of intermediaries in emerging scenario.

Chapter 4 deals with the present marketing channels used by the insurance companies and the future strategy which may be formulated in the liberalised economic environment. The paper has recommended the basket approach to personal insurance products, taking assistance of financial consultants and adapting 'piggy riding approach' in promoting sales. It has also pleaded for tie up with consumer durable manufacturing units, financial institutions, stock brokers, co-operative banks, automobile dealers, corporate agents, non-governmental organisations etc. Tie up with professionals has also been recommended for efficient marketing.

Chapter 5 discusses marketing strategies for insurance products in the emerging scenario in India. It has been argued in the paper that low insurance penetration and density reflects upon the vast untapped insurance market in India. The paper points out that the future of insurance market will be influenced by the convergence of financial services, the rise of E-commerce and the emergence of new distribution channels.

Chapter 6 discusses the nature, pattern and process of product design in an emerging market with special reference to India.

Chapter 7 examines various issues involved in innovating new products in general insurance industry, particularly in the present competitive environment. The paper traces the development of insurance products right after the general insurance industry was nationalised in 1973.

Chapter 8 examines the issue of pricing of insurance products in liberalised economies and lessons which can be drawn for Indian insurance industry. The paper traces out the role of price factor in the development of financial structure of general insurance business right from early days and points out that the concept of adequate price for marine insurance has been evident from ancient times.

Chapter 9 examines investment policy of general insurance industry with particular reference to Indian insurance industry. Part one of the article deals with the need for capital investment, principles governing these investments and financial planning required as a prelude to taking investment decisions. Part two examines the opportunities that may be existing in the market while investing the funds. Part three evaluates the regulatory mechanism under which investments are carried out and part four traces the growth of investment in Indian insurance industry and future challenges and opportunities in this area.

Chapter 10 describes the importance of building up an optimum investment portfolio as a tool to improve the financial strength of insurance companies. With the globalisation and deregulation of insurance sector, there will be need to improve efficiency and profitability of investment portfolio. Chapter 11 examines present status, opportunities and challenges in health insurance segment of general insurance in India. India spends about 6 per cent of GDP on health expenditure. Private health care expenditure accounts for as much as 4.25 per cent of GDP and rest is government funding. At present, the insurance coverage is negligible. The paper has discussed the role of regulator in the development of health insurance. The experience of USA and Germany in health experience has also been examined.

Chapter 12 attempts to examine the present status of agriculture insurance in the world, its role in accelerating agricultural development, forms and scope of agriculture insurance, constraints to its growth in developing economies, and risk management techniques in agriculture insurance with particular reference to crop insurance. The growth of agriculture insurance in India with special reference to crop insurance has been evaluated. Chapter 13 on insurance intermediaries discusses the role of intermediaries in the present set up and the role they are expected to play in a free competitive environment based upon international experience.

4

Future of Marketing in Non-life Insurance

S.K. Kanwar

Prior to the nationalisation of insurance business in 1972, there were 106 companies, including the branches of foreign insurance companies, operating in India. They provided a kind of service restricted mainly to trade, commerce and industry. Besides, they were also providing the requirements of statutory insurance. The marketing set up of the said companies, spread over the country, were limited to the branch operations and a system called Inspectorates. The agency system was not a well developed intermediary.

Very few companies practised structured training programmes for their employees and agents. Therefore, the inspectors and agents were ill-trained and ill equipped to educate the customers and provide the right insurance covers for the right requirements. Continuation of such a situation, however, came to an end with the nationalisation of general insurance industry in 1972. All the 106 Companies were taken over by the Government and constituted into 4 subsidiary companies under the ownership of General Insurance Corporation of India.

Since then, the Government intervention and the policy guidelines led to establishing a systematic marketing set up, on the lines of LIC of India. The marketing set up was constituted, at the base level, the agents, supervised by development officers who, in turn, were serviced in the matter of documentation and claim settlement by the branches/divisional offices. Further, as a matter of mandate of the nationalisation of the industry, it was a conscious decision to create branch network in almost all the districts of India. Unlike, the olden days, the potential customers could now find servicing offices of the general insurance companies, in practically in all districts of the country. Down the line, development officers (earlier known as inspector) and agents are even found at *tehsil* and block levels.

Exponential growth of branch network of four Government

owned companies reached a strength of over 4000 and sales officers, i.e. development officers, reached a figure of 13,000. There are as many as 1.5 lakh part time agents working for the state undertakings.

No doubt, this is an achievement, worth commending, on the part of the nationalised set up, which has helped to carry benefits of the general insurance to the nook and corners of the country.

Despite this massive formation of marketing network, the penetration of general insurance industry in the lower end of the marketing remained unsatisfactory. The 4 companies, generate a gross direct premium of about 9,000 crore of which only 2% are from the rural insurance products like Cattle, JPA, GPA, *Kisan* package etc. There are 2.5 million mediclaim policy holders in a vast country like ours. Despite the high rate of road accidents in the country, consciousness for accident insurance remain to be very low and personal accident policies are not yet popularised amongst the lower and middle class.

At the time of nationalisation, the Government of India intended that low cost mass-based insurance schemes should be popularised. However, this has not happened in reality. One of the reasons attributed to our failure is the poor retail network and skewed service conditions of sales officers called development officers, in the nationalised industry. One of the aberrations of the marketing policy of the nationalised industry was to keep the agents out of the purview of canvassing business which were financed by either banks, financial institutions etc. It is well known that the need for general insurance products, are in extricably linked to the world of finance. Therefore, the army of agents were deprived of income by servicing a large segment of business emanating through banks, NBFCs, project finance, hire purchase and leasing etc. The inspectors, having high targets to meet their cost of operation, themselves concentrated on commercial sector and corporate sector business.

The actual implementation of marketing policy of the general insurance industry has been responsible for keeping the clientele from the household and personal insurance sector neglected. Indeed, considering the burgeoning middle class, we are virtually sitting on a gold mine of business. While 50% of policy holders of LIC come from rural sector, the common man failed to get the flavour of the general insurance service, as no one has approached them. There has been no strategic co-operation between LIC and GIC, and they have failed to synergise their respective strengths. The so-called low cost mass insurance schemes failed to pick up, paradoxically, because they are low cost. The sales officials/agents did not feel motivated to mop up individual policies as the average premium collection per document did not give them enough income. However, the industry as a whole, sold a large number of group accident schemes to low income groups, like fishermen, agriculture workers, municipal workers, railway passengers, railway policemen, village artisans and organised groups in housing societies etc. Even banks/some NBFCs/co-operatives extended the benefits of accidental insurance to their loanees, beneficiaries and members. Some enlightened employers have also group JPA/GPA accident insurance schemes and various health insurance group policies for their employees. However, the vast majority of unorganised labour have remained outside the benefits of such schemes. Even traders, shopkeepers, self employed have not been adequately protected by insurance.

While we have seen some success in group schemes, on the other hand, some well intentioned schemes have also failed to pick up, because of the absence of right kind of intermediaries For example, *suhana safar*, a low cost personal insurance scheme for domestic travellers in groups, could not be launched in the market as the industry, did not permit under its rules, agency licence to the travel agents. The scheme itself was otherwise duly designed after market survey by a leading agency.

Besides, the other reason for slow development has been the cumbersome procedures for claim settlement. By and large, the impression is that the claim recovery from insurance companies are not hassle free.

It is a sad commentary on the management of nationalised industry that it has failed to simplify the procedure for a mass market, despite the avowed goal of nationalisation, i.e. to carry the benefits of general insurance to every house and homes.

While LIC of India grew by leaps and bounds, to touch upon lives of individuals, the personal insurance sectors of general insurance industry did not create the market mainly by neglecting to create a dynamic agency force.

There was, however, some attempt to develop Rural Agency Scheme in 1970s and early in 1980s. All banks, sponsoring their rural finance schemes made insurance cover a requirement. This move, on the part of banks, provided the much needed boost to the rural insurance scheme and support to the agency force. It was, unfortunately, a short-lived growth curve in rural sector. The banks exempted many of their rural finance schemes, from the requirements of insurance. The agency force that was slowly coming up, in the rural sector, started drying up. The rural branch network of state owned companies started shifting from non-traditional rural insurance to traditional forms of insurance like motor vehicle insurance. Presently, the so-called rural branches and rural development officers are mainly producing motor insurance premium. It does no credit to the marketing ability of the powerful state sector insurance industry that their network failed to nurture the market and capture a share of rural savings, on the lines of LIC's success story.

There was a glimmer of hope when the nationalised sectors experimented with Direct Agents Branch Scheme in the late 1980s. The strategy was undoubtedly focused and the results were extremely profitable. This experiment, unfortunately, did not receive the support of the management to the desired extent. There were as many as 70 branches till last year in the four companies, with varying degrees of success. While a well meaning marketing strategy has been neglected in the state owned insurance companies, the new regulations by IRA has emphasised the need for developing agents, as the driver of Indian market in future.

The New Dawn

Amongst so many changes in Indian economy, we are also expecting far reaching changes in the insurance sector as well.

For the last 40 years in life insurance and 28 years in general insurance, the customers of insurance services have been provided service by monopoly companies. Although the monopoly has lent financial strength and ownership of the Government on the plea side, they failed in the area of customer service. The insurance sector, particularly, non-life, is a highly commercial activity. The system of

Government ownership came in the way of making the companies market savvy. High potential employees failed to deliver the expected service, as they were bound by the rigid rules and regulations.

Government companies could not push through enough of internal reforms to remain market sensitive. They were tardy on technology and upgradation. The mindset up of their employees was not customer friendly. The writings on the wall was there ever since Malhotra Committee Report was published in 1994. In the absence of political consensus, the reforms in the insurance sectors had to wait till 1999. Now, we have a set of regulations governing the industry, both for the existing and new players.

Thus, thanks to the commitment of the IRDA, licence for the new insurance companies have been issued. Such companies however, have a daunting task ahead. They have to meet the high expectations of the market place. Monopoly markets have come to its end. It is now to be seen how the new players take on the challenge of the market place.

The Way Forward

Having experienced, the deficiencies of marketing under the nationalised set up, the newly licensed insurance companies are now faced with the challenge of appropriate channels of distribution, which is the key to the success of marketing insurance products, in a vast country like ours. As we have observed, historically speaking, neither during the period preceding nationalisation, i.e. prior to 1972, not after nationalisation for last 28 years, no good model exists in the matter of agency system in non-life market. The public sector companies relied on a variety of distribution system like, direct marketing from office to office, development officer as a semi-wholesaler/retailer and part time agents as casual retailers and distributors. Thus, the entire distribution machinery in non-life was unfocussed.

Uniqueness of Non-life Insurance

Unlike, life insurance business, non-life insurance is unique in the sense that the products/business is rather non-homogeneous. The range of product could vary from a small business/risk like poultry farm to the highly complicated risk like communication satellite and petro-chemical risks. Such a variety of market cannot possibly be handled by a single kind of intermediary. Therefore, world over, brokers have been acknowledged as the right medium of distribution. Because, brokers could aggregate the variety of risks in the market, pre-process the requirements of the mixed clientele and place the business proposals with appropriate underwriters. The underwriters have also the expertise to service various niche/segments in the market. In such an arrangement, the customers are satisfied that they are getting their right advice at their doorstep and the delivery mechanism is rather prompt and accurate, of course, at a price.

In India, however, we have not experienced, in the system of brokers in insurance market. Neither in the pre-nationalised period, nor after nationalisation, broking was ever introduced as a credible distribution channel. The chain of offices under the nationalised set up dovetailed the role of the brokers into their working. Insurance offices were expected to provide expert advice and guidance through development officers. However, the development officers were not thoroughly trained and supervised for fulfilling the role expected of them. Thus, the monopoly insurance services fell short of the desired level of the satisfaction, in the absence of customer focused approach.

Now, Which Way ?

It is said that successful companies are market driven, which means that customers would decide what products to buy, from whom and at what price?

Keeping to the market realities, as stated above, a good marketing strategy would do well to research the products range and the channels of distribution available and determine the right mix of distribution mechanism for pushing their product line. Whatever the customers want they must get. It is up to the good marketers to choose the channel to deliver the desired service at the doorstep of the customers. As they say, a successful company seeking to expand its market share, as to beat its path to the door of the customer.

Anyone familiar with insurance would know that insurance world over, has been sold rather than purchased. It only means that there is more selling efforts necessary in insurance market than in any comparable service market. For instance, insurance buying is not yet a priority in the budget of an individual. Even in the commercial market decision on insurance is mainly on driven on the conditionality financial transactions. The hi-tech area is, however, more focused on risk management and appropriate insurance covers. No hi-tech project can ever neglect insurance.

Some people feel that general insurance products are not well known. They need to be heavily advertised to create awareness. Success in insurance marketing cannot be achieved largely by advertisement and publicity. At the most, continuous and careful planning in media publicity could build the brand image of the insurance companies. Creative product publicity could create awareness on the benefits amongst the customers and potential buyers. Advertisement and publicity alone cannot provide stimulus to the buyers of insurance. What is most needed in insurance buying is one to one selling efforts. This is possible by developing a strong agency force and broking mechanism.

The customers in insurance are to be influenced by educating them, i.e. about do's and don'ts of insurance packages. They have to be drawn to participate in customising the product for their own good. The customers have to be well informed about their rights and obligations, while taking the policy and at the time of lodging the claims.

This consultancy approach in insurance sales is peculiar, for insurance is, after all, a legal contract which must insure identity of mind, at the time of concluding the contract. Both the insurer and the insured have to understand what is the risk associated with the business and how best the same could be protected by insurance product and at the appropriate price, commensurate with the risk. Much of the misunderstanding on insurance claims could be removed, if appropriate exercise is done at the time of pre-sale. Unfortunately, in most insurance transactions, the parties to the contract are rushed. There is very little application of mind.

Choice of Distribution Mechanism

Considering the nature of the insurance sales directions, the insurance companies have to determine the structure and quality of distributive channels. It is again dependent upon the business strategy of the companies for penetration into specific segments of the market. For examples, if an insurance company is planning to enter the personal insurance market in a big way, the intermediaries like full time agents would be more appropriate. Because, personal insurance development requires building up qualitative long term and one to one relationship. The customers require repeat calls by the agents to carry the conviction with the buyers. After sales service is critical to the personal insurance market, the agents must know claims procedures and guide the customer. The back office must support their agents in servicing the claims. A satisfied individual customer, could spread the good word around, for the company, and could prove to be the best advertisement medium. This would eventually result in lots of new customers, by reference, from the satisfied customers. For example, if an insurance company plans to enter the marine insurance market (both export or import), the right selection of intermediaries from within the export/import trade could serve the clientele better than by using agent who are specialising in personal/domestic insurance.

The character of the market would determine the type of intermediary and accordingly, preparations are to be made for appropriate recruitment and training strategies, before actually placing the intermediaries in the identified market segments.

There is yet another kind of strategy for penetrating the market.

The Basket Approach to Personal Insurance Product Selling

There are a number of financial products available in the market. They are mutual fund investment, small savings like postal department products, life insurance, pension schemes, company fixed deposits/debentures, small savings in banks/co-operatives/NBFCs etc.

Presently, individual customers are being solicited by agents from a variety of institutions representing their products as stated above. For instance, a young employee/professional in the early stage of his career is being sold a life policy by LIC agent. Certainly, it is the right age for taking life insurance policy. If he happens to be a travelling executive, he also needs a personal accident policy, for which, an agent from general insurance company, is approaching him for insurance. As he grows up in his profession and gets married, he needs householder policy to cover his personal assets. An agent from general insurance sells him such policies. Similar things are happening as and when he has more savings and the agents of individual mutual funds and other financial companies are pushing their intermediaries to reach out to such individuals. Thus, you will see an individual needs a variety of products which is a kind of basket of needs and he needs an advisor for specific products, at different points of time, during his productive life cycle.

In overseas markets, individuals under similar situation are being serviced by financial consultants. They are privy to the individual's needs and requirements. They know the intricate tax laws and are better equipped to advise them continually on various aspects of savings, security and investment products.

It is a Kind of One Stop Shop

Is the time ripe now in India to facilitate the emergence of such recognised financial consultants?

The distribution channels for insurance companies have got too structure themselves, according to the kind of policy holder/clientele base, they plan to cultivate. They must be focused to ensure professionalism. Accordingly, the recruitment strategy for agents/consultants/brokers have to be designed. The training and updation of such professionals have to be carefully worked out and budgeted as a component marketing cost on long term basis. Agency manager has a crucial role to play and it is no doubt challenging.

Piggy Riding Products for Sales Promotion

This is a well known approach, in the consumer durable and non-durable market. However, financial products and insurance products are resorting to the piggy riding approach in promoting sales, in a limited way. Linkage with credit cards is a clear example of this new marketing strategy in insurance. Such approach widens the distribution channels.

Some of the other ways known to be effective in widening the reach of distribution channels are as follows:

1. Tie up with C & F agents.

2. Tie up with consumer durable manufacturing companies like refrigerators, air-conditioners, water pumps, televisions, air coolers etc.

3. Tie up with stock brokers.

4. Extension/service counters at industrial estates, export processing zones, super markets could be called useful as call centres and franchisee arrangements.

5. Tie up with co-operative banks/RRB for effective rural sector marketing.

6. Kiosks at shopping malls.

7. Major railway stations, S.T. stands, extension counters.

8. Car/two wheeler dealers.

9. Tie up with mutual funds and NBFC.

10. Corporate agents, for example banks and others.

Of all these above channels for distribution, banks and financial institutions are going to play a massive role of mobilising business and creating awareness. They are fortunate to have a valuable data base of their existing clients, which could be profitably utilised for pushing insurance products. However, such institutions are more incentive driven in their approach. The insurance companies have to carefully nourish them not merely as point of sale but much more, by a careful vendor development programme.

The role of the social services organisation like NGO for rural marketing has not been fully utilised. This would be a new and durable channel of distribution of rural products.

Top co-operative banks and co-operative societies, housing societies are almost captive markets and they could prove to be source of a wealth of business potential.

Various associations of professionals like chartered accountants, cost accountants, medical professionals, project consultants, financial consultants could prove to be extremely useful, in creating awareness amongst their clientele.

Other miscellaneous avenues of sales are as follows:
- Real estate agents.
- Travelling agents.
- Builders network.
- Money charger/courier services.

- Various *mahila samaj* for households.
- Demat network/depositories.
- Religion associations/social services organisation.

Despite the availability of a variety of channels of distribution in our country, insurance service has not been fully focused and credibly firmed up. The current size of non-life business is not much to be proud of compared to advanced country, . even comparable to the South East Asian Countries. The contribution of non-life premium in India, to the country's GDP is barely .06%. Some of the problems associated with unsatisfactory insurance service could be listed as follows:

1. Absence of hi-quality man power in marketing area.

2. Absence of R and D, resulting in poor launching of products. Most insurance products, do not satisfy the real needs of the customer groups

Weak Links in the Chain of Marketing

1. Absence of full fledged IT support, i.e. activation between customers and the servicing centre.

2. Absence of on line service.

3. Absence of dedicated back office support, to marketing services absence of effective MIS system.

If only new companies could take care of all the above within the quickest time possible, they could pose a serious threat even to existing players, despite their strong network.

The new players could ill-afford to ignore the strength of the nationalised companies. The state companies must make a fresh beginning and overcome their handicaps to good marketing.

The future of marketing in insurance, in our country holds out exciting possibilities and promises to benefit the customers. The consumer, however, is going to be the referee to determine in what measures, both, the existing and new players are going to come up to their expectations.

Let us watch the future scenario with hope and expectations.

5

Marketing Strategies for Insurance Products in the Emerging Scenario

A. N. Poddar

Today, organisations are competing in complex business environment characterised by continuous changes in economic, social, technological, politico-legal and regulatory factors. The 1990s ushered in an accelerated trend in liberalisation and globalisation of the Indian economy. The insurance sector along with other elements of the financial infrastructure has been touched and influenced by the process of liberalisation and globalisation. The external environment has not only affected the demand side of the insurance sector but also caused changes in the internal process of the insurance service providers. The realisation that the ability of a company to mobilise and utilise its intangible or invisible assets is far more decisive than investing and managing physical and tangible assets has dawned in the minds of captains of the industry.

Although the size and the growth rates of the Indian economy have been quite impressive in the last decade, the insurance industry in India is still having a low penetration (non-life premium has a 0.71% share in Gross Domestic Product and the corresponding share of life premium is 1.90%) as compared to countries like USA (corresponding figures stand around 5%), UK (3% and 9% respectively), Japan (3% and 9% respectively). The per capita insurance premium in India is also well below the levels of advanced countries. All these indicate that there is a huge untapped potential in the Indian insurance market. According to a recent study by C.K. Prahalad and Kenneth Lieberthal the demand side of the emerging Indian market can be analysed in terms of the following Market Pyramid and could be compared with China and Brazil:

	Purchasing power parity (US$)	Population (million)		
		India	China	Brazil
Tier 1	Greater than $20,000	7	.2	9
Tier 2	$10,000 to $20,000	63	60	15
Tier 3	$5,000 to $10,000	125	330	27
Tier 4	Less than $5,000	700	800	105

It is interesting to note that the emerging markets in terms of different tiers as depicted in the picture represent not only quantitative elements of purchasing power but also qualitative dimensions of dynamic and changing life style of different groups of people. The Indian insurance market in the non-life sector has the traditional composition of private sector corporate accounts (20%) public sector accounts (20%) and organised business (60%). The emerging socio-economic scenario would be creating a tremendous amount of paradigm shift through emergence of personal lines of insurance and retailing will feature in a big way.

According to a Report by Pricewaterhouse Coopers, the future of insurance market will be influenced by three new developments:
- The convergence of financial services
- The rise of e-commerce
- The emergence of new distribution channels

As for the customer the key concern will be service and customisation as against mere price.

Marketing strategies for insurance products in the emerging scenario could be understood in terms of the following steps:

R → STP → MM → I → C

where,
- R = Market research

- STP = Segmentation, targeting, positioning
- MM = Marketing mix
- I = Implementation
- C = Control

Having done market research and finalising on segmentation, targeting and positioning the strategy would focus on the marketing mix which could be elaborated by way of the 4 Ps;

Having done market research and finalising on segmentation, targeting and positioning the strategy would focus on the marketing mix which could be elaborated by the following 4 Ps:

Product	Price	Place	Promotion
Variety	Rate	Channel (D/I)	Sales promotion
Design	Discount	Coverage	Advertisement
Brand	Allowances	Location	Publicity
Services	Payment terms	Inventory	P R

The Indian insurance market is likely to witness a sea change in the realm of all the 4 programmes. The customer driven market would result in lot of flexibilities and innovations in product, pricing, distribution channels and communication mechanisms. The IRDA with its developmental and regulatory guidelines is likely to promote competition, fairness, and reliability and at the same time protect insured against excessive, inadequate or unfairly discriminatory rates. While efforts for strengthening the existing distribution channels and making them more effective will continue, introduction of new intermediaries like insurance brokers, new avenues like bancassurance and utilisation of electronic media and internet would call for new strategies. Communication to create more awareness and greater demand for insurance products will continue to assume high importance. At the same time, unfair or misleading advertisements will be discouraged and necessary checks and controls will be in place.

On the whole, the focus of emerging strategies would centre on the following Value Propositions:
- Reduce costs.
- Increase profitability.

- Reduce time to market.
- Improve customer intimacy.
- Retain customers for life.
- Enable electronic business.
- Establish strong partnerships.

While determining the implementation methodology of marketing strategy it should be kept in mind that insurance as a service has got four characteristics:
- Intangibility
- Inseparability
- Perishability
- Variability

Each of the four characteristics gives rise to certain unique requirements that deserve careful attention while formulating marketing strategies.

Intangibility
- No patent protection is possible for services.
- It is difficult to display and communicate services and service benefits.
- Service prices are difficult to set.
- Quality judgement by customers may be subjective.

  The Two dimensions of quality judgement are process quality (judged by the customer during the service) and output quality (judged by the customer after the services is performed).
- Some services involve performances/experiences.

Inseparability
- The consumer may be involved in the production of services.
- Centralised mass production of services is difficult.
- If a popular employee leaves a firm, customers may switch to the new company where that person works.

Perishability
- Services cannot be inventoried
- The effects of seasonality can be severe
- Planning employee schedules can be complex

Variability

- Standardisation and quality control are hard to achieve.
- Services may be delivered by employees who are beyond the immediate influence of management (at the customer's home, on the road etc.)
- Customers may perceive variability in service quality from one occasion to the next occasion, even if such variability does not actually occur.

The ultimate test of a marketing strategy would be whether it leads to achieving the value propositions narrated earlier. In one word, the issue boils down to relationship building with the customer. The successful insurance organisations anywhere in the world focus not merely on offering zero defect products but also ensuring zero defection of customers. The basic factors determining service quality of an insurance company could be summarised under 10 heads:

Tangibles: facilities, appearance of personnel, tools or equipment, physical representation of service (such as a plastic credit card)

Credibility: Trustworthiness, believability, and honesty

Competence: Possession of required skills and knowledge

Access: Approachability and ease of contact

Reliability: Performing service at designated time, dependability of performance, accuracy in billing, and correct record keeping.

Responsiveness: Timeliness of service

Courtesy: Politeness, respect, consideration, and friendliness of contact personnel

Communication: Keeping customers informed, in language they can understand, and listening to customer comments

Understanding: Making an effort to understand the customer

Formulation of a marketing strategy is more a process than an event. Environmental factors like macro-economic parameters, regulatory norms and themes, technology, infrastructure, legal set up, competition by way of new entry, degree of globalisation need be scanned and considered in framing the likely scenarios. For instance, whether a company would adopt a strategy for market penetration or market development or product development or would go in for diversification could be determined by analysing all the relevant data in terms of the Product-Market Scope:

Product-Market Scope

	Market	
PRODUCT	Existing	New
Existing New	Market Penetration Product Development	Market Development Diversification

With complexities multiplying in the market place, the maturity levels of the markets and the product life cycles keep changing. Existing products may face obsolescence from sources like demand-side, supply-side or technology. An analysis of products with reference to market growth rate and market share (growth/share matrix) will offer clue for product strategies.

- Products with high relative share in low growth markets (nick named cash cows) will produce healthy cash flow.
- Products with low relative share in low growth markets (dogs) will often be cash traps.
- Products with high relative share in high growth markets (stars) usually will require large amounts of cash to sustain growth but have a strong market position that will yield high reported profits.
- Products with low relative share in rapidly growing markets (question marks or wild cats) require large cash inflows to finance growth:

	High Market Share	Low Market Share
High Market Growth	Star ★	Question Mark ?
Low Market Growth	Cash Cow	Dog

Borrowing the basic framework from the BCG, insurance companies may harvest or divest the "dogs", utilise the "cash cow" to make "question marks" into "stars".

The emerging insurance business scenario in India is characterised by significant changes, many of which may be radical, and some may be different in both qualitative and quantitative terms from the past practices and customs. With the elements of production and distribution activities undergoing a metamorphosis in the insurance market in India, the intensity of industry competition and profitability are likely to be determined by five competitive forces:

- Entry
- Threat of substitution
- Bargaining power of buyers
- Bargaining power of suppliers
- Rivalry amongst current competitors

These forces will act upon a company's ability to survive and grow. For example, there is a possibility of catering to specific markets, product-wise or geographical area wise by a company. Introduction of risk based capital could make the entry and eventually operational norms quite different. Application of IT and BPR are likely to change the scales and speed of market operations. All these require a company to adopt an appropriate competitive strategy to cope successfully with the five competitive forces. Experts like Michael E. Porter have identified three internally consistent generic strategies, which can be used singly or in combination:

- Overall cost leadership
- Differentiation
- Focus

The notion underlying the concept of generic strategies is that competitive advantage is at the heart of any strategy, and achieving competitive advantage requires a company to make a choice.

Cost leadership is perhaps the clearest of the three generic strategies. In the Indian general insurance parlance, it suits the requirements of section 40C of the Insurance Act which makes this strategy all the more imperative.

Three Generic Strategies
Competitive Advantage

	Lower Cost	Differentiation
Broad Target	1. Cost Leadership	2. Differentiation
Narrow Target	3A. Cost Focus	3B. Differentiation Focus

Competitive Scope

In a differentiation strategy, a company seeks to be unique in its industry along some dimensions that are widely valued by the customers. May be the lowest cycle time for settling a claim under, say, mediclaim policy could be a differentiating factor.

In a focus strategy, a company selects a segment or group of segments in the industry and tailors its strategy to serve them to the exclusion of others. The focus strategy has two variants. In cost focus a company seeks a cost advantage in its target segment, while in differentiation focus a company seeks a differentiation in its target segment.

It is only after a thorough, continuous and pragmatic SWOT analysis and appropriate financial implications review that a company should identify the generic strategy. Achieving cost leadership and differentiation simultaneously has an element of inconsistency because differentiation is usually costly. Moreover, every type of generic strategy has a definite exposure to risk. The reality is that barriers to imitation are never insurmountable. Therefore, the strategy needs a constant evaluation and monitoring.

As Porter opines, the essence of formulating a competitive strategy is relating a company to its environment. We have already analysed different elements in the marketing mix through which the company relates to the customers as well as the environment. Needless to say, the essence of an effective marketing strategy lies in combining the degree of flexibility with the extent of focus in a dynamic and changing market place. And, for an insurance company the marketing strategy involves in mobilising and utilising its intangible or invisible assets which will enable the company to :

- develop customer relationships that retain the loyalty of exiting customers and enable new customer segments and market areas to be served effectively and efficiently;
- introduce innovating products and services desired by targeted customer segments;
- produce customised high-quality products and services at low cost and with short lead times;
- mobilise employee skills and motivation for continuous improvements in process capabilities, quality, and response times; and
- deploy information technology, data bases, and systems in an optimum manner.

The marketing strategy cannot be taken up in isolation. All the major elements of the organisation, viz., structure, systems, processes, staff, skills, managerial styles and, above all, the shared value should be appropriately integrated in implementation of the strategy. The basic tool for diagnosing competitive advantage and finding ways to enhance it is the value chain, which divides a company into discrete activities it performs in designing, producing, marketing and distributing its products. For, in the ultimate understanding the marketing strategy is an integral part of the business value design the company exists for. A business value design is the totality of how a company selects its customers, defines and differentiates its offerings, defines the tasks it will perform itself and those it will outsource, configures its resources, goes to the market, creates utility for customers and finally, captures profit. It is the entire system for delivering utility to customers and earning profits from that activity.

A strategy worth the name must take into account both the disaggregative as well as the aggregative aspects of the business value design of the company.

The competitive advantage of a company may stem from the many discrete activities in the value chain. Each of these activities can contribute to a company's relative cost position or create a basis for a differentiation. Thus, the disaggregative aspects are important contributors to the strategy formulation process.

Coming to the aggregative aspects, each generic strategy implies different skills and requirements for success, which commonly translate into differences in organisational structure and culture. Cost leadership usually implies tight control systems overhead minimisation and pursuit of scale economies. But for a company attempting to differentiate itself through a constant stream of creative new products, these implications may not be consistent. Speaking of company culture, differentiation may be facilitated by a culture encouraging innovation, individuality and risk taking while frugality discipline and attention to detail may facilitate cost leadership. Culture can powerfully reinforce the competitive advantage a generic strategy seeks to achieve, if the culture is an appropriate one.

Marketing strategies in the insurance sector would revolve round products and companies and their thrust areas would be a function of environmental, regulatory, competitive and technological factors in a dynamic continuum.

6

Product Design In an Emerging Market

H. Ansari

A common axiom holds that 80% of a product's cost is determined during the first 20% of development. In other words, if insurers make a few wrong turns at early stage, it won't take long for product development costs to skyrocket. Conducting design research early in the development process helps eliminate unnecessary costs. When the product is intended to enter the global market, the insurer must further consider the variances of each country in which the product is to be sold.

In today's global economy, cross-cultural research is fast becoming a valuable tool for insurers trying to determine product viability. At the very simplest level, cross-cultural research involves studying respondents from more than one culture. The dilemma is that culture has a broad range of definitions; as a result, interpreting cultural differences is extremely vulnerable. Products catering to the rural, social and unorganised sectors, as also the health sector, are particularly sensitive to cultural influence due to differences in social and medical practices throughout the world. Insofar as health insurance is concerned, consumers might have a choice between private practice and socialised medicine or between holistic and clinical approaches to medical treatment. Patients also receive treatment in different environments, from doctors' offices to urban hospitals to rural clinics. A company's failure to acknowledge cultural differences in medical practices often limits its product's marketability. Cross-cultural research provides the key to unlocking these potential-marketing barriers.

Like all research, cross-cultural studies provide qualitative and quantitative data that can be translated into a broad-based analysis of user needs. Quality cross-cultural research assesses and analyses differences in perception, context, and in the use of products in selected states or geographic regions. Just as successful product developers wouldn't attempt to design and develop a new product without first performing comprehensive research, an enterprise shouldn't enter the market without proper cross-cultural research. Information on how products are perceived in different geographic locations greatly increases the likelihood of nation-wide success.

Preventing Mistakes

It is much easier for an insurer to penetrate the market when it is armed with the right information. Unfortunately, in the rush to get to market, some insurers take the plunge and then find out that their lack of cultural information creates a flurry of potential marketing disasters. Following are some of the most common mistakes made by insurers in their rush to international markets.

Boardroom Design: Product design often revolves around profits, marketing, engineering, or product aesthetics without involving end-users in the process. The problem while creating the widest and then looking for a market should be obvious. Research should test every assumption so that product viability is based on quantitative results. Design driven by consumer needs, as opposed to design in the corporate boardroom, ensures greater product acceptance and longevity.

Copycat Mentality: Another tendency of boardroom product design is the copycat product that mimics the competitors. This stifles creativity and ultimately limits a company's growth. In this paradigm, products are relegated to a commodity market where real differences are hard to find and premium becomes the deciding factor. Obviously this is not where insurers want to be, since it means constantly reducing profit margins to stay competitive. A better option is to differentiate a product through usability and functionality. A comprehensive matrix that includes cross-cultural, design, marketing, end-user perception, and usability research provides a basis for creative thinking that's grounded in reliable data.

Feature Creep: Features are not synonymous with functionality. In fact, unnecessary features can be a liability instead of a benefit. "Feature creep" is the result of trying to make one product fit every need. For example, one client may ask for a particular feature, while another client wants a different feature; eventually, all the features overwhelm the product's usability. This happens in every product category, and rural, social and unorganised and health sectors, are particularly susceptible because they need to work in a host of different social environments and cultures. Features necessary in one country may not be important in another. Instead of adding different features for each country, cross-cultural research discovers which features can be whittled down to one solution, which can be eliminated, and which are necessary country-specific variances. The goal is to obtain this information early in the product development process when all possibilities are open.

Oversimplification: When consumer and product studies are conducted among respondents in different cultures, they are often done superficially, arriving at overly simplistic cultural attributions. Catastrophic marketing mistakes occur when design, pricing, or marketing decisions are based on generalised conclusions about ethic and national groups. It is not enough to report the differences; there needs to be an understanding of why the differences exist. Differences in economies, governments, education, occupations, ethnicity, gender, social class, and family systems should be analysed for their effect on research results.

The Research Process

To achieve maximum benefit for the design process, the cross-cultural research team should be included in development discussions as soon as there is the desire to pursue a new insurance product, and should continue to be included at every step of the way. Using cross-cultural as well as actuarial inputs early in the development process allows the research team to find enhancements that may add little or nothing to the cost, but contribute significantly to the perceived value and profit margin, e.g. cross-cultural research should uncover the process of interaction between the medical practitioner and the patient. Levels of technology vary, but the proposed product must be geared to maximise the process of this interaction.

Define the Procedures: All scientific study requires a precise research methodology consisting of systematic procedures for designing the study, gathering the data, and analysing the findings. Like other market research, cross-cultural research uses traditional

market slicing by age and gender, but it goes further to include data on cultural effects, socio-economic conditions, and distribution channels in order to address the concerns unique to each state. In defining the procedures, insurers should take the following steps:
- Begin research planning with line managers by clearly identifying the overall research objective. Confirm the consistency of the objective in each of the national market.
- Define all aspects of the procedural operations to ensure reliability in the data collection process. The same instructions should be followed during each interview, questionnaire, and observation. Follow a standard questionnaire to collect data on consumer response.

Incorporate Study Control: An objective in all scientific study is to minimise the variables so as to obtain clean, reliable data. The analysis and interpretation of cross-cultural results require a thorough investigation of extraneous factors to minimise their impact on results. Study control is difficult to obtain when crossing state borders. However, with the numerous variables that exist, cross-cultural studies require diligent control of all aspects within the sphere of influence. Control of the methodology and neutralisation of the language differences are critical to obtaining reliable data.

To help facilitate the data-gathering process, training of the researchers and data collection methods should be standardised. Researchers should be trained on the background, the product being studied, the research objectives, and the specific procedures to be carried out during interviews and observations.

Cultural Similarities

At the same time while they are researching for cultural differences, insurers must be careful not to overlook similarities across cultures; they shouldn't assume there would be major differences. Differentiating a product for a certain group may create more problems than it solves. Adaptations of a current design means more money spent on retooling, pricing, and marketing. Research may uncover a universal solution that meets the needs of all cultures.

Often, the main objective for the insurer is to come to a global decision on a new product design. Countries are sampled for cultural variances with the purpose of achieving a sample broad enough to generalise the insurer's particular national market. This type of research is not intended to develop state-specific products.

Interpreting Differences

If the objective of the insurer is to understand national markets, the broad research parameters would have made a perfect setting for the frequent mistakes made by its marketing decision makers. When the objective is country specific, the regional differences need to be investigated for a deeper understanding of cultural, and national influences by including data on cultural effects, socio-economic conditions, and distribution channels. These studies must also address the similarities in findings across cultures and consider them in marketing decisions.

Health insurance product success is particularly dependent on an understanding of protocol, procedural differences, purchasing habits and mortality and morbidity rates. For instance, across cultures there are different perceptions as to what constitutes a disposable or what represents a capitalised expense. Some countries can capitalise an expensive piece of medical equipment but not afford disposable, or vice versa. For insurers, the solution to the sale lies in the bundling. The new product can be bundled with the existing product as a rider. In another purchasing paradigm, the premium can be "earned" through the purchase of a specified policy. In the United States and other capitalist countries, the competition of the open market elevates the importance of profitability. Conversely, profitability is not an issue for socialist and communist countries.

When a company understands the reasons behind regional differences, it has the information necessary to properly position its product in the market. For example, a study found that users and purchasers in the United States were less concerned about the price of a medical insurance than were respondents in England. Instead of mistakenly generalising about more frivolous purchasing habits of American consumers, one would have to further investigate the healthier and insurance industries in the United States and England to understand the underlying financial concerns. The researchers would not only need to understand how the industries vary by country, but

Product Design in an Emerging Market

also how procedures vary in the private and public sectors.

Cultural rules and social norms must be understood in order to make an accurate analysis of results. Users and purchasers in Japan, for example, may report finding a product more appealing than consumers in Germany. But before jumping to conclusions and rolling out a large marketing campaign in Japan and a small campaign in Germany, further analysis is necessary. An understanding of Japanese culture would need to be considered when comparing Japanese responses to those in cultures where respondents are less inclined to emphasise the same social standards.

Respondents in all countries except the United States may consistently respond negatively to the largest size model of a medical insurance. Instead, development teams must analyse why in this country differences exist. For example, insurance offices of Germany, France, Japan, and England are smaller on average than typical US offices. Space limitations might be less of a concern in US insurer's offices, but that does not necessarily mean that US respondents prefer largest investments. Again, the trick is to discern the meaning behind the cultural variable.

Counting the Costs

The cost of cross-cultural research depends on the number of subjects and venues included, as well as the degree of complexity and rigour required. The depth and breadth of the actuarial research, the competitive analysis, and the market analysis determine the costs. In assessing the value of cross-cultural research, it is important to remember that the earlier research is integrated into the process, the more cost-effective it is.

One way to hold down the cost of cross-cultural research is to use internal resources to the fullest extent. First insurers should assess the resources within their own organisation. Do they have the time and capabilities to undertake some or all of the research process? In-house researchers and marketing, engineering, and design team members can help articulate goals and design strategies.

Premium Rating and Product Design

The Indian insurance market is changing rapidly because of

deregulation, new foreign entrants and increasing consumer awareness. Innovative product design, new marketing techniques and timely product launches are required to stay ahead of the competition. Sophisticated premium rating and the flexibility to respond quickly to changing market trends are increasingly recognised as the key to meeting this challenge. Where existing tariff structures are likely to change in future, it is essential to start collecting statistical data well in advance so profitable rating structures for the new environment can be designed. Actuaries in insurance practice who have extensive experience of designing products and rating structures for many different classes of business shall, therefore, play a key role in the near future.

Analysis of the Market: The first step in the process is to determine the exact nature of the market and the requirements of the customer base. This will include:
- estimating the size of the current and potential market.
- analysing market trends and profitability.
- determining the products and rating methods used by the competition.
- evaluating competing products in terms of price and cover.
- investigating who actually makes the decision to buy a particular type of product.
- identifying the principal reasons for buying the product.
- comparing the benefits of different distribution methods and advising on the most effective methods for remunerating sales distribution channels.

Analysis of Data: Accurate premium rating depends critically on collecting relevant data in an appropriate format, and then analysing this data using the right statistical techniques. The insurers can address these central issues by:
- advising on the design of databases and the collation of statistical information.
- analysing claims experience to determine the effect that rating factors have upon the risk.
- comparing these theoretical results with the relativities implicit in the existing rating structure, and interpreting the results.
- considering the possible effect upon the portfolio of introducing

particular rating changes.
- providing financial projections of future results, based on the calculated premium rates
- undertaking sensitivity analyses.

Statistical Techniques: As insurance markets become more sophisticated and as computing power increases, companies are using more advanced statistical techniques to analyse their business and design premium rating structures. For example, companies are using generalised linear modelling techniques to fit premium rating models for classes of business that have large numbers of possible rating factors, such as motor insurance. Such models can be used to determine the risk factors that discriminate most effectively between good and bad risks, and to produce rating schedules based on these risk factors. In addition, these statistical techniques can be used to investigate the effect upon policyholder retention of measurable factors including the change in proposed premium and the competitiveness of the premium. Such analysis can provide valuable insights into how best to manage future rating changes.

Statistical techniques can also be used to model and price excess-of-loss reinsurance contracts. In this case simulation methods are generally used, based on fitted claim numbers and amounts distributions. Aggregate models can be considered to assess whether the excess-of-loss premium charged is sufficient to cover the expected costs of claims, brokerage and an adequate loading for adverse contingencies and profit. The international insurers who have promoted the Indian insurance companies have considerable experience of using such statistical techniques having carried out statistical premium rating analyses in the countries where they operate world-wide.

File and Use System

An insurance product is a bundle of utilities, which means every thing the buyers receives, including psychological utilities as well as tangible and intangible dimensions. The standardisation of product, price, and service which has been a hallmark of commercial lines of insurance over all these years, is a result of the needs for sound statistical and actuarial prediction, and setting prices that maintain solvency. Standardisation is also a result of the drive toward mass selling and marketing. Conventional insurance regulation reinforces standardisation. If regulators approve policies and premium schedules before insurance can be sold, rapid changes or deviations in product, price, or marketing practices are unlikely to occur.

In developing the growth trajectory for the marketing of innovative and new products by insurers in the liberalised market the regulatory authority envisages to establish deep and direct linkages between the insurance companies and the policyholders by understanding what exactly would offer a policyholder adequate protection and yet allow the insurance companies to remain creative under the "File and Use" system. Companies should develop products that fulfil new aspirations but still meet old needs.

The purpose of the file and use system is:

1. to protect policyholders and public against the adverse effects of excessive, inadequate or unfairly discriminatory rates;

2. to promote price competition amongst insurers so as to provide rates that are responsive to competitive market conditions;

3. to prohibit price fixing and other anti-competitive behaviour amongst insurers;

4. to provide regulatory procedures for the maintenance of appropriate data reporting systems;

5. to provide regulatory controls in the absence of competition;

6. to improve availability; fairness and reliability of insurance;

7. to authorise essential co-operative action among insurers in the rate making process and to regulate such activity to prevent practices that lend to substantially lessen competition;

8. to encourage most efficient and economical market practices.

Today with the emergence of complex computer programmes, individualised insurance relationships have become possible. The opportunity to custom design insurance packages for customers carries with it the power to design broader financial services packages. While the duty of the regulator to oversee the package would be minimised, oversight problems in ensuring sound premiums and management of reserves in order to protect solvency and prevent discriminatory pricing would increase. Therefore, self-regulatory guidelines need to be formulated and established by insurers. The regulator under the 'file and use' system shall not approve each and every customised package. While the duty of the regulator to oversee the package would be minimised, problems in ensuring sound premiums and management of reserves in order to protect solvency and prevent discriminatory pricing would increase. Therefore self-regulatory guidelines need to be formulated and established and encouraged.

In the emerging scenario in the country, no policy of insurance shall be used or delivered to any person nor shall any proposal, rider or endorsement be used in connection therewith until a copy of the form and the classification of risks and premium rates have been filed with the regulator. Upon request supporting/supplementary information shall also be required to be filed. Any filing made shall be deemed as approved (unless not approved by the regulator) within a period of thirty days after the date of filing.

Supplementary rating information would include any manual or plan of rates, classification, rating schedule, minimum premium, policy fee, rating rule, underwriting rules, and any other similar information needed to determine the applicable rate in effect or to be in effect. Supporting information shall include the experience and judgement of the filer; the interpretation of any other data relied upon by the filer; descriptions of methods used in making the rates; certificate from a solicitor that the policy wording used in the contract are not in violation of the laws in vogue; or any other information required. Within the specified period of thirty days after filing of a form, the regulator may disapprove the form if the benefits provided are unreasonable in relation to the premium charged, or it contains a provision or provisions which are unjust, unfair, inequitable, misleading, deceptive or encourage misrepresentation of the policy.

Rates shall not be excessive, inadequate or unfairly discriminatory. In determining whether rates comply with the standards set forth due consideration should be given to past and prospective loss and expense experience; catastrophe hazards; a reasonable provision for profit and contingencies; loading for levelling premium rates over a reasonable period of time, reinsurance arrangements, and all other relevant factors, including the judgement of the insurer.

Data reporting ensures that the experience of all insurers is made available at least annually in such form and detail as is necessary to aid in determining whether rating systems comply with the rating law/tariff wherever applicable. Experience shows that regulatory demands for data customarily increase when there are market problems.

Every insurer must record and report its loss and expense experience and other data and to submit returns, on prescribed form/s, showing its direct underwriting results. The regulator shall annually compile and review all such reports submitted by insurers to determine the appropriateness of premium rates for insurance. The regulator's findings and the filings shall be published and made available to any interested insured or citizen.

Every insurer shall establish specific standards, including standards of full and fair disclosure, that set forth the manner, content and required disclosure for the sale of insurance policies which may cover but shall not be limited to terms of renewability, initial and subsequent conditions of eligibility, non-duplication of coverage provisions, coverage of dependants, pre-existing conditions, termination of insurance, probationary periods, limitations, exceptions, reductions, elimination periods, requirements for replacement, and recurrent conditions etc. No policy or contract shall be delivered or issued for delivery which does not meet the prescribed minimum standards for the categories of coverage listed or does not meet the requirements set forth or if the benefits provided therein are unreasonable in relation to the premium charges.

By the time an insured discovers a particular insurance product is unsuitable for his needs, it may be too late for him to return to the market place to find a more satisfactory product. The uniqueness of an insurance product shall always have to be kept in mind in developing advertisements. False information, advertising, filing statements before the regulator, or any public officer, or knowingly making, circulating or placing before the public directly or indirectly any false material statement shall be treated as an unfair trade practice.

Packaging is very much part of product's attributes, and companies expend considerable effort in developing packaging that is recognisable and distinctive as well as functional. Primary considerations in labelling are providing information to the consumers and the use of multiple languages. Detailed product information must be provided, policy wordings should be simplified and warning messages included. Insurers should also provide instructions for proper product use, in which case readability and the quality of communication matter.

Conclusion

New product design and development must identify the similarities and differences of various cultures. This understanding shall allow companies to capitalise on commonalties or respond to differences appropriately. A well-designed product would answer most consumer needs. The needs of different cultures, populations and regions may not be able to be homogenised into one product. However, a country-specific variation of a product may be required. The question insurers need to ask themselves is - if it is better to discover the need for country-specific variations before the design phase or after the prototypes have been created. The more thoroughly a product is researched in the early stages, the fewer mistakes occur in the more expensive development phase. The user-centric approach of cross-cultural research eliminates ill-fated proposals early in the game. The streamlined development process ensures that better products get to market faster and more economically.

The 'new' order changeth yielding place to new. With the opening up of the insurance market in India, there shall be a continuous scramble for business. Insurance companies shall be increasingly rafting global and local tides simultaneously. They shall bring their vast experience of best practices to the table. As more and more people buy insurance, the demand for products and services is likely to expand. Customers shall become more discerning, and demand higher levels of service and value for money. The insurers and the regulator shall be responsible in the transformation of the insurance industry in the coming years. Adapting to change, responding to customers, and constantly looking for ways to innovate can ensure its accomplishment. At the same time integrity will go a long way in improving credibility and enhancing public confidence in the insurance system.

7

Some Issues in Product Development

B.D. Banerjee

One of the major issues in the overall liberalised scenario in the insurance sector is distinctly to be in the area of development of new products. While the importance of this area of a company's operation, particularly in the non-life sector can never be over emphasised, it is also a fact that this being a continuous activity is very crucial to determine the overall profitability and growth of any insurer. In fact, one of the major reasons given out for opening up of the insurance sector has been an oft repeated criticism that the sector has not been pro-active, in terms of development of products suited to consumer needs and wants. This may be true in some lines of business, but cannot be accepted as a generality.

The development of any enterprise draws its inspiration from the overall environment in which it has to function. This includes economic and social factors and more importantly the legal framework (Acts and Regulations), which the insurance industry is supposed to be working under. This framework in India is provided by the General Insurance Business Nationalisation Act (GIBNA), section 19(2) of which mandates the functions of any general insurer as:

"Each acquiring company shall so function under this act as to secure that general insurance business is developed to the best advantage of the community"

Product Development: Evolution Since 1972

It can be observed from the above principles under which the functions of a general insurer are being defined that any activity of product development should be carried out in the best interests of the community. From this point of view, the product development since 1973 has been directed towards meeting this goal by the Indian insurance sector. It is not that the General Insurance Corporation along with its four subsidiaries in the last three decades of operation have not developed new products or have not tried to meet the aspirations of the customers. It is a fact that presently there are more than 150 products on shelf in the four subsidiary companies of GIC.

The industry has been able to develop a plethora of new products, both in rural based covers as well as personal lines of insurance. Development of rural based covers in the industry since early 1970s has been one of the hallmarks of the general insurance industry. These products were not only unique in nature but had the advantage and privilege of meeting the economic and social objectives of the Government of India. One may recollect that even today there is a programme of development in the vast rural sector of India funded and financed by the Government. The programme works more like a movement and is known as Integrated Rural Development Programme (IRDP). The broad objectives of the programme has been towards alleviation of poverty and providing employment opportunity to our rural populace.

The general insurance industry, has in the past, served well these objectives by developing products suited to the beneficiaries of IRDP and service them also in the best interest of the community. It is possible that while providing a service and developing products for these lines of business, some aberrations may have creeped in the business principles on which these products were developed. However, with the passage of time, it was felt necessary to bring in the interest of the community over and above the business principles. This was possible as industry had developed business portfolios which could subsidise the profitability compromised in the development of rural based covers.

In addition to these, the industry did try to work out a solution for developing health care products as well. Mediclaim, overseas mediclaim and travel related products were introduced by the industry in 1980s. These products along with the traditional and non-traditional covers took care of the personal needs of a vast segment of population and indeed are quite popular to stand the test of time.

Other segments, which were more industrial in nature were covered by products like developing an Industrial All Risk Policy, a policy solely devoted to taking care of virtually all-possible risks to which an industrial hazard is exposed to. This policy was introduced in 1995 after having extensive consultations with various industrial organisations like chambers of commerce, industry associations etc. Presently, the product has been sold to nearly 80-85 clients from India, Oriental being the leader with 50% market share. While it may be agreed that 5 years may be rather too a short period to evaluate and review a product, considering the fact that insurance is a long term business, it is also true that this product has been serving well the needs of our industrial market segment, and yet not been fully utilised by eligible industries.

In the area of project insurance, particularly in the construction phase, the industry was able to introduce one of the popular products in industrial market taking care of the delayed start-up/advance loss of profits need of the clients. This was made possible with a fillip from liberalisation, which started in the Indian economy in early 1990s, is the financing of reforms went more and more in the hands of the private sector, there arose a need to cover anticipated loss of profits or delays in start- up due to various insurable perils. This cover goes a long way in not only meeting the requirements of the industrial entrepreneurs, but also takes care of the requirements of lenders as well. These products like industrial all risk, are like any comparable sophisticated industrial products.

Opening up of the financial services sector in the economy saw the general insurance industry developing covers for various stock exchanges, brokers, custodial services and depositories as part of their scheme to cover financial risk. With an extremely cautious approach, as is necessary, the Indian insurance market is serving the stock exchange, depositories etc. since last five to six years.

In addition to these covers, the industry was also able to develop products for segment on women (Rajrajeshwari Mahila Bima Yojna) and that for the girl child known as the Bhagyashree Girl Child Policy. The experience of developing products since 1973 has shown that the initiatives taken by the industry were in consonance with the governmental policy considerations. These are only a few instances of Indian market responsiveness to changing needs to protect development which includes the effort to package various risks under an umbrella cover. Notable among those are Fire 'A', 'B' and 'C' types. Motor policies on comprehensive terms, Householders and Shopkeepers Comprehensive Policy (with even LOP cover for small traders), office umbrella policies and so on. Latest in this innovation is the Mega Risk packaging in 1999, which has covered even different classes of insurance, under our policy with flexibility in terms and conditions and its applicability in time, with the practice followed in international markets.

Changing Scenario

Now with the IRDA Act in place and the sector having been opened to private participation including foreign multinationals the responsibility to develop new products is not limited to the four nationalised companies. Various regulations required for the new players to function have also been defined thereby making an overall environment conducive to developing new products and competition. In a way, the responsibility of product development now and in times to come will be on the market forces and it will be on these forces that the success or failure of reforms will depend. It is necessary for the new players to be equally conscious of the requirements of GIBNA and derive the benefits of a consequent social commitment. It will therefore be imperative on the part of the new players to meet the aspirations of the people or what the GIBNA defines as *the best interest of the community*.

Consumer Megatrends

If we try to look at the major changes in the socio-economic profile of our country, we come across the following trends by 2005:
- More than two thirds of our population will be literate.
- Close to half the population will be very young and in the age group of less than 20 years
- More than 30 m household will be earning in excess of USD 10,000 p.a.
- 165-180m homes will provide a vast pool of consumers for the market
- IT penetration and international linkages, internet will be widespread. It is expected that PC penetration will be 1 in 50 by 2008, from the present 1 in 500.

It can very easily be ascertained from the above facts that the maximum impact in terms of developing new products in this new socio-economic order will be felt by the players in the field, viz. consumers as users of service, insurers as providers of these services, reinsurers as supporters to the entire activity of providing a service, and various intermediaries responsible for representing either the customer or the insurer. Since our basic concern is trying to decipher the implications for insurers, the first thing that strikes us is that insurers as service providers will be required to develop distinctive insights into ongoing economic and social changes.

What this means from the point of view of a strategic business analyst is that the organisation will require to discern consumer megatrends. These trends will go a long way in determining the broad outline in which product development takes place. Discerning consumer megatrends leading to development of products therefore becomes a very natural business process. After the product is developed, it is required to be priced appropriately, awareness created about its existence, efficiently distributed so that the consumers can take advantage of its existence, and serviced effectively in order to ensure that the trial purchase repeats itself thereby developing into a long term business relationship. We must not forget that insurance is a business of relationship, essentially long term in nature. As a part of the marketing activity, therefore, it is imperative that the service provider develops this relationship in a positive way.

The process of marketing, therefore, becomes an exercise in product innovation. Innovation itself is defined as new ways of doing a thing. From the point of view of an insurance organisation this may mean two different activities:

- creating need for a product which already exists, and/or
- creating awareness of a product which hitherto did not exist, leading to development of a need.

What is required of an insurer is to identify that element which triggers this need. In other words, the dormant need has to be prominent through a marketing technique and acumen. Once this stimulant is identified the process of innovating a product begins rather automatically.

Policyholder Expectations

Identification of this need of the consumer which acts as a stimulant for product innovation itself flows from the process of analysing consumer megatrend. These involve analysing major economic and social shifts in an economy that affect business environment, directly or indirectly. These changes are themselves created by shifts in demographic profile, changes in consumer behaviour and preferences, qualitative changes in environment and future trends that these expectations are likely to take at the micro level. They can be termed simply as *policy holder expectations*. Identifying the expectations of policyholders or the aspirations of a customer of an insurance service would then involve the following steps:

- provide knowledge for initiating development of products.
- convert knowledge into products which offer value to customers.
- envisaging goals simultaneously at three horizons:
  (a) growth of current business.
  (b) expanding into related fields.
  (c) options for future growth.

It has been experienced that when new products are developed, the available product itself undergoes a change, and old products phase out. While this may be true of the manufacturing sector the service industry does not necessarily follow the same process. International experience shows that companies should develop new products which fulfil the aspirations of the customers (policyholders' expectations), but, at the same time, do not disregard their fundamental needs. Considering this by way of an example, when Industrial All Risk Policy was developed in the market, it did not, in any way, reduce the importance of the traditional products satisfying the need of the customer (to get protection).

The insurance industry did not phase out the fire and machinery breakdown products along with their consequential loss extensions. Even if we take the example of the IAR policy to be an experiment, which succeeded, we have in actual life scenario the rates of fire business actually being reduced in the market with the development of IAR portfolio. This is a good illustration of how with new product developments taking place on a continuous basis, the old ones themselves keep on developing within their own parameters of price, promotion or place.

Similarly, as office umbrella policy developed for a specific market segment, it did not ipso-facto reduce the importance of a fire cover or an electronic equipment policy cover. Market is abound with such examples where products continue to cater to their target market segments while at the same time new products continue to get developed for niche markets. It all depends on the overall marketing philosophy of an organisation. What is important is that the organisation identifies the policyholder expectations in the right manner and derive necessary trends and parameters to initiate the process of developing new products, on a continuos basis.

Role of Technology

From the above sequence of development it can be observed that no product development takes place in isolation. It has to be supplemented by a series of knowledge trends and along with environmental factors that make the entire process of product development a continuous one. Technology is one such element, which provides an edge to developing suitable products in an emerging scenario. It is also a crucial element in competitive scenario, particularly when e-commerce is likely to be the order of the day. Technology as a distribution tool may be at present in a nascent stage but has a great potential for providing a platform to develop cost effective supply chain. Needless to mention that this will be done by using state of art technology.

In the long-run, as internet and e-commerce penetration in an emerging economy reaches a stage of maturity, technology will be used for creating new products as well as delivering value for money insurance products. Looking further ahead, the servicing of the product will also be done with the help of state-of-art technology. We have already experienced the advantages of office automation in streamlining the overall operations of an insurance company. This will be extended to other areas of operation as well, new product development be one such important tool.

Insurance companies have been one of the biggest users of state-of-art technology particularly in the field of information technology.

The advantage of being technologically efficient leads to minimising distribution costs and increases greatly the speed of providing efficient service. Technological development has come along with facilitating interactive media, enabling the companies to take better marketing decisions. Such decisions, more appropriate to conditions of the market, have originated primarily due to a better understanding of the market. We have seen in the recent past the results of this better understanding by development of customised products, better segmentation of markets and better-targeted promotional campaigns.

The Product Itself

Looking at the product itself, an insurance product is nothing else but a bundle of utilities. It promises a service in the event of specified perils operating on a risk. This promise by way of an insurance contract becomes operational after a consideration is paid in the form of premium. This bundle of utilities can take the form of developing either standardised products or products customised to various market segments. Both have their own advantages and disadvantages. The Indian market till now has been characterised by availability of standardised products at standardised rates, terms and conditions. There have been products, which have been developed for niche consumer markets but they have been far and few. The market constantly tries to balance the pros and cons of a standardised versus customised products.

Developing a standardised product is inexpensive, faster and achieves economies of scale in mass selling. Contrary to this, customisation involves expensive development costs but allows the insurance companies to develop flexible individual insurance relationship. In an emerging scenario this is very important. With the growth of the Indian insurance market there is a strong likelihood that the market will experience more and more product development catering to particular segments of the market (niche markets) thereby allowing the companies to develop better relationship with their own customers. It is a fact that the product life cycle of an insurance product is shortening over a period of time. The implication of this is either to extend the product life cycle by innovating on the existing product or devise new and customised product after taking into account market requirements.

Internationally, the move is towards single premium and single insurer. The Indian market also has experienced this trend in the form of developing package policy for mega risks. This policy is available for mega risks after taking into consideration certain risks parameters, which qualify them for such products. They take care of the operational risks and are a combination of fire and engineering covers, which are developed in conjunction with marine or other commercial portfolio. The final package or a repackage depends on every individual case. The market has in this way not only reviewed the existing products but has also repackaged the same realising consumer megatrends. The only way this can go further is to expand its customer base and target market segments hitherto untouched. The market has also been providing opportunities in various other fields to which slowly the insurers are becoming pro-active.

Here, it would be appropriate to mention a word of caution. While adapting the products to suit consumer needs one may also have to take into account the judicial thinking which is available to us in the form of judgements in various legal forums like courts, consumer redressal forums and very recently ombudsman. What is necessary for an insurer now is also to take into considerations these judicial imperatives while developing a product in terms of conditions, exclusions etc.

Product Development: Role of Tariffs and After

Hence it can be seen that any product launch is to be preceded by extensive domain research, legal vetting, actuarial vetting and a test marketing exercise. The Indian regulator at different forums have categorically stated that insurers will be free to develop products on their own without having any regulatory interference. The only condition is that a life insurer will develop products in the life portfolio and a non-life insurer will concentrate only in the non-life sector. The policyholder expectations are, therefore, possible to be identified and met in devising appropriate covers. As far as pricing for developing products is concerned, the market has till now been used to tariffs, governed by the Tariff Advisory Committee (TAC). It should be understood well that in last three decades of market

Some Issues in Product Management 137

development, the process of product development has been rather a slow process.

Insurers have also concentrated on developing standardised products but have seldom concentrated on the emerging requirements of the market. The industry may have been able to achieve economies of scale but other parameters of product development have been rigid. This inflexibility governed by TAC has been reflected in the products by devising tariff prices, which were rigid, and not being responsive in terms and conditions as per requirements of the market. Only very recently TAC has brought a fair amount of transparency in its working by making the tariff a public document. This has allowed the tariff itself a fair amount of simplification thereby leading a better and transparent understanding of the terms of contract both by the insured and the insurer.

The emerging market trends indicate that tariffs may have to make way for non-tariff regime over a period of time. Tariff regime with regulations provide stability to the market as the prime concern of the regulator will be the solvency of any insurer. As soon as the market becomes fairly stable and insurers develop their own capacity to write business one can reasonably expect that the regulatory trend will be towards phasing out of tariffs. It is at this stage that there is going to be a real test for the market forces to meet the aspirations of an average customer. The test will also be for the regulator to ensure that the policyholder's expectations are synergised with the product development exercise. This entire process will actually determine the success of reforms in insurance. The non-tariff products, as and when they develop, either in standardised form or by being customised will have the following broad features:
- simplicity
- quality: fit for use
- customisation
- easy accessibility
- speed
- customer friendly documentation
- relevance to risk

Intermediaries

Another feature that the market is going to experience is the emergence of intermediaries in developing business as well as servicing clients. Insurance contract presently allows only one form of intermediary, an agent. Agent will represent an insurance company in front of a customer. Customers are presently indirectly represented before the insurance company by way of industrial associations or chambers of commerce. While this had taken care of the industrial insurance aspirations of a customer, the mass base in personal lines, health care and rural still remain underrepresented. It is expected that in due course of time intermediaries will also emerge as insurance brokers. The broker fraternity will have an immense responsibility to contribute to new product development. While this market force is yet to emerge it is clear from the trends available in other emerging economies that they play an important role in communicating and representing the aspirations of customers. They help in becoming genuine advisers to the customers thereby not only helping them to access the relevant products but also help insurance companies becoming aware of market requirements. Brokers will have an additional requirement of servicing the customers in the area of claims.

The draft regulations of brokers have been introduced in the market and from what the contents speak of the brokers will have a tremendous responsibility by not only representing the customer interests but also this is being ethical in practice.

Efficiency in Allocation

Various players in the process of product development as well as the overall environment initiated by GIBNA 1972, it is very difficult that market forces will take care of the best interests of the community. Regulatory intervention may therefore be required to ensure that the market develops as per the spirit of the overall economic policy of the Government of India. Allocative efficiency of insurance companies may, therefore, be a matter of concern while developing products. Since market forces may not automatically ensure the best interests of the community, it is for the regulatory forces to impress upon the players that those in need of risk protection should get it. It has been the experience world-over that health care insurance is available and service is provided to those who are healthy and wealthy.

India's vast population which lives in rural areas may have to be serviced by the emerging players by providing appropriate covers to those who actually require to be serviced. In this scenario the market should not only be competitive but also efficient in allocating services. From this point of view the rural and social obligations enunciated by IRDA deserve a special mention. Regulator has prescribed minimum standard obligations of insurers which have necessarily to be complied with in the market. It has also been specified that these obligations are for the next five years and can be reviewed after this time period. Product development will accordingly have to be directed towards meeting these goals.

Adverse Selection

Insurers also have a natural tendency to write only good risks. Within a particular market segment it is possible that different insureds may end up paying different premiums. A case in point is that of health insurance. The market forces will have to see that while developing products the possibility that a group of policyholders may be discriminated against any payment of premium be avoided. A sense of equity in pricing and providing terms will have to be developed while insurance services are directed towards developing niche market products. It is possible that product development may in the long run also see actuarial intervention.

Transparent Disclosure

While revising the product after developing it, it is the duty of the insurer to facilitate public understanding. This would indicate that the provisions of the product which may be misleading or potentially confusing are eliminated. Minimum product standards may have to be set up by each insurer while developing new products. From this point of view, disclosure norms brought out by the regulator as well as the norms on *file and use* are important.

Pricing

The most important aspect of developing products is pricing. It should be understood in no uncertain terms that price should not be excessive, inadequate or unfairly discriminatory. An excessive price may lead to losing potential customers and may invite legal action for charging excessively. Inadequate price may not be acceptable from the point of view of maintaining solvency of an insurer, particularly the one who has a very recent operation. The regulatory authority in India have also made it clear time and again that while they may not interfere in pricing of a product except that it should carry an actuarial survey of its ability to serve the customer, their prime concern will be the solvency of the insurer. This will be necessary to be taken into account while developing products. Ability-to-pay approach from the point of view of customers is, therefore, important and essential. It would also be desirable to obtain actuarial opinion and adopt actuarial standards in developing new products.

Conclusion

In sum, the essential components of product development can be listed as under:
- Consumer megatrends
- Policyholder expectations
- Technology
- Product
- Allocatively efficient
- Ability to pay pricing
- Minimum product standards
- Non-discrimination
- Maintaining policyholders rights and obligations

Choosing the right option through Research and Development and response study, balancing the operation with right kind of marketing which should include underwriting and pricing and being always competitive and focused to customer needs with constant updating of knowledge and database are the true qualities of product development in the emerging scenario.

8

Pricing of Insurance Products in Liberalised Economies: Lessons for India

R.D. Samarth

1. Introduction

As indicated by the title of this paper, an attempt has been made to discuss the various aspects which Insurance Regulatory and Development Authority (IRDA) will have to take into consideration in planning its strategy to monitor the pricing of Insurance products in new environment of liberalisation to ensure on the one hand healthy growth of our insurance industry on sound financial basis and on the other to ensure that policyholders get fully adequate, secure insurance service at economic cost to meet their socio-economic, technological needs.

The scope of this paper is restricted to discuss the problems of pricing of insurance products in general insurance arena of our insurance market. However, as per my perception, the basic issues involved in terms of price of insurance products and its impact on growth and stability, security and profitability, interests of stakeholders and shareholders are identical for both life and non-life insurance sectors of our market.

It may be mentioned that the issues of pricing of all products and diverse services required to fulfil community needs have become intricately complex in the present phase of restructuring of human society when the established socio-economic-political models of 19th and 20th centuries have either totally collapsed or have been radically transformed under the impact of relentless forward movement of its technological vector at galloping pace in post-1950 decades. As the offshoot of this dynamic macro-environment, theories pertaining to the perfect operation of a free market as envisaged by Adam Smith or ideally stable operation of economy in Marxist utopia have no more status of infallible elixirs.

Problems of pricing of products of insurance sector in general and general insurance in particular have become relatively compared to other commercial-financial service sector products, all the more complex, since insurance sector has to fulfil the role of simultaneously stabilising the unstable characteristics of human society's socio-economic-technological development.

Consideration of each and every constituent aspect of the pricing problem of general insurance product will require comprehensive discussion. However, within the constrains of the form for this article, it has been attempted to highlight the significant issues linked with every aspect and hope that it makes meaningful contribution to the discussion amidst the insurance professionals, policyholders and controllers of insurance business to evolve through consensus the right type of price strategy for ensuring, as stated earlier, vigorous growth of our general insurance industry on sound financial basis fulfilling its objective of contributing to the promotion of socio-economic-technological progress of India in 21st century.

2. Historical Role of Price Factor in the Development of Financial Basis of General Insurance Business

General insurance started in its primitive form of marine insurance 3000 BC in the form of a Bottomry Contract defined under Hamurabi's Code. As per the provisions under this historical code, the financier of the trade venture undertaken by a commercial entrepreneur was prohibited from the recovery of his financial loss from the trader, arising from the failure of the venture owing to the acts of God but was allowed in the event of a successful venture, to charge the trader the rate of interest on advanced loan, as per his discretion in excess of normal limits of interest rates stipulated under Hamurabi's Code for loan transactions.

Pricing of security risk in this primitive marine insurance form was thus the beginning of free market in global trade, linking the Western consumers' markets with the exporting centres in the East through the clearing house of International trade in Babylonia. Manusmriti (200 BC) provided Indian version of primitive marine insurance, stipulating that "The trader should be made to pay (taxes or duties) to the State for providing *Yogakshema* (risk and safety) taking into consideration the terms of purchase, sale, the length of journey, expenses and incidentals. The concept of adequate price for marine insurance in primitive form either through a private entrepreneur or through the state enterprise, is thus evident from ancient times.

The financial basis of the insurance contract, which was started in inceptive marine insurance contract form in 13th century by Italian traders as an add-on feature for commercial contract for export of goods was fully developed by Lloyds Marine underwriters and later on by British Fire Insurance company underwriters in 19th century to stabilise the instability in the operation of fire insurance companies. Basis of pricing of fire insurance is well defined in the extract from the article by J.M. McCandish in 1900 (Vol.III FCII), *"The prudent Fire office creeps along from year to year feeling its way, watching the ever varying contingencies which affect it, raising and lowering its rates as growing experience dictates, and having to deal with hazards which it can measure very imperfectly, it so deals with them as to attain a high degree of safety"*.

Early approach of fire and marine underwriters to the issue of pricing of risks was appreciated and supported by Adam Smith in 1776 in following words, *"That the chance of loss is frequently undervalued and scarce ever valued more than its worth, we may learn from a very moderate profit of insurers. In order to make insurance, either from Fire or Sea risk, a trade at all, the common premium must be sufficient to compensate the common losses, to pay the expense of management and to afford such a profit as might have been drawn from an equal capital employed in any common trade"*.

Underwriting of fire insurance business by British and European insurers progressed on this basic principle of generating surplus after payment of agency commissions and claims and incurring of administrative expenses lead to the development of tariff markets. Monopoly pricing of fire insurance was, however, challenged by British policyholders after the historical event of Tooley Street Fire in June 1861 which lead to the amendment of London mercantile tariff and establishment of Fire Office's Committee to monitor changes in premium rates of various types of industrial risks developing during the phase of industrial revolution. The same approach of pricing insurance risks was adopted by underwriters of miscellaneous accident business, which developed to meet socio-economic technological needs of new society emerging in Europe and UK as the by-product of Industrial Revolution.

It is worth noting that whereas Adam Smith supported the development of insurance practice, Karl Marx criticised it concluding that this practice does not result in covering the ultimate financial and production loss of community in spite of compensation of financial loss of an individual commercial company. As per his assessment, instability of community owned production economy by accidental hazards can be effectively covered by community investment in elimination or reduction in frequency and quantum of such losses through collective ownership and control of loss fund. Contribution of parties for such a fund was to be generated by right estimation of loss exposure of their risks. In spite of diverse approaches, it should be noted that either insurance premium or loss fund contribution was to be linked with risk exposure.

Mutualisation of insurance sector also emerged from the same approach of sharing of surplus generated by charging right type of price for risk and sharing the loss or surplus amidst the policyholders and insurers who had had direct stake in the ownership and management of mutuals as compared to the shareholders of stock companies whose interest was only in terms of security of their capital and adequate returns thereon.

From the above discussion it can be seen that pricing of insurance products is interlinked primarily with the risk factor involved and secondarily with the ownership norm of insurance industry. By the end of the 19th century insurance industry developed in Britain, Western Europe and USA market norm subject to widening statutory control through insurance legislation. Price control of insurance products, particularly pertaining to covers for social insurance risks like employer's liability and medical insurance remained under vigilance of governments of all states.

The basic financial equation of the operation of general insurance market in the 19th century Western World and its affiliated colonial markets was:

Premium − [(Claims + Expenses + Commission) + Reserve Strain] = Underwriting Surplus

Pricing of the insurance product was expected to generate underwriting surplus by all insurers irrespective of whether they were members of tariff association or operated as non-tariff insurers. Investment income generated from insurance funds was regarded as a welcome add-on to the underwriting surplus but not taken into consideration in the pricing of the general insurance products which exclusively depended on claims ratios and commission expenses outgo of insurers. Stabilisation of global general insurance sector was achieved on this pricing basis developed fully by the first quarter of 20th century through statistical techniques.

It is worth noting that global recession of 1930 did not jeopardise financial health of general insurance sector in developed countries. It is also worth noting that as per UK Government Committee's reports from 1925 onwards excessive price was charged by insurers for workmen's compensation insurance and hence finally this business was taken over by post-War Labour Government in 1945. The Labour Government also started National Health Insurance Scheme keeping this sector out of private insurance operation. Post-war French Government also nationalised four leading insurance companies with the objective of control of pricing of Insurance products and ensuring security for policyholders. Even in USA after experience of 1930 recession, stiff statutory control was imposed on pricing of insurance products and solvency provisions.

3. Transformation of Basic Operational and Structural Norm of Global General Insurance Sector in Post-war Decades (1950 – 2000)

During the post-war (1950-1990) decades, global general insurance industry underwent structural and operational transformation under the impact of macro-environment transformation as shown below:

A. Western General Insurance Market: Developed Markets

1. Excessive competition for business leads to decline of premium rates (price for insurance products) to inadequate level generating underwriting loss on long term basis (1975–90).

2. Returns on investment in stock/security market promoted cash flow basis for development of general insurance business.

Investment income became the primary source of profit compensating underwriting loss arising from inadequate pricing.

3. Formation of captives, pools, self-insurance schemes supported by global reinsurers promoted shift from conventional to non-conventional insurance systems.

4. Concentration of business in limited number of megasize companies. Medium size and small companies could not withstand the practice of competition and had to survive on limited volumes of business from their niche market sectors.

B. Japanese General Insurance Market: Developed Market

1. Pricing of general insurance products in post-war development of Japanese general insurance industry on tariff basis ensuring underwriting surplus in the region of 0.5% - 2% enabled growth of Japanese general insurance industry from the level of US$ 0.5 bn in 1950 to the level of US$ 80 bn in 1990 on sound financial basis with huge accumulated reserves.

2. Concentration of business with limited number of mega size companies was the outcome of Japanese corporate structure which tied corporate portfolios to their group insurance companies. Even though personal insurance sector developed through new products like Saving Linked Insurance Schemes contributed in post 80 decades 70% to Japanese general insurance business, stiff competition at economic price resulted in concentration of business in mega size companies with huge financial reserves ensuring higher investment returns on saving linked part of premium.

3. Tariff controlled Japanese general insurance started in 1991 transformation into free market norm under pressure of globalisation and with the completion of this process in 1998 the impact is seen in the decline in market premium growth rate and decline or disappearance of underwriting surplus in traditionally surplus market of Japan. Japanese general insurance market is passing through difficult period of transition owing to liberalisation of market and discontinuation of tariff system. If this market is not in a position to recover its consistent underwriting surplus in the region of 2% and generates consistent underwriting loss at the level of 5% like Western developed markets, it will be necessary for Japanese insurers to increase their traditional investment returns in the region of 4% to the

adequate level to absorb underwriting loss and produce cumulative surplus which will give satisfactory returns to shareholders of insurance companies. In this difficult environment there will be further concentration of business in 4–5 mega size domestic companies and possibility of take over or exit of a large number of medium – small size companies from Japanese general insurance market. There are trends of significant increase in future in the share of USA and Western European mega-size insurance companies in Japanese market which up till now is less than 2% of the total volume.

C. Market of Countries in Communist Block: States in Transition

Under the impact of collapse of communist system in USSR and Eastern Europe, their nationalised general insurance markets transformed into free or mixed norm market. This process caused virtual collapse of Russian insurance sector which in pre-liberalisation period was regarded financially sound for reinsurance business though limited in volume of direct non-marine insurance business. Chinese insurance market transformed with remarkable smooth pace into mixed norm market, with predominant share of 80% controlled by public sector company and business written at price, ensuring underwriting surplus in the region of 10%, preparing thereby a sound financial base for development of business from the level of 0.5 bn US$ in 1978 to the level of 4 bn US$ in 1999. Control on pricing of insurance products to meet adequately claims, commission and expense outgo and slow pace of opening of market to foreign insurers has ensured smooth transition of Chinese insurance industry from nationalised form into liberalised mixed norm as against the collapse of USSR's general insurance sector owing to the excessively rapid pace of transforming nationalised industry into totally free market norm.

D. Third World Insurance Sector

Third World insurance sector, which had emerged in post-colonial period, predominantly in localised and nationalised norm, adopted financial basis of underwriting surplus from the colonial insurance companies operating in these markets. Even though earlier double digit growth rates of these markets declined to marginal level in the economically recessionary decade of 80s, underwriting surplus on non-motor business of these markets generated by tariff rating of risks remained at satisfactory level. However, with the opening of these markets in the decade of 90s and discontinuation of tariff pricing, underwriting surplus levels are fast vanishing and the commercial and financial operation of medium and small size companies is jeopardised as there is little scope for generating investment incomes to compensate underwriting loss and generate surplus for adequate return on insurance investment.

These markets from Africa, Latin America, Middle-East and South Asia will have to find out a solution to this crisis if they have to avoid take over of this industry by financially strong and technically advanced developed insurance industry of Western Europe and USA. Insurance markets in Far-East and ASEAN Region developed very fast owing to double digit economic growth rates in the decade of 80s and are now developing characteristics of developed markets and likely to get integrated in global frontierless market.

From the above review, we can conclude that the:

Basis of pricing of insurance products in diverse sectors of global market has been linked to their macro-environment and socio-economic model. For developed markets, premium rates or price of insurance product is now totally integrated with financial operation of insurance funds. Cyclical fluctuation in the pricing of insurance products operates but the curve emerges from the imposition of investment returns on claims ratios in successive years, Basis of pricing of insurance products in the markets of states in transition and developing world, will be also increasingly integrated with investment income returns unless controllers of insurance take steps to see that there is generation of underwriting surplus at least at the level of 5% to ensure steady accumulation of financial reserves of domestic industry at the adequate level to increase its capacity for retention of market premium at reasonable level and limit outgo of premium through reinsurance to financially strong developed markets. Financially weak general insurance industry of states in transition and Third World cannot avoid in due course take over or control by mega size units of developed insurance sector. As per my perception, global general insurance industry will transform in tune with global macro-environment.

4. Pricing of Insurance Products in Indian General Insurance Market in Post-liberalisation Period

Based upon historical review of the role of price factor in the transformation of general insurance from its inceptive norm as bottomry contract in 3000 BC to the 21st century advanced norm of integral part of financial risk management, we have to consider now the price strategy which IRDA will have to plan for the operation of Indian general insurance sector in post-liberalisation period. As regards evolving price strategy for insurance sector, following aspects will have to be taken into consideration:

A. Underwriting Aspect

IRDA will have to take a firm decision whether it expects the insurers to develop business at price adequate to generate underwriting surplus or whether it accepts the operational norm of developed markets, which are now operating on cash flow basis generating cumulative surplus with investment income.

As shown by R.E. Beard, T. Pentikainen and E. Pesonen in their treatise on Risk Theory, if safety loading 'l' in insurance premium 'P' is non-positive then shareholders and reserve fund required by insurers to support premium growth of company should increase at least proportionately to the square root of the premium income. If safety loading 'l' in insurance premium is positive, then the reserve fund required by insurer to support premium income 'P' can be limited to a maximum given by 'Pl'.

Based upon the basis adopted by IRDA in fixing solvency provisions for Indian insurers, they will have to take a decision on fixing benchmarks for underwriting surplus for various types of portfolios, to monitor operation of insurance companies in the market. IRDA will have to decide whether to accept the approach taken by controllers of insurance in USA, to ensure that adequate in flow of funds is available for insurers reserves for supporting their business and if it is provided then not to take cognisance of the underwriting deficit of insurers in judging solvency position. It is felt that in the present stage of development of Indian general insurance sector, we should not adopt the approach of controllers of insurance in developed markets of ensuring only injection of adequate funds to support insurance market development.

Our premium growth in the next decade is expected to grow to the level of Rs. 20,000 crore from the present level of Rs. 8,000 crore and for supporting this growth reserves should be generated from underwriting surplus and not to be injected from external domestic or financial sources which may not be either available or can be utilised for investment in building other sectors of our socio-economic development. Limitation of 26% level of foreign insurers' participation in joint-venture companies will have to be raised to substantially higher level if domestic investment of funds is not available to support premium growth from solvency aspect. Financial health of our insurance industry should not be linked with foreign funds flow unless we are prepared to accept total integration of our domestic industry in the global insurance market dominated by developed insurance sector. Pricing of our insurance products should, therefore, at this stage of our development should ensure underwriting surplus under all portfolios. The level of underwriting surplus for various types of portfolios should be fixed taking into consideration the following aspects:

B. Technical Aspect

Neil Doherty has lucidly discussed problem of interlinkage of insurance premium and risk management in his treatise on Insurance Pricing and Loss Prevention: *"The conflict between the collective and individual interests of insureds arises when premiums fail to discriminate between insureds. Premiums thus tend to be averaged within a rating class with low risk insureds paying more than is appropriate on actuarial grounds and high risk insureds paying something less. This system provides an effective subsidy from low to high risk insureds and a move to a more efficiently discriminating rating system would consequently shift rates in favour of low risk insureds. This approach of insurance pricing to minimise if not totally eliminate unfair discrimination and ensure equity in premium rating imply a positive social valuation on movements in this direction".*

There has generally been a gap in communication between the technical managers and finance managers of our public or private corporate sector on the approach to the role of risk management and loss prevention in ensuring avoidance of loss and adequacy of security cover in its unfortunate occurrence. Insurers will have to play very active role in giving the benefit of economic price for insurance of our high-tech industrial sector and marine hull risks on par with global market but at the same time ensure that risk management of our corporate clients also rises to the level of developed markets.

Even though underwriting surplus of our fire and engineering portfolios shows satisfactory average level in the region of 20% with the escalation in the present marginal commission cost to 15% level in post-liberalisation period, there will be steep decline in this underwriting surplus. Claims ratios on high risk portfolio like petrochemical sector show increasingly fluctuating trend and pricing of this sector needs vigilant monitoring by IRDA from risk management aspect. Underwriting surplus under our Fire and Engineering portfolios should be retained at the minimum level of 5% in spite of increase in commission cost and expected reduction in premium rates under competitive pressure.

C. Commercial Aspect

Commercial aspect of pricing of insurance products is particularly applicable to premium rates under our marine portfolio. Export growth of our country is vitally important for supporting foreign exchange earning, which also compensates foreign exchange outgo on imports which are bound to increase in frontierless global market under WTO regime. Marine insurance rates of our market should, therefore, be competitive with global rates to make it possible for our traders to export on CIF and import on C and F terms. Even during era of nationalised industry, we did not prohibit arrangement of marine insurance overseas under CIF contracts for our imports and C and F contracts for our exports. At least 50% foreign trade turnover is, as per my estimation under overseas insurance policies.

With the right type of marine rate matching global level, there is substantial scope for development of our marine cargo portfolio which generates satisfactory underwriting surplus. It is perceived that 75% of our road transit trade is not insured and there is, therefore, scope for the development of marine business on substantially large turnover of inland transit trade. Linkage of risk management with pricing of marine cargo insurance will enable us to develop right type of commercial basis for marine cargo premium rates. However, IRDA will have to ensure that underwriting surplus of marine cargo sector which at present is at 20%, is kept at least at 5% in spite of increase in commission cost and decline in premium rates under competition pressure for ensuring healthy growth of marine business utilising hidden potential available for this expansion from our expanding trade turnover. IRDA cannot impose price on free market, particularly in marine sector which is intrinsically non-tariff market but they must fix some benchmarks for underwriting surplus under marine cargo business for monitoring the quality of underwriting control of companies.

D. Financial Aspect

Financial aspect in the pricing of our insurance products is intimately linked with the operation of our global direct foreign operation and reinsurance business. The operation of our direct foreign insurance sector as well as reinsurance arrangement of our target risk insurance in overseas market, it is felt that we have been too rigid in our approach to the financial operation of our foreign branches and reinsurance operation. If Indian insurance industry wants to develop further our well developed overseas direct operation, we must play the game according to the rules of foreign markets. It will not be possible for our underwriters to write business at price to ensure underwriting surplus in developed markets like UK, Western Europe, Australia or North America. These operations must be supported through judicious utilisation of our foreign operation funds and moving them through flexible schemes to earn adequate investment income to generate cumulative surplus on our foreign operation justifying returns on investment of funds for meeting solvency requirements in these markets.

New global scenario is bound to expose our foreign operation to the crisis of underwriting losses arising from inadequate prices and, therefore, right type of financial strategy is needed to support our foreign operation.

In the case of arranging reinsurance for our petrochemical, hull, aviation, satellite risks we must take maximum advantage of global competition for good risks. Our corporate clients from these sectors must get economic price for their insurance with good security. Continuity and long term relations in insurance world, should be given due consideration but to get the right price with adequate security in global reinsurance market will require far more flexibility in our reinsurance connections and financial expertise by our executives, in time to come.

Financial aspect of pricing of insurance products sold and bought by us in overseas market will have paramount importance in new environment.

Financial aspect of pricing of insurance products will be also important in developing in our domestic market new products like saving linked insurance schemes. If vast potential for development of personal insurance sector is to be tapped, we have to follow example of Japan in introducing saving linked insurance products at the right price and giving attractive guaranteed returns on saving linked part of premium. With percentage of our domestic savings to GDP at the level of 22% and with expected development of 20% population in middle income strata there is vast scope for developing this new type of portfolio. Financial management of insurance funds will play an important part in computing the right type of price for insurance products like householders risks, personal accident insurance to be developed in this category with saving linked component.

E. Social Aspect of Pricing Risks for Welfare of Community

In this era of globalisation and free markets it is worth reminding ourselves that even in the developed markets of USA and Europe, underwriters have not as yet succeeded in finding out the right solution for pricing liability insurance, motor insurance, medical insurance and crop insurance. As can be seen from the articles in insurance journals (Ref: Bests' Review-1992) of developed countries, there is contradiction in the attitudes of controller of insurance and insurers on the theme of the right price at which the insurers should be expected to fulfil their social obligations of providing community protection for their essential socio-economic needs.

IRDA will have to play an immediate important role in evolving the right solution to the problem of raising motor premium in our market to the level which ensures at least a break-even position for insurers as compared to the 30% underwriting loss which this portfolio constituting 35% of our total business generates. With the opening of the market to private sector and joint-ventures of foreign insurers, it will not be possible for IRDA to compel insurers to write motor insurance at regulated maximum price. It will be gross injustice to public sector insurance companies, if they are compelled by Government to write business at price which jeopardises their financial position.

Subsidisation of motor insurance by other non-motor portfolios cannot be justified when monopoly of public sector insurance corporation to write profitable non-motor business is lost. Right price for motor insurance, subject to right type of management of motor portfolio to ensure at least break-even position should be the strategy to be developed by IRDA through consensus of insurers, vehicle owners, transport operators and all other agencies like traffic control, vehicle manufacturers and repairers, legal profession, medical profession, etc. involved in this sector. There is no right price for motor premium in the society which is ruled by lack of integrity, consciousness, and commitment for social obligations at all levels. Example of Japan in solving the problem of right pricing of motor insurance by evolving a scheme for meeting T.P. liability claims through co-ordination between Government and insurance industry is a good example to follow. Litigation oriented systems of the Western World have been a failure to provide a satisfactory commercial solution to the problems of motor T.P. insurance.

New portfolios of medical insurance and crop insurance are expected to be developed by Indian insurers in new scenario of liberalisation with social commitment. If this business is to be developed on subsidy basis at national level, it can be done only through independent Government corporation. If insurers are expected to write this business on commercial basis, IRDA will have to evolve a right type of price strategy to ensure that these schemes do not start on unsound basis and end in a failure. There is lot of scope for commercial development of medical insurance in India for the developing market of 20% population with purchase price or covered under employer's schemes. Pricing of products for this class of clients should be left to insurers.

Rural sector insurance development for big/medium size units can also be developed on commercial basis by insurers as per their discretion at the right practice. But social welfare and crop insurance schemes for 70% of rural sector population which is either at marginal subsistence level or below poverty line, can be done only through independent Government corporation and not public sector or private sector insurance companies. In our welfare state our government has to fulfil responsibility of providing social welfare, security, health care and nutritional needs of 70% low income strata of our society. Investment of funds of commercial insurance sector in social welfare oriented government schemes under statutory provisions is justifiable contribution expected from our insurers to national goals. But for success or failure in operating these schemes planned to fulfil national socio-economic objectives, the responsibility will rest upon Government corporation formed with this specific objective.

5. Conclusion

Based on the world experience it is but natural that Indian insurance industry will transform into structural norm in tune with political-socio-economic transformation of our country. When this final transformation of our macro socio-economic model and micro insurance model into communitised form takes place, the problem of the right price for insurance products and service will get resolved. Till then we will have to continue efforts for evolving an integrated price strategy for ensuring growth of our general insurance sector in post-liberalisation period preserving the positive financial/technical features of our nationalised insurance sector and correction of distortions which have developed in its price strategy and other operational characteristics.

9

Capital Investment of General Insurance Industry: Issues and Challenges

D.C. Srivastava and Shashank Srivastava

Insurance, by definition, is an activity through which insurance companies indemnify the losses of the policyholders in lieu of the premium received by them from the policyholders. The losses to be covered and the period during which they are covered are clearly spelled out in policy documents. Thus the principal function of insurance companies is to meet the losses of the policyholders as and when they occur in consideration of premium received by them. The principal function of insurance in no way speaks about the investment operations of insurers. Investment as an activity and as a function of insurer is thus incidental to its main function, but assumes primary importance during the course of carrying out underwriting business. The present paper attempts to highlight the importance of investment function in the insurance business, the principles governing investment decisions, financial planning for these investments, existing opportunities for investment in money or capital markets, growth of insurance operations and regulatory framework governing investment decisions.

The paper has been divided into four parts. Part I deals with the need for capital investment by insurers, principles governing these investments, and the financial planning to be carried out as a prelude to taking investment decisions. Part II concerns itself with the opportunities that may be existing in the market while investing the funds. Part III examines the regulatory mechanism under which investments are carried out and Part IV traces out the growth of investment over a period of time and future challenges and opportunities in this area.

Part I

Need for Capital Investments by Insurers

The insurance companies receive premiums while extending the covers and carrying out underwriting business. The flow of funds to the insurance companies is on a sustained and continuous basis depending upon the policy period, which in case of non-life policies is mostly on an annual basis. The liability to pay the claims out of these funds arise at periodical intervals. Since there is a time-lag between the receipt of premium on the one hand and claims payment on the other, during the intervening period, insurance companies amass huge funds which they are in a position to invest. They build up such a large pool of funds, that they have been called as economy's 'investment reservoirs'. The investment made by these companies yield regular income and constitute an integral part of the financial activities of insurers.

There happens to be closed link between the principal activity of underwriting business on the one hand and the investment operations of insurers on the other. Competitive environment in the insurance sector leads to cut-throat competition amongst different firms resulting into price cut and lower premium income, which adversely affects the underwriting results. In many countries, it has even resulted into underwriting losses. The negative and adverse effects of competition on underwriting operations can be countered by the efficient and productive investment policies generating maximum investment income to these companies. However, since invested funds belong to the policyholders and claims have to be met out of these funds immediately as soon as they arise, it is essential that insurers should take sufficient cash reserves to meet claim obligations. In most of the countries, investment operations are subjected to supervisory regulations so that the interests of the policyholders are protected and investments are not made in unproductive channels. The efficiently carried out investment policies help in meeting solvency margin requirements on the part of these companies.

Principles Concerning Investment Decisions

The investment operations by the insurance companies are carried out from the accumulated funds of the policyholders. Insurers have to meet their claim obligations out of these funds and thereby protect the interests of the policyholders. For meeting the above objective, capital investment by insurance companies should be based upon the following principles.

1. Safety of Investment: The insurance companies are required to immediately fulfil their obligations of claim payment as soon as the loss arises. They should not default in their obligations. It requires that investment to be made should be safe and secure. The implications are that the value of investment portfolio of an insurance company should always match the commitments it has to meet while carrying out insurance business. The safety of investment will mainly mean that as and when the existing assets, in whatever form they have been held (land, share, security, debentures etc.) mature, the money received by the insurers should match the money spent in acquiring these assets. Inflationary rise in prices are normally not taken into account while matching the above funds.

However, it is important to bear in mind that capital assets are basically unsafe. It is not possible to measure safety in precise terms and should always be conceived in relative terms. For instance, while it is possible to calculate exactly the yield on fixed interest security since on maturity full value of security is realised, it is not possible to calculate the dividend in advance that a share will yield. It is quite possible that the market price of share at a particular point of time may be lower than the price at which it was initially purchased.

2. Yield/Profitability of Assets: The investments should not only be safe but should also produce high yield and be profitable. The investments should generate high and sustained yield while conforming to safety and liquidity parameters. They should also be in consonance with the situation prevailing in the capital market. The return on investment reflects upon the soundness of the investment policy and also determines its competitive strength vis-à-vis other insurance firms. As against safety which cannot be measured precisely and is expressed in relative terms, the profitability of investment can be measured and is expressed as a percentage between an assets yield (interests, dividends, rental income) and its book value.

There is a possibility of conflict between the objectives of safety on the one hand and profitability on the other. Normally assets yielding high rate of return are susceptible to high level of risks. It implies that in majority of cases high level of yield produces negative and adverse affect on safety and vice versa. Thus it is quite likely that an investment decision to advance a loan or to purchase a share may be justified in the short run based upon its high yield but in the long run it may prove to be questionable decision and may turn out to be non-performing asset (NPA). In the long run, due to change in economic structure or other changes in the economy, the debtors may find it difficult to redeem the debt and the companies may also become insolvent. From this angle, the evaluation of assets in terms of their riskiness and yield is of crucial importance while taking investment decisions. It is possible that the short term yield oriented approach may result into long term losses and may negatively affect the financial strength of insurance companies.

3. Liquidity: Another principle governing investment decision is preserving liquidity of assets. The debt instruments in the market possess different degree of liquidity. It is imperative for insurance companies to always hold certain proportion of assets in their portfolio which are highly liquid in nature and could easily be converted into cash. This is essential for an insurance company since it may be required to fulfil its claim obligation at any point of time in an unrestricted manner.

A conflict may also arise in pursuing the goals of liquidity and profitability. For instance property insurance covers necessitate holding large proportion of easily convertible assets since these covers are exposed to sudden major losses. Generally short term investments yield high return than long term investments.

4. Diversification and Spreading: As mentioned earlier, there is invariably a conflict between pursuing simultaneously the goals of safety, profitability and liquidity. Most of the high yielding forms of investment are subjected to large risks. The conflict may be resolved, to certain extent, by following the principle of diversification and spread. It implies that a investor should diversify his investment portfolio through a mix of assets of different variety. The assets could be of different maturity period, of different levels of liquidity and of different profitability. It is also required that there should be geographical spread of investments and it should not be confined to few selected locations. No single type of investment should predominate the portfolio of investors. Investment should have different debtors, and should be made in variety of forms. Even within each type of instrument, there should be variations in the sense that assets of different maturity dates may be held by the insurer.

The objectives of diversification and spread are basically to protect the investments in their entirety and combat one sided investment policy. Through the technique of economic models, it has been possible to determine the appropriate relationship between risk and profitability in a portfolio of assets. These models have enabled the investors to arrive at optimum combination of the assets in such a fashion that no other combination will generate less risk for a specific yield or a higher yield for a specific degree of risk.

5. Congruent Coverage: The principle of congruent coverage should be followed by those insurance companies who have business operations abroad and also be reinsurers who have to settle claims in foreign currency. It implies that insurers operating abroad and reinsurers should always hold assets in the same foreign currency where its liabilities may arise. It prevents the insurance companies from the losses originating from fluctuations in exchange rates. Thus if the value of a foreign currency increases, there will be increased liability but simultaneously there will also be enhancement in the value of assets held in that foreign currency.

Part II

Financial Planning and Investments

The above principles of safety, profitability and liquidity set out the broad framework within which investment policy should be framed. However, the actual investment policy will have to be tuned as per the prevailing business conditions and environment of the insurance companies. That necessitates carrying out financial planning by insurers. The financial planning helps in quantifying the funds that would be available for investment, the types of assets in which investments have to be made, the risks to which investments are exposed to and the nature and pattern of the portfolios in terms of mix and spread.

Firstly, the financial planning helps in actually identifying the size of funds which will be available for investments. Broadly for an insurer, investment funds are arrived at after deducting from the total premium, the existing and potential claim liability and management expenses. The interest income from the investments already made and the proceeds from the sale of assets, if any, are also available for investment. The underwriting experience of insurance companies indicates that the claim liabilities arise shortly in respect of those companies which have large number of low premium covers for masses compared to those companies whose business broadly covers large projects. The insurers with low premium mass oriented policies need funds at a very short interval to meet claim liabilities and are not in a position to place large proportion of their funds as investment. In contrast, insurance companies with large projects in their business are capable of deploying their funds as investment. For these companies, there is also financial compulsion to invest their funds and earn investment income which go to meet the claims liabilities, which are large in nature as and when they arise.

Secondly, financial planning also helps to determine the distribution of funds between short term, medium term and long term assets. The insurers whose nature of business is such that claims arise at short intervals will have to place their funds in short duration liquid assets. For instance in India, the funds collected from motor business are required to be paid as claims at short intervals and quite frequently. The claim ratio in this business is also quite high. These companies will have to invest in short term assets so that they could be converted into cash as soon as claims liabilities arise. On the other hand, companies having underwriting business of the nature where claims liabilities arise in the long run have the leverage of investing in long term assets with high risk content.

Thirdly, the investments made by a insurance company are exposed to several risks. The company is required to identify these risks, find out the probability of their occurrence and should take measures to prevent or minimise these risks. In particular, the company should safeguard the price of assets and interest rate earned on it. The risk to investment may arise from various corners. These could be primarily commercial and market risks. Commercial risks are those which arise owing to debtors inability to pay back the loan. Such risks are normally more in case of long term loans where repayment schedule is after a long time and also in case of firms with doubtful integrity. There could also be market risks to investment. These risks emanate from unforeseen changes in market prices, in particular through fluctuations in interest and exchange rates. The movements in financial markets particularly in share markets are most uncertain. Most of the forecasts on these movements turn out to be wrong. The financial markets are effected by hosts of factors which could be either economic or non-economic in nature. Although it may be relatively easier to predict movements in major macro economic variables such as inflation, economic growth, balance of payments, labour markets, exit policy etc. but it is very difficult to precisely predict movements in financial markets since these markets are primarily guided by non-economic factors which may be psychological and political in nature. Recently, there has been emergence of new forms of investment which protect other investments against negative movements in market prices or interests rates (hedging).

Insurers could also use the technique of option to protect the adverse effect on shares caused by the fall in its market value. The technique of option implies that the buyer of an asset (say shares) pays a premium to the seller to acquire the right to purchase or sell the asset at a fixed rate. As against the technique of option, the method of 'future' binds both seller and buyer to fulfil the sale deeds in future at pre-determined point of time.

The decision regarding mixing of assets of different varieties in the portfolio of insurers depends upon several factors such as nature of business of insurance companies (whether engaged in life or non-life business), the structure of domestic capital market, prevailing political, economic and social environment etc. The insurers have wide choice to select from the assets being traded in the market. These could be in the form of short-term investments, fixed interests bearing securities, shares, real estate, mortgages etc. The insurance companies whose business is subjected to wide fluctuations tend to invest in short term securities and such debt instruments which can be converted into cash at a short notice. For instance, companies with maximum of property insurance and motor insurance may have to invest in short term assets. These securities are not susceptible to interest risk and are safe. These securities also ensure high rate of profitability. Such fixed interest bearing securities are traded in the form of open market loans, mortgage bonds, municipal (local authority) bonds, optional binds, zero bonds etc.

Part III

Insurance companies command large accumulated funds which are built up over a period of time as they have to generate reserves for payment to the policyholders in case of occurrence of loss. These funds are built up from the premium collected by the insurer against the commitment to cover the identified losses. Policyholders have, therefore, legitimate claim over these funds. It is but imperative that these funds should be used judiciously so as to ensure safety, profitability, and liquidity. There may be temptation on the part of insurers to block these funds in high quick yielding securities which in the long run may turn out to be unsafe. They may turn out to be non-performing assets (NPA). The interests of policyholders is marred in this process as the insurance companies may fail to fulfil their commitments to meet the losses. They may also not be able to maintain required level of solvency margin.

Further, in certain economies there may also be need for mobilising investment in socially oriented projects or in infrastructure projects which may be required for creating conducive investment environment. For meeting these objectives, in some of the countries Government/regulatory authorities have imposed certain restrictions on the capital investments to be made by insurance companies. These restrictions have been either in the form of framing broad guidelines under which investment policy has to be structured or binding the insurers to invest only in selected well defined assets which in turn may be required to be kept for meeting solvency margin.

In India, the investment policy of insurers is regulated under Section 27 (a+b) of the Insurance Act, 1938. The main provisions of the Act are given as under:

No insurer carrying on general insurance business shall invest or keep invested any part of his assets otherwise than in any of the following approved investments:

(i) approved securities;

(ii) securities guaranteed as to principal and interest by the government of the United Kingdom;

(iii) debentures or other securities for money issued with the permission of the state government by any municipality in a state;

(iv) debentures or other securities for money issued by any authority constituted under any housing or building scheme approved by the central or a state government, or by any authority or body constituted by any central act or act of a state legislature;

(v) first mortgage on immovable property situated in India under any housing or building scheme of the insurer approved by the authority (Insurance Regulatory and Development Authority) or a state government.

(vi) immovable property situated in India or in any other country where insurer is carrying on insurance business;

(vii) fixed deposits with banks included for the time being in the Second Schedule to the Reserve Bank of India Act, 1934 (2 of 1934) or with co-operative societies registered under the Indian Co-operative Societies Act, 1912 (6 of 1912), or under any other law for the time being in force, the primary objective of which is to finance other co-operative societies similarly registered;

(viii) debentures of or shares in co-operative societies registered under the Indian Co-operative Societies Act, 1912 (2 of 1912), or any other law for the time being in force;

(ix) debentures secured by a first charge on any immovable property, plant or equipment of any company where either the book value or the market value, whichever is less, of such property, plant or equipment is more than twice the value of such debentures;

(x) first debentures secured by a floating charge on all its assets or by a fixed charge on fixed assets and floating charge on all other assets of any company which has paid dividends on its equity shares

Capital Investment of General Insurance Industry 165

for the three years immediately preceding or for at least three out of the four or five years immediately preceding the date of the investment;

(xi) preference shares of any company which has paid dividends on its equity shares for the three years immediately preceding or for at least three out of the four or five years immediately preceding;

(xii) preference shares of any company on which dividends have been paid for the three years immediately preceding or for at least three out of the four or five years immediately preceding and which have priority in payment over all the equity shares of the company in winding up;

(xiii) shares of any company which have been guaranteed by another company, such other company having paid dividends on its equity shares for the three years immediately preceding or for at least three out of the four or five years immediately preceding;

Provided that the total amount of shares of all the companies under guarantee by the guaranteeing company is not in excess of fifty per cent of the paid up amount of preference and equity shares of the guaranteeing company;

(xiv) shares of any company on which dividends of not less than four per cent including bonus have been paid for the three years immediately preceding or for at least three out of the four or five years immediately preceding;

(xv) first mortgages on immovable property situated in India or in any other country where the insurer is carrying on insurance business;

Provided that the property mortgaged is not leasehold property with an outstanding term of less than fifteen years and the value of the property exceeds by one-third, or if it consists of buildings, exceeds, by one-half, the mortgage money;

(xvi) such other investments as the authority may by notification in the Official Gazette, declare to be approved investments for the purpose of this section.

Investments in assets as specified between i to xvi have been categorised as investment in approved assets. It has also been laid down that subject to the conditions contained in the Act, an insurer may invest or keep invested any part of his assets otherwise than in an approved investment specified in i to xvi above if

1. after such investment, the total amounts of such investments of the insurer do not exceed twenty five per cent of his assets, and

2. the investment is made or in the case of any investment already made the continuation of such investments is with the consent of all the directors, other than the directors appointed under Section 34C.

3. An insurer shall not invest or keep invested any part of his assets in the shares of any one banking company or investment company more than -

a. ten per cent of his assets, or

b. two per cent of the subscribed share capital and debentures of the banking company or investment company concerned, whichever is less.

4. An insurer shall not invest or keep invested any part of his assets in the shares or debentures of any one company other than a banking company or investment company more than :

a. ten per cent of his assets, or

b. ten per cent of the subscribed share capital or debentures of the company, whichever is less.

5. An insurer shall not invest or keep invested any part of his assets in the shares or debentures of any private company.

6. An insurer shall not keep more than ten per cent of his assets in fixed deposit or current deposit, or partly in fixed deposit and partly in current deposit with any one banking company or with any co-operative society.

7. No insurer shall directly or indirectly invest outside India the funds of policyholders.

8. The authority may specify by the regulations made by it, the time, manner and other conditions of investment of assets to be held by any insurer.

In the general insurance industry, the Government had laid down the broad guidelines for insurance companies for investment of their funds. These powers have been delegated to IRDA after the passing of IRDA Act. These guidelines are as under:

(a) Central Government securities being not less than 20 per cent.

(b) State government securities and other approved securities, bonds, debentures of public sector undertakings inclusive of (1) above not less than 30 per cent.

(c) Loans to HUDCO, state governments for housing and for purchase of fire fighting equipment and special deposit with Government of India 15 per cent (subsequently special deposits with Government of India were taken apart from the above category for the purpose of investment).

(d) Market sector investments 55 per cent.

Thus, in general insurance industry, 45 per cent of investment is in the form of directed investment and the rest of 55 per cent can be placed in the market. It has also been laid down that investments to be made in the market should only be in approved securities, and the Act itself defines as to what type of securities could be treated as approved securities. As per the Act, the investment in unapproved securities should not exceed 25 per cent of the total assets and should have consent of all the directors of the company except those directors who have been appointed under Section 34C of the Insurance Act, 1938. Section 34C of the Act empowers the IRDA to appoint additional directors on the board of an insurance company.

It has also been prescribed under Section 28B of the Act that every insurer carrying on general insurance business shall every year within 31 days from the beginning of the year, submit to the IRDA, a return in the prescribed form showing as at the 31st day of March of the preceding year the investments made out of his assets referred to in Section 27B and every such return shall be certified by a principal officer of the insurer. It has also been made mandatory under the Act that every insurer shall also submit to the IRDA, a return in the prescribed form showing all the changes that occurred in the investments during each of the quarters ending on the last day of March, June, September and December within 31 days from the close of the quarter to which it relates, and every such return shall be certified by a principal officer of the insurer.

The insurer is also required to submit a statement, where any part of assets are in the custody of a housing company, from that company, and in any other case, from the chairman, to directors and a principal officer , if the insurer is a company or from the principal officer of the insurer, if the insurer is not a company, specifying the assets, which are subject to a charge and certifying that the other assets are free of any encumbrance, charge, hypothecation or lien.

Are These Restrictions Justified ?

Although there is a near unanimity of opinion that some restrictions in one or other form should be imposed on investment decisions of insurers, but the extent to which these restrictions should be imposed have been debated. Insurance companies collect the funds from the policy holders in the form of premium with the promise to meet the losses arising in future. Since essentially, the funds belong to the policyholders, it is imperative that the funds should be used in efficient and safe manner so that insurers are able to meet their liabilities to the policyholders immediately as soon as they arise. The assets to be created out of these funds should be able to meet the liabilities which have been created while collecting these funds. Further the yield from the investment is one of the important factors determining the price of insurance products. Although, there is a need to ensure safety and liquidity of the assets, but high ceiling on mandated investment reduces the freedom of the insurance companies to deploy the funds in high yielding securities.

There is a need to gradually reduce the proportion of mandated investment in the investment portfolio of insurers. Malhotra Committee Report has rightly pointed out that in the current economic scenario, the extent of mandated investments needs to be reduced. The reasons advanced by the Committee for reduction in mandated investments are as under:

(a) Despite an upward trend in the interest rates on government securities, the returns on mandated investments of insurance companies are distinctly lower than those on heir non-mandated investments.

(b) It has been the policy of the government to reduce the fiscal deficit which in turn implies lower borrowing from the market. In pursuance to the above policy, the statutory liquidity ratio for banks is being gradually reduced. The budgetary support to the public sector is also being reduced and they are being encouraged to access the financial markets for their funds.

(c) The policy of the government had been to increase the coupon rates on Government and approved securities as to bring them at par with market clearing levels. The move will automatically make Government securities attractive as compared to non-government securities. In that case there may not be any necessity to statutorily prescribe any limit for mandated investment on the part of insurance companies. These companies, on their own, may find these securities attractive and may prefer to invest in them.

Further, it is also necessary that the list of 'approved investments' as outlined in the Act may be withdrawn. In fact, these are in the nature of 'prudential norms' and may be notified as regulations by the IRDA instead of being incorporated in the Act itself. The list of approved investment dates back to 1938 when the Insurance Act, 1938 became effective. Since then, the financial market has undergone revolutionary changes and several new debt instruments have been innovated. The 'approved investment' list needs to be changed and modified at frequent intervals commensurate with changes in the financial market. Malhotra Committee Report (page 49) has rightly pointed out that "Sections 27A and 27B of the Insurance Act contain many provisions setting out the eligibility of various type of investment as 'approved investment'. These are in the nature of prudential norms which may be taken out of the Act. The insurance regulatory authority may reformulate them and modify them from time to time as may be necessary, in the light of evolving financial markets. The revised prudential norms may be notified as regulations. It is important in this connection to mention that for the sake of safety of investments on insurance companies, debt instruments should preferably be rated by credit rating agencies of standing, and term loans should be to companies of investment grade".

It may concluded that present regulations governing investments of insurer are at a higher side and needs to be reduced in a competitive and liberalised economic environment. Insurance companies should be given greater freedom and discretion to invest their funds and build up their 'equity portfolio' as per their own wisdom. Reduction in mandated investment may be necessary and in order to prevent investment in unsound securities, several other indirect methods may be used. One such method may be to make it obligatory for insurer to place their investments in securities of those companies which obtain higher ratings from reputed credit rating agencies. Similarly, the list of 'approved investment' needs to be modified as per the development in financial market and should also be taken out from the Act. However, reduction in controls should be such as not to result in weakening of financial strength of these companies and turning them into insolvent units. A judicious balance between decontrolling on the one hand and solvency of investment funds have to be worked out.

Part IV

In this section, the growth of investment, investment income and yield on investment of general insurance industry have been examined. Further, the challenges before the insurance companies in conducting their investment operations in a competitive market environment have been analysed.

There has been significant growth of both investment funds and investment income over a period of time. Table 1 reflects upon the growth of investment operations over a period of time. The salient features of investment operations are given below:

1. The total investments which were to the tune of Rs. 354.73 crore in 1973 have increased to Rs. 21923.96 crore in 1999-2000, recording an increase of about 61 times during the above period. During the last 5 years, the compound growth rate of investment funds was 12%.

2. The investment income increased from Rs. 20.5 crore in 1973 to Rs. 2473.95 crore in 1999-2000 amounting to about 120 times jump between the above period. The compound growth rate of investment income during the last 5 years amounted to 10.5%. Figure 1 depicts the growth of investment income over the period of time.

3. The yield on investment has varied between 12 to 13 percent during the last five years. Of course compared to yield of 6.5 per cent in 1973 it has gone up to 12.07 per cent in 1999-2000. The yield on directed and market sector investment during the last five years reveals that up to 1996-97, it was lower on investments in directed sector compared to investments in market sector. For instance, it was 8.77, 12.67 and 12.28 per cent in directed sector investment while for the market sector it was 16.43, 13.2 and 12.96 per cent during the years 1995-96, 1996-97 and 1997-98 respectively. However, since

Table 1 : Investment, Income and Yield of GIC and Subsidiary Companies, 1995-96 to 1999-2000

(Rs. Crore)

Year Ended 31.3.2000	1973 Invt. (Rs.)	1973 Income (Rs.)	1973 Yld. (%)	1995-96@ Invt. (Rs.)	1995-96@ Income (Rs.)	1995-96@ Yld. (%)	1996-97 Invt. (Rs.)	1996-97 Income (Rs.)	1996-97 Yld. (%)	1997-98 Invt. (Rs.)	1997-98 Income (Rs.)	1997-98 Yld. (%)	1998-99 Invt. (Rs.)	1998-99 Income (Rs.)	1998-99 Yld. (%)	1999-2000 Invt. (Rs.)	1999-2000 Income (Rs.)	1999-2000 Yld. (%)
Directed Sector	--	--	--	3796.9	424.0	8.77	4582.1	531.0	12.67	5628.1	643.4	12.28	6592.3	771.5	12.96	8052.5	920.1	12.56
Market Sector	--	--	--	8598.8	1075.7	16.43	9803.7	1216.2	13.21	11100.1	1337.8	12.96	12457.7	1489.3	12.64	13871.3	1553.7	11.80
TOTAL	354.7	20.5	6.5	12395.7	1499.7	13.2	14385.9	1747.2	13.00	16728.2	1981.2	12.73	19050.0	2260.8	12.64	21923.9	2473.9	12.07

1. @ As per the revised guidelines, from 1.4.1995, special deposits and loans to GIC HF are not included in socio-oriented sector hence the low yield.
2. Directed sector includes investment in Government of India securities, State Government securities, Government guaranteed bonds, loans to State Governments, for housing and purcahse of fire fighting equipments and loans to HUDCO.
3. Market sector includes debt, equity, term loan, investment in special deposit with Govenment of India and units of GIC Mutual Fund, Unit Trust of India. It also includes investment in money market instruments viz., call, CP, CD, FD.
4. (Yld.) Income as a percentage of average of opening and closing investment.

172 Indian Insurance Industry: Transition and Prospects

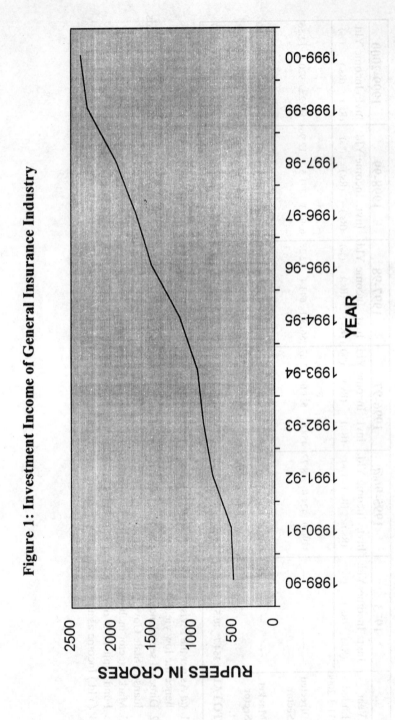

Figure 1: Investment Income of General Insurance Industry

1998-99, the yield on directed investment has exceeded that of yield on market sector investment. It was 12.96 and 12.56 per cent in directed investment as compared to 12.64 and 11.8 per cent in market sector during the years 1998-99 and 1999-2000 respectively. This could have been as a result of the Government policy to enhance the coupon rates on government securities and also due to depressed stock market in general. Figure 2 portrays the above trend.

4. Market sector investment spreads over different types of assets and securities. These could be in the form of special deposits with Government of India, taxable or tax-free bonds, equity shares of public sector or non-public sector units, debentures, preference shares, term loans and investment in money market. The yield on equity shares of non-public sector units ranged between 13.8 per cent in 1994-95 to 9.3 per cent in 1998-99. The yield on equity shares of public sector units was one of the lowest ranging between 2.4 per cent to 3.1 per cent between the years 1994-95 to 1998-99. The debentures commanded higher yield compared to equity shares. The yield on term loans was also relatively higher. Table 2 and Figure 3 indicate the yield on these investments.

Future Challenges

The opening of the sector will lead to intense competition amongst insurance companies to sell their products at lower prices. Insurance products are subjected to high price elasticity of demand. There is every likelihood that the price-war may be carried out to the extent that these companies start incurring underwriting losses. Unless these losses are countered by investment income, these companies may be forced to close down and stop their operations. It will make them financially weak and they may not be able to maintain solvency margins. Investment decisions will have to be taken by professionally skilled personnel in the field. Despite the fact that the underwriting losses of the existing companies have been compensated by the investment income, yet these companies have failed to develop expertise in investment department. In future, for increasing competitiveness and be able to survive in the industry, insurance companies will have to ensure maximum yield from investible funds within the parameters of safety and liquidity.

174 Indian Insurance Industry: Transition and Prospects

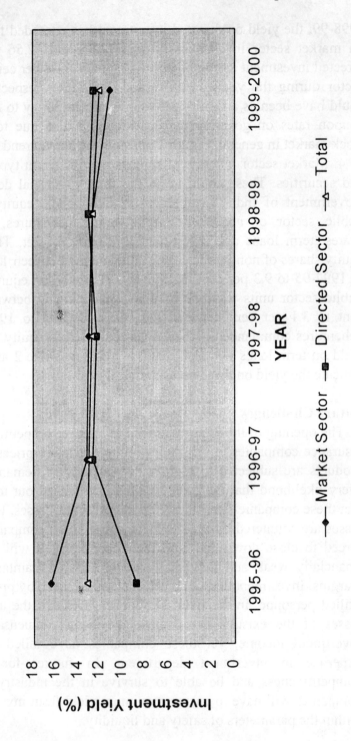

Figure 2: Investment Yield (%) of General Insurance Industry

Table 2: Category-Wise Investment, Income and Yield of GIC and Subsidiaries

(Rs. crore)

	1994-95	1995-96	1996-97	1997-98	1998-99	Average
SOCIALLY ORIENTED INVESTMENTS						
I. Central Govt. Securities						
Investment	1,793.22	2,214.30	2,646.81	3,166.35	3,654.31	2,695
Income	193.91	244.07	297.86	358.97	426.40	304
Yield %	11.5	12.2	12.3	12.4	12.5	12
II. State Govt. & Other Approved Securities and Bonds, Debentures of PSUs						
Investment	1,021.59	581.61	861.13	1,166.10	1,489.50	1,024
Income	107.78	67.57	100.97	144.17	181.91	120
Yield %	11.4	8.4	14.0	14.2	13.6	12
III. Loans to HUDCO, State Govt.'s for Housing & Purchase of Fire Fighting Equipment and Special Deposit with GOI						
Investment	3,439.93	1,001.01	1,074.17	1,295.70	1,435.06	1,649
Income	332.07	112.37	132.18	140.58	163.35	176
Yield %	10.7	5.1	12.7	11.9	12.3	11
MARKET SECTOR INVESTMENTS						
I. Special Deposit with GOI						
Investment	0.00	1,939.75	1,879.75	1,817.75	1,737.75	1,475
Income	0.00	238.43	229.66	221.79	211.72	180
Yield %	0.0	12.0	12.0	12.0	11.9	10
II. Bonds Taxable *						
Investment	0.00	335.16	440.05	365.16	556.88	339
Income	0.00	38.27	62.21	69.87	70.41	48
Yield %	0.0	22.8	16.0	17.4	14.5	14
III. Bonds Taxfree *						
Investment	0.00	446.79	498.35	475.27	382.61	361
Income	0.00	40.26	48.18	51.13	44.76	37
Yield %	0.0	18.0	10.2	10.5	14.5	11
IV. Equity Shares (PSU) *						
Investment	0.00	402.39	402.26	316.95	324.24	289
Income	0.00	11.02	10.71	8.65	9.32	8
Yield %	0.0	5.5	2.7	2.4	3.1	3
V. Equity Shares						
Investment	1,838.40	2,067.54	2,270.38	2,618.00	3,039.06	2,367
Income	225.55	262.85	295.48	335.81	260.59	276
Yield %	13.8	13.5	13.6	13.7	9.3	13
VI. Debentures						
Investment	924.59	1,273.08	1,613.15	1,910.84	2,372.81	1,619
Income	144.52	152.96	225.11	264.42	316.18	221
Yield %	15.4	13.9	15.6	15.0	14.7	15
VII. Preference Shares						
Investment	48.54	127.60	139.39	159.38	184.76	132
Income	5.90	7.55	10.69	9.33	8.51	8
Yield %	12.2	8.6	8.0	6.2	4.7	8
VIII. Term Loans						
Investment	413.39	587.91	670.35	1,001.10	1,144.80	764
Income	60.22	82.04	101.10	133.24	150.98	106
Yield %	15.6	16.4	16.1	15.9	14.1	16
IX. Money Market						
Investment	875.70	1,418.64	1,890.11	2,435.80	2,702.72	1,865
Income	100.99	242.32	233.09	263.85	453.82	259
Yield %	12.7	21.1	14.1	12.2	19.2	16
TOTAL INVESTMENTS						
Investment	10,355.36	12,395.78	14,385.90	16,728.40	19,024.50	14,578
Income	1,170.94	1,499.71	1,747.24	2,001.81	2,297.95	1,744
Yield %	12.3	13.2	13.0	12.9	12.7	13

* Included under State Govt. Securities as per the old guidelines and shown separately from the year 1995 - 96 onwards as per revised guidelines.

176 Indian Insurance Industry: Transition and Prospects

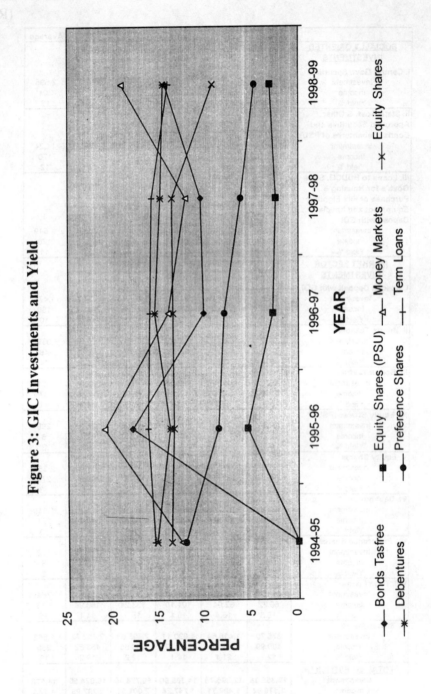

Figure 3: GIC Investments and Yield

10

Investment Management of Non-life Insurance Companies

A.P. Pradhan

A continuing integration of the Indian and the global economy and sound economic growth have created ground for opening of the insurance sector. A shift in regulatory control towards solvency and operations control have raised the need for competitive benchmark performance levels in insurance sector. It would, therefore, be appropriate and timely to appreciate the dynamics of Investment functions of non-life insurance industry in the context of emerging changes.

The investment activities of non-life insurance industry in India are highly regulated with a statutory framework and flow of guidelines in respect of pattern of directed investments. Like the insurance companies world over, the investment portfolio plays a key role in determining the financial strength of a non-life insurance company. The investment portfolio contributes significantly to the overall profitability of the Company. Prevailing tariffs in major class of business, domestic not leave opportunity for sustainable underwriting surplus in insurance business. During the last few years underwriting deficits are causing a drain on overall profitability by taking away a substantial part of investment earnings. In an adverse alarming situation the shrinkage in earnings would disturb the safe liquidity position.

In the event that an insurer has created adequate reserves to meet its obligations towards policyholders, earnings on investment are the key element in the overall financial health of an insurer. Earnings generated through underwriting and non-insurance related earnings constitute such strength of support needed for the core business. Earnings determine surplus available for capital growth, enlarge capacity to venture into products development, maintenance of solvency, ability to withstand adverse conditions and finally create an impression about the survival of the insurer. The dual effect on surplus inflicted by underwriting losses on one side and falling investment return in a volatile securities market on the other, highlight the need for increased accumulation to provide stability. For Insurance companies, surplus serves two purposes viz. financing the creation of statutory reserves as required by increasing premium volumes and absorbing the fluctuation of values of investment portfolio. In the matter of relationship between investment income and underwriting profit, the fact that now the insurers will operate in a competitive market will have a critical implication. In financial markets, they will compete for acquisition of investment and capital assets and in insurance market they will compete for premium income for funding these investment. The competitive forces will compel the insurers to settle with market price in both these markets.

In non-life insurance business investment income has traditionally been considered separate from underwriting income. Returns from investment operations have been considered to belonging to the company and its owners rather than to the policyholders. Insurers have asserted that investment returns reimburse the insurance company for an advance credit given to the policyholder in the form of premium discount. It has been argued that owners must be rewarded for using their capital to establish and maintain the return on such investment at the cost of not investing these funds in alternative enterprise of similar risk is considered appropriate. Further attractive return on equity are necessary to attract new capital for growth in the industry.

Asset creation process in the form of netting out of claims outgo from premium collection and net reinsurance flow is peculiar to non-life insurance. Actively collecting inflows from both business and investment income, parking them in short term investment avenues, converting them into permissible long term avenues, holding them till maturity or recycling them and actively reshaping the marketable portfolio altogether constitute major activity profile of investment management. Cash Management provides a challenge in reducing transaction costs which are involved in initiating and completing a transaction to avoid delay in handling the funds. In non-life insurance business, high cash reserves are needed to meet unexpected claims.

Such motive for high reserves creation has to be related to value of risks underwritten and should be increased when the value of retained risk rises. Experience of past two decades has shown that the demand for cash over and above that needed for meeting current transaction even for exceptional liquidity are met from the normal inflow of premium.

However, with the introduction of mega risk policies, need for up front cash outgo on even small to medium size would put pressure on investment managers to opt for precautionary approach. In a large insurance company having wide geographical spread of operating offices, capturing of cash receipt calls for availing of the best of the banking mechanism for quicker process of availability of funds for earning highest income on floats. Electronic funds transfer is introducing the changes in the nature of banking with the introduction of modes available to customer to pay their bills. The use of credit and debit cards, ATMs, banking at home systems via telephone or computer are expected to provide net work environment to cash managers. Management of short term funds aim at lowest float commensurate with liquidity needs and earning highest return through various money market instruments. Conversion of parked funds into long term avenues like sovereign and corporate debts, securities, equity and preference shares and other marketable securities need an up to date knowledge of market dynamism and a strong system support to pre-empt and respond to market development. In market related interest and pricing regime coupled with volatility, the ability of management to maintain and control the desired balance between liability and assets plays a greater importance. Managers of funds are exposed to be assessed with reference to benchmarks relevant not only to insurance sector but also to other financial market participants.

Insurers ability to finance its present and projected business from internally generated cash flow covers investment philosophy of management, asset portfolio mix and quality, matching of assets and liabilities, level of return on investment, cash flow and liquidity. Added to it is a capital market related sensitivity of net assets to fluctuations in market value of risk investments such as in equity shares. Investment strategy, hitherto primarily driven by regulatory requirements need to be replaced by a structured long term portfolio management perspective with more flexible market responsive investment strategy with clear cut objectives of building manageable asset portfolio to provide quick adaptability to volatile debt and equity markets. A large size sovereign and corporate debt portfolio built up through acquisition from primary issues and locked for maturity need to be converted into market oriented in a phased manner to seize the available market opportunities. The cost of such conversion should be kept at minimum level through operational efficiency. It is pertinent to realise that both life and non-life insurance industry holding large portion of sovereign debt can have a sizeable impact on price determination of this portfolio.

As large investment institutions, non-life insurance companies shall not ignore their role in capital market. A high percentage holding of corporate equity and preference shareholding and debt calls for active role in capital market. Institutionalised capital market with evolution of professionalised intermediary set up and sophisticated infrastructure in primary and secondary markets provides an opportunity to insurance companies to attain higher returns through efficient portfolio management in a well regulated capital market. The market is competitive and wide enough to provide the desired risk return profile to the investment portfolio through variety of new instruments having rating mark and fairly good marketability. In dealing with equity, a balance between insurance exposure and proportion of assets invested in equity need to be maintained. A history of underwriting losses emphasises the need to have a cautious approach in having equity dominated investment portfolio which is exposed to market risk. While recognising the need for risk diversification through sectoral exposure and spreading the portfolio over large number of scripts, such diversification shall not result in excessive fragmented holding resulting in administrative hurdles in monitoring the performance of large number of scrips and inhibit action in case of underperforming ones.

Investment Management is expected to aim at achieving higher knowledge of the risk index of the portfolio arising from credit risk, liquidity risk and interest risk in respect of each individual instrument. The management would thus demand a better control over risk-return parity of individual instruments and portfolio as a whole. The management need to be fully seized of the quality of portfolio and take quick measures to strengthen control over performance of the portfolio in an environment of market volatility and competitive pressure. Investment manager shall need to be quick to inject such strategic direction in management of investment portfolio.

The insurance companies will be required to initiate measures to streamlining operations and increase profitability and towards this significant efforts need to be made for building investment portfolio having profitable composition. A critical appraisal of the investment portfolio to assess whether it could support the modified needs of core business operations and withstand the fluctuations in the financial market is necessary. Asset composition would be expected to be comprising of a maturity profile which would be the best combination to enable it to timely honour its liabilities which are uncertain in nature and at the same time earn maximum overall return on investment. The need for growth in underwriting capacity through capital formation would invite pressures for creating resources within the company.

After the arrival of globalisation and deregulation of insurance sector, presence of competition in core business would bring pressure on management to improve efficiency and profitability of investment portfolio. Deregulation and liberalisation of insurance industry are accompanied by extensive regulatory framework. Investment Regulatory norms are emerging in extensive form covering both operational framework and disclosure requirements. Prudential norms in investment exposures would provide insulation from high risk investments. Provisioning norms would minimise the undisclosed erosion in asset valuations. With new players entering the insurance sector, there will be pressure on incumbent players to reshape investment portfolio not only to match their liability profile but also to assure a sustainable income flow.

11

Health Insurance in India: Opportunities, Challenges and Concerns

Dileep Mavalankar and Ramesh Bhat

1. Introduction

Over the last 50 years India has achieved a lot in terms of health improvement. But still India is way behind many fast developing countries such as China, Vietnam and Sri Lanka in health indicators (Satia et. al. 1999). In case of government funded health care system, the quality and access of services has always remained major concern. A very rapidly growing private health market has developed in India. This private sector bridges most of the gaps between what government offers and what people need. However, with proliferation of various health care technologies and general price rise, the cost of care has also become very expensive and unaffordable to large segment of population. The government and people have started exploring various health financing options to manage problems arising out of growing set of complexities of private sector growth, increasing cost of care and changing epidemiological pattern of diseases.

The new economic policy and liberalisation process followed by the Government of India since 1991 paved the way for privatisation of insurance sector in the country. Health insurance, which remained highly underdeveloped and a less significant segment of the product portfolios of the nationalised insurance companies in India, is now poised for a fundamental change in its approach and management. The Insurance Regulatory and Development Authority (IRDA) Bill, recently passed in the Indian Parliament, is important beginning of changes having significant implications for the health sector.

The privatisation of insurance and constitution IRDA envisage to improve the performance of the state insurance sector in the country by increasing benefits from competition in terms of lowered costs and increased level of consumer satisfaction. However, the implications of the entry of private insurance companies in health sector are not very clear. The recent policy changes will have been far reaching and would have major implications for the growth and development of the health sector. There are several contentious issues pertaining to development in this sector and these need critical examination. These also highlight the critical need for policy formulation and assessment. Unless privatisation and development of health insurance is managed well it may have negative impact of health care especially to a large segment of population in the country. If it is well managed then it can improve access to care and health status in the country very rapidly.

Health insurance as it is different from other segments of insurance business is more complex because of serious conflicts arising out of adverse selection, moral hazards, co-variate risks and information gap problems. For example, experiences from other countries suggest that the entry of private firms into the health insurance sector, if not properly regulated, does have adverse consequences for the costs of care, equity, consumer satisfaction, fraud and ethical standards. The IRDS would have a significant role in the regulation of this sector and responsibility to minimise the unintended consequences of this change.

Health sector policy formulation, assessment and implementation is an extremely complex task especially in a changing epidemiological, institutional, technological, and political scenario. Further, given the institutional complexity of our health sector programmes and the pluralistic character of health care providers, health sector reform strategies in the context of health insurance that have evolved elsewhere may have very little suitability to our country situation. Proper understanding of the Indian health situation and application of the principles of insurance keeping in view the social realities and national objective are important.

This paper presents a review of health insurance situation in India, the opportunities it provides, the challenges it faces and the concerns it raises. A discussion of the implications of privatisation of insurance on b health sector from various perspectives and how it will shape the character of our health care system is also attempted. The paper following areas:
- Economic policy context.

- Health financing in India.
- Health insurance scenario in India.
- Health insurance for the poor.
- Consumer perspective on health insurance.
- Models of health insurance in other countries.

This paper is partly based on a deliberations of a one day workshop (IIMA 1999) and a conference held at IIM Ahmedabad (IIMA 2000) in 1999-2000 on health insurance involving practising doctors, representatives from government insurance companies, medical associations, training institutes, member-based organisations and health policy researchers. Workshop and conference were part of the activities of Health Policy Development Network (HELPONET) and is supported by the International Health Policy Programme. The paper also draws on several published and unpublished papers and documents in the area of health insurance.

2. Economic Policy Context and Imperatives of Liberalisation of Insurance Sector

There are several imperatives for opening of the insurance and health insurance sector in India for private investment. Here we review these imperatives.

Economic policy reforms stated during late eighties and speeded up in nineties are the context in which liberalisation of insurance sector happened in India. It was very obvious that the liberalisation of the real (productive) and financial sector of the economy has to go hand in hand. It is imperative that these sectors are consistent with policies of each other and unless both function efficiently and are in equilibrium, it would be difficult to ensure appropriate economic growth. Given these facts liberalisation of both sectors has to proceed simultaneously.

Indian economic system has been developed on paradigm of mixed economy in which public and private enterprises co-exist. The past strategies of development based on socialistic thinking were focusing on the premise of restrictions, regulations and control and less on incentives and market driven forces. This affected the development process in the country in serious way. After the economic liberalisation the paradigm changed from central planning, command and control to market driven development. Deregulation, decontrol, privatisation, delicensing, globalisation became the key strategies to implement the new framework and encourage competition. The social sectors did not remain unaffected by this change. The control of government expenditure, which became a key tool to manage fiscal deficits in early 1990s, affected the social sector spending in major way. The unintended consequences of controlling the fiscal deficits have been reduction in capital expenditure and non-salary component of many social sector programmes. This has led to severe resource constraints in the health sector in respect of non-salary expenditure and this has affected the capacity and credibility of the government health care system to deliver good quality care over the years. Given the increasing salaries, lack of effective monitoring and lack of incentives to provide good quality services the provider in the government sector became indifferent to the clients. Clients also did not demand good quality and better access, as government services were free of cost.

Under this situation more and more clients turned to the private sector health providers and thus the private sector health care has expanded. Given the socialistic political thinking and populist policy it has been generally difficult for any government to introduce cost recovery in public health sector. Given that government is unable to provide more resources for health care, and institute cost recovery, one of the ways to reduce the under-funding and augment the resources in the health sector was to encourage the development of health insurance.

Another imperative for liberalisation of the insurance sector was the need for long-term financial resources on sustainable basis for the development of infrastructure sector such as roads, transports etc. It was realised that during the course of economic liberalisation, the funds for development of the infrastructure also became a major constraint. Country certainly needed infrastructure development. For this, the finances are major constraint. In these investments the benefits are more social than private. The major concern was how these finances can be made available at low costs. In past the development of social sector was financed using government channelled funds through various semi-government financial institutions. Under the liberalised economy this may not be possible. One hope is that if the insurance sector develops rapidly under privatisation then it can provide long term finance to the infrastructure sector.

The financial sector, which consists of banks, financial institutions, insurance companies provident funds schemes, mutual funds were all under government control. There was less competition across these units. As a result these institutions remained significantly less developed in their approach and management. Insurance sector has been most affected by the government controls. Government had significant control on the policies these insurance companies could offer and utilisation of the resources mobilised by insurance companies. One can see that most of the insurance products (e.g. life insurance products) were promoted as mechanisms to improve the savings and tax shelters rather as risk coverage instruments. Other segments of the insurance products grew because of the statutory obligations (e.g. Motor Vehicle, Marine and Fire) under various acts. The management and organisation of insurance sector companies remained less developed and they neglected new product development and marketing. Thus one of the hopes in opening of the insurance sector was that the private and foreign companies would rapidly develop the sector and improve coverage of the population with insurance using new products and better management.

Last imperative for opening of the insurance sector was signing of the WTO by India. After this there was little choice but to open the entire financial sector - including insurance sector to private and foreign investors (Dholkia, 1999).

3. Health Sector and its Financing: Present Scene and Issues for the Future

During the last 50 years India has developed a large government health infrastructure with more 150 medical colleges, 450 district hospitals, 3000 community health centres, 20,000 primary health care centres and 130,000 sub-health centres. On top of this there are large number of private and NGO health facilities and practitioners scatters throughout the country. Over the past 50 years India has made considerable progress in improving its health status. Death rate has reduced from 40 to 9 per thousand; infant mortality rate reduced from 161 to 71 per thousand, live births and life expectancy increased from 31 to 63 years. However, many challenges remain and these are life expectancy 4 years below world average, high incidence of communicable diseases, increasing incidence of non-communicable diseases, neglect of women's health, considerable regional variation and threat from environment degradation. It is estimated that at any given point of time 40 to 50 million people are on medication for major sickness in India. About 200 million workdays are lost annually due to sickness. Survey data indicate that about 60% people use private health providers for outpatient treatment while 60% use government providers for in-door treatment. The average expenditure for care is 2-5 times more in private sector than in public sector.

India spends about 6% of GDP on health expenditure. Private health care expenditure is 75% or 4.25% of GDP and most of the rest (1.75%) is government funding. At present, the insurance coverage is negligible. Most of the public funding is for preventive, promotive and primary care programmes while private expenditure is largely for curative care. Over the period the private health care expenditure has grown at the rate of 12.84% per annum and for each one per cent increase in per capita income the private health care expenditure has increased by 1.47%. Number of private doctors and private clinical facilities are also expanding exponentially. Indian health financing scene raises number of challenges, which are :

- increasing health care costs.
- high financial burden on poor eroding their incomes.
- increasing burden of new diseases and health risks.
- neglect of preventive and primary care and public health functions due to under funding of the government health care.

Given the above scenario exploring health financing options becomes critical. Health Insurance is considered one of the financing mechanisms to overcome some of the problems of our system.

4. Health Insurance Scene in India

Health insurance can be defined in very narrow sense where individual or group purchases in advance health coverage by paying a fee called *premium*. But it can be also defined broadly by including all financing arrangements where consumers can avoid or reduce their expenditures at time of use of services. The health insurance existing in India covers a very wide spectrum of arrangements and hence the latter, broader interpretation of health insurance is more appropriate.

Health insurance is very well established in many countries. But in India it is new concept except for the organised sector employees. In India only about 2 per cent of total health expenditure is funded by public/social health insurance while 18 per cent is funded by government budget. In many other low and middle income countries contribution of social health insurance is much higher (see Table 1).

Table 1: Percentage of Total Health Expenditure Funded Through Public/Social Insurance and Direct Government Revenue

Country	Social health insurance	Government budget
Algeria	37	36
Bolivia	20	33
China	31	13
Korea	23	10
Vietnam	2	20
India	2	18

Source: As cited in Naylor et. al. 1999.

It is estimated that the Indian health care industry is now worth of Rs. 96,000 crore and expected to surge by Rs. 10,000 crore annually. The share of insurance market in above figure is insignificant. Out of one billion population of India, 315 million people are estimated to be insurable and have capacity to spend Rs. 1000 as premium per annum. Many global insurance companies have plans to get into insurance business in India. Market research, detailed planning and effective insurance marketing is likely to assume significant importance. Given the health financing and demand scenario, health insurance has a wider scope in present day situations in India. However, it requires careful and significant effort to tap Indian health insurance market with proper understanding and training.

There are various types of health coverage in India. Based on

ownership, the existing health insurance schemes can be broadly divided into categories such as:
- Government or state-based systems.
- Market-based systems (private and voluntary).
- Employer provided insurance schemes.
- Member organisation (NGO or co-operative)-based systems.

Government or state-based systems include Central Government Health Scheme (CGHS) and Employees State Insurance Scheme (ESIS). It is estimated that employer managed systems cover about 20-30 million of population. The schemes run by member-based organisations cover about 5 per cent of population in various ways. Market-based systems (voluntary and private) have Mediclaim schemes which cover about 2 million of population. There are many employers who reimburse costs of medical expenses of the employees with or without contribution from the employee. It is estimated that about 20 million employees may be covered by such reimbursement arrangements. There are several government and private employers such as Railway and Armed forces and public sector enterprises that run their own health services for employees and families. It is estimated that about 30 million employees may be covered under such employer managed health services (Ellis et. al. 1996).

General Insurance Corporation (GIC) and its four subsidiary companies and Life Insurance Corporation (LIC) of India have various health insurance products. These are Ashadeep Plan II and Jeevan Asha Plan II by Life Insurance Corporation of India and various policies by General Insurance Corporation of India as under. Personal Accident Policy, Jan Arogya Policy, Raj Rajeshwari Policy, Mediclaim Policy, Overseas Mediclaim Policy, Cancer Insurance Policy, Bhavishya Arogya Policy and Dreaded Disease Policy (Srivastava 1999).

The health care demand is rising in India now a days. It is estimated that only 10 per cent of health insurance market has been tapped till today. Still there is a scope of rise up to 35 per cent in near future. The most popular health insurance cover is Mediclaim Policy. This policy is discussed below:

5. Mediclaim Scheme

The government insurance companies started first health insurance in 1986, under the name mediclaim, thereafter mediclaim has been revised to make it attractive product. Mediclaim is a reimbursement base insurance for hospitalisation. It does not cover outpatient treatments. First there used to be category-wise ceilings on items such as medicine, room charges, operation charges etc. and later when the policies were revised these ceilings were removed and total reimbursements were allowed within the limit of the policy amount. The total limit for policy coverage was also increased. Now a person between 3 months to 80 years of age can be granted mediclaim policy up to maximum coverage of Rs. 5 lakh against accidental and sickness hospitalisations during the policy period as per latest guidelines of General Insurance Corporation of India. This scheme is offered by all the four subsidiary companies of GIC. Mediclaim scheme is also available for groups with substantial discount in premium.

The current statistics on health insurance indicate that out of 1 billion population only about 2 million of population is covered by Mediclaim scheme. The reason for lack of popularity of this scheme could be several. The health insurance products are generally complicated and it is suggested that GIC and its subsidiary companies who deal in non-life insurance market which is dominated by mandated insurance such as accident, fire and marine, do not have expertise in marketing health insurance and therefore this scheme is not popular. Health insurance also represents very small percentage of overall business of GIC and its subsidiaries hence they have also not focused their attention in this area. The GIC companies have little interest and means to monitor the scheme. It should also be recognised that because of technicalities of health service business there are number of cumbersome rules which have hampered the acceptance of the scheme. It is also reported that in number of cases the applicants of older ages have been refused to become member of mediclaim scheme due to unnecessary conservatism of the companies.

Another area of less popularity of the Mediclaim is the lack of appropriate marketing efforts in selling these products. To popularise the schemes it is important that proper marketing is done. To make the scheme more acceptable government has exempted the premium paid by individuals from their taxable income. This provides 20-40% subsidy on the premium to taxpayers.

Mediclaim has provided a model for health insurance for the middle class and the rich. It covers hospitalisation costs, which could be catastrophic. But given the premium is on higher side it has remained limited to middle class, urban tax payers segment of the population. There are also problems and negative unintended consequences of this scheme. There are reported fraud and manipulation by clients and providers, which have implications for the growth and development of this sector. The monitoring systems are weak and there are chances that if the doctor and patient collude with each other, they can do more harms to the system. There is also element of adverse selection problem as the scheme is voluntary. As the scheme reimburses charges without limit, it has also pushed up the prices of services in the private sector. Our analysis of mediclaim data from one centre indicates wide variation of charges for same operation in the same city. Anecdotal evidence from doctors also indicates that charges are increased if patients are insured. All these effects will tend to increase the prices of private health care thus hurting the uninsured.

6. Employee State Insurance (ESI) Scheme

Under the ESI Act, 1948, ESI Scheme provides protection to employees against loss of wages due to inability to work due to sickness, maternity, disability and death due to employment injury. It also provides medical care to employees and their family members without fee for service. When implemented for the first time in India at two centres namely Delhi and Kanpur simultaneously in February, 1952 it covered about 1.2 lakh employees. Presently, the scheme is spread over 22 states and Union territories across India covering 91 lakh employees and more than 350 lakh beneficiaries. The Act compulsorily covers (a) all power using non-seasonal factories employing 10 or more persons; (b) all non-power using factories employing 20 or more employees and (c) service establishments like shops, hotels, restaurants, cinema, road transport and news papers are covered. ESIC is a corporate semi-government body headed by Union Minister of Labour as Chairman and the Director General as chief executive. Its members are representatives of central and state governments, employers, employees, medical profession and parliament.

The financing of the scheme is done by Employees State Insurance Corporation (ESIC) which is made up of contributions from: (a) employees who contribute at the rate 1.75 per cent of their wages (if daily wage is Rs. 25 or less, his contribution is waived); (b) employers who contribute at the rate of 4.75 per cent of total wage bills of their employees to contribution on behalf and for employees having daily wage of Rs. 25 or less; and (c) State Governments contribute 12.5 per cent of total shareable expenditure worked out by prescribed ceiling on expenditure which is Rs. 600 per insured person per annum and expenditure incurred outside/over and above the prescribed limit.

The State Government runs the medical services of this scheme of social insurance meant for employees covered under the ESI Act 1948. This scheme, compulsory and contributory in nature, provide uniform package of medical and cash benefits to insured persons is implemented through special ESI hospitals and diagnostic centres, dispensaries and panel doctors. The existing facilities under the ESIS are listed in Table 2.

Table 2: Existing Infrastructure under ESIS in India

Particular	
Number of centres	632
Number of insured persons/family units	84,45,000
ESI hospitals	125
Number of ESI hospital beds	23,334
ESI dispensaries	1,443
Insurance medical officers	6,220
Insurance medical practitioners	2,900

The delivery of medical care is through service (direct) system and/or panel (indirect) system. It provides allopathic medical care, but medical care by other systems like ayurvedic and homeopathy in the states is also provided as per the state government decision. The medical care consists of preventive, promotive, curative and rehabilitative types of services are provided by the scheme through its own network or through arrangements with reputed government or private institutions by concept of proper referral system and regionalisation.

Preventive services include immunisation, maternal and child health, family welfare services. Promotive services include health education and health check-ups camps. Curative services include dispensary care, hospital care, maternity care, supportive services including diagnostic centre, drugs, dressings, surgical procedures, dental care, prosthesis and other appliances. Rehabilitative services include physical rehabilitation, economical rehabilitation, and provision of artificial aids (social, psychological rehabilitation).

Even though the scheme is formulated well there are many problem areas in managing this scheme. Some of the problems are:
- large number of employers try to avoid being covered under the scheme.
- a large number of posts of medical staff remains vacant because of high turnover and lengthy recruitment procedures.
- there is duality of control.
- rising costs and technological advancement in super speciality treatment.
- management information system is not satisfactory.
- there is low utilisation of the hospitals.
- the workers are not satisfied with the services they get.
- in rural area the access to services is also a problem.

Some of the state governments have to subsidise the scheme heavily even though the ESI Corporation which is the financial arm of the system, has much surplus funds. All these problems indicate an urgent need for reforms in the ESI scheme (Vora, 2000).

Some of the options for reforms in ESI scheme could be making the scheme autonomous, managed by workers and employers while government only retails controls through a guiding framework as is the case with German Sickness Funds. Secondly, the scheme should be made open for non-organised sector through fixed income based contribution. This will extend the benefits of the scheme to many more people. The government should set the patient care standards and monitor outcomes as well as patient satisfaction. The management of the health facilities also needs to be improved substantially. The financial management of the scheme also needs improvement.

7. Health Insurance for Poor by NGOs

With 70 per cent of population in India living in rural areas and 95 per cent of work-force working in unorganised sectors, and disproportionately large percentage of these populations living below poverty line, there is strong need to develop social security mechanisms for this segment of population. This need for security is further increased because the poor are the most vulnerable for ill health, accidents, death, desertion, social disruptions such as riots, loss of housing, job and other means of livelihood. There are some efforts in this direction of providing social security to the poor by a few NGOs. The most prominent among them is that of Self-Employed Women's Association (SEWA). The other scheme by government insurance companies developed to focus on poor is called Jan Arogya Bima Policy which was introduced in 1995 and covers expenditure up to Rs. 5000 for a premium of Rs. 70 per annum.

It is estimated that about 5 million people are covered under various NGO insurance schemes. The experience from other countries suggest that in developed countries such as USA, UK, the health insurance have grown out of small non-profit schemes. A large share of health insurance market in USA is in not-for-profit sector. There is need in India to promote these schemes as they address the needs of the poor. Over the last few years in India small and big NGO's like Tribhuvandas, SEWA, ACCORD etc. have implemented the insurance schemes. Many of these schemes are designed to meet the needs of the poor segments of the community. They have developed several innovations such as:

- mechanism of monitoring the performance.
- pricing of various services.
- integration of various risks in one single product.

- linking of insurance schemes with savings.
- coverage of many services not included in market based schemes such as maternity services, transportation, coverage of risks such as from riots floods etc.

Some NGOs have developed special linkages with public health systems, private facilities and also accessed resources through insurance companies.

7.1 SEWA's Health Insurance and Social Security Schemes for the Poor: Poor women are the most vulnerable sections of a developing society. SEWA, a membership based women workers' trade union, has developed an initiative to protect the poor women from financial burdens arising out of high medical costs and other risks. Each member has option to join the programme by paying Rs. 60 per annum and it provides limited cover for risks arising out of sickness, maternity needs, accidents, floods and riots, widowhood etc. The scheme is also linked with saving scheme. Members have the option to either deposit Rs. 500 in SEWA bank and interest on this deposit will cover the annual premium or pay annual premium of Rs. 60. The scheme has 30,000 members and is expected to grow to 50,000.

In the beginning the SEWA started this programme with support of one of the public sector insurance companies. The experience of SEWA has been that the insurance companies are not well equipped to handle the present day complexities of health insurance particularly in context of lower income group needs. Given the bureaucratic rigidities in settling the claims, procedures, which one has to follow, and poor monitoring mechanisms make it difficult for the poor to continue with these schemes. For example, the patients belonging to lower income groups opting for the schemes would need systems which are simple, flexible, prompt, relevant, having less paper work and have fewer tiers. The design of the product including what it covers, scope of coverage and at what premium are important considerations for people belonging to lower income groups.

SEWA experience suggests that the design of the insurance products have to be integrated with several add-ons that may be priced differently. For example, health risk coverage should include sickness as well as maternity aspects. SEWA experience illustrates that other aspects of risk which need coverage include natural and accidental death of women and her husband, disablement, loss because of riots/flood/fire/theft etc. The overall premium has to be low. There has been lot of emphasis and education in the community on understanding the concept of insurance. This awareness is growing. The linkage with the providers has been critical aspect in keeping this cost of scheme down. At the same time the member has complete choice in selecting the provider but the reimbursement is limited. It has been observed that costs in private are more than 5 times than what they are in public sector hence developing linkages with the public facilities are therefore critical. This also depends on quality of care at public facilities. The overall experience of SEWA's health insurance has been encouraging. Women have started to seek health care and have been asking to enlarge the scope of the scheme. The scheme has tried to address the special needs of women health by allowing the other systems of medicine, which is quite popular in various places and paying for maternity related expenses which are not covered by Mediclaim scheme. The scaling up of the scheme and increasing the coverage is the most important management and organisational challenge. Recent study of the members of the SEWA scheme by Gumber and Kulkarni (2000) also indicate its usefulness.

7.2 Other NGO Health Insurance Schemes: Over the last several year there has been efforts to develop health insurance by various small NGOs. Some of the prominent among them have been ACCORD in Karnataka, Tribhuvandas Foundation, Aga Khan Health Services, India (AKHSI) and Nav-Sarjan in Gujarat, and Sewagram medical college Maharashtra. ACCORD works with tribal population in forested areas of Karnataka, AKHSI works with Ismaili population in North Gujarat, Tribhuvandas Foundation works in villages of Kheda district where there are strong milk producing unions of Amul Dairy Co-operative, Nav-Sarjan works with schedule castes in 2000 villages of Gujarat. Ranson (1999) has reviewed NGO efforts in India in this field. There are some common features of NGO schemes. The coverage of these schemes vary and most use their own health workers to provide primary care and have tied up with hospital to provide secondary care. Premiums are low, generally fixed and not related to risk. Most schemes have limited coverage and some also provide wider services besides health and treatment. All these organisations had good track record of services in the community and then added on health insurance on their existing activities hence they did not have to establish credibility with the community. The key feature among them was low premium and low coverage. These NGOs have shown that it is possible to develop a model of health insurance for the poor without much subsidy. The experience also suggests that if a credible NGO exists then it is not difficult to develop health insurance as an add on benefit. What is unclear and need to be researched is that what amount of total health expenditure does these scheme covers for the poor given that their coverage is limited.

7.3 Consumer and Social Perspective on Health Insurance: With the liberalisation of insurance and entry of private companies in this business, it is very important that specific interventions are developed which focus on increasing the consumer awareness about insurance products. One of the major challenges after privatisation of insurance would be how to develop such mechanisms, which help making consumers aware about the various intricacies of insurance plans. As of now information, knowledge and awareness of existing insurance plans is very limited. This is also shown by the study of Gumber and Kulkarni (2000) among the members of SEWA, ESIS and mediclaim schemes. With Consumer Protection Act coming in force, it has become easy for aggrieved consumers to complain and seek redressal for their problems. Consumer organisations such as CERC of Ahmedabad have been helping consumers to get due justice in disputes with the insurance companies. Their experience would be varying valuable in guiding development of health insurance plans that are transparent and just.

Many a times the insurance claims are rejected due to some small technical reasons. This leads to disputes. Most of the time the conditions and various points included in insurance policy contracts are not negotiable and these are binding on consumers. There is no analysis on what is fair practice and what is unfair practice. Given that insurance companies are large and almost monopoly setting the consumers are treated as secondary and they do not have opportunity to negotiate the terms and conditions of a contract. Many times insurance companies do not strictly follow the conditions in all cases and this create confusion and disputes (Shah M, 1999).

The most important area of dispute and unfair treatment is the knowledge and implications of pre-existing conditions. A number of cases of litigation are disagreement on these pre-existing conditions. These problems also arise because of lack of specification of number of areas and properly spelling out the conditions. This is also because some chronic conditions such as high blood pressure and diabetes can increase and risk of many other disease of organs such as heart, kidney, vascular and eyes diseases. The patients with these pre-existing conditions are denied claims for treatment of complications. This is not fair and leads to disputes.

Health insurance is typically annual and has to be renewed yearly. Policy which is not renewed in time lapses and a new policy has to be taken out. Medical conditions detected during the intervening period are treated as pre-existing condition for the new policy, which is not fair. This is seen as major issue as it changes the conditionalities about what constitutes pre-existing conditions. Courts, however, have ruled that even if there is delay in renewing the policies, it should be considered as renewed policy. In case two doctors give different reports one favouring consumer and other insurance company, the insurance company generally follows the later opinion. There are several such consumers related issues, which need to be addressed in health insurance.

One of the planks on which the insurance has been deregulated is the gain in efficiency and passing on these benefits to the consumers. It is very unrealistic to assume that insurance companies will be able to gain efficiency, which helps them to reduce the price of schemes. At least one should not be expecting this thing happening in the short run. But providing full information to the consumers and dealing with claims in a just and expeditious manner is the minimum expected outcome of the deregulation process. Consumer organisations have to play very active role in future development of the health insurance sector in India.

There are several social issues such as exclusions of sexually transmitted diseases, AIDS, delivery and maternal conditions etc. These are not socially and ethically acceptable. Insurance companies must take care of all the risks related to health. The companies may charge additional premium for certain conditions. Secondly the present mediclaim policy premiums are high and do not differentiate between people living in urban and rural areas where the costs of medical care are different. Thus the present policy is less attractive to poor and rural people. The tax subsidy provided to the mediclaim is also going largely to the rich who are the taxpayers. The newer health insurance policies have to improve upon the shortcoming of the existing policies.

8. Impact of Health Insurance on Structure and Quality of Private Provision

The experiences in liberalising the private health insurance suggest that it has undesirable effects on the costs of health care. The costs of care generally go up . Given the present system of fee for service and current scenario of health infrastructure in private sector, the development of insurance will need improvements in quality and change in structure. The new investments to improve quality will result into high cost and therefore increase in prices of insurance products. There would be developments in the direction of exploring options of managed care, which would help in reducing the costs. The developments would be needed in the direction of strong information base and accreditation system for providers. The structure of the health sector will have to change from multiple-single doctor hospitals and clinics to large hospitals and polyclinics, which provide services of multiple specialities and can operate at large scale. This will allow them to provide high quality professional care at competitive prices. As one of the responses to these issues Third party Administrators (TPA) are rapidly emerging in India. Here we can learn from the models, which have emerged elsewhere. But their applicability to Indian situation needs to be examined carefully. These aspects of the health sector will need detailed study.

We lack adequate information base to operate insurance schemes at large scale. The insurance mechanism prevalent in many developed countries has their history. Health reforms experiences in many countries are replete with the suggestion that the systems cannot be replicated easily. Self-regulation is an important in an market driven system. The regulation from outside does not work. Implementation of regulation in this sector is difficult. We significantly lack mechanisms, which would ensure self-regulation and continuing education of providers and various stakeholders. The accreditation systems are hard to implement without mechanisms to self-regulate. For example it took 35 years in US to put the accreditation system effectively in place. For example, it has been difficult for many states in India to put nursing homes legislation in place. Given the deterioration on standards in medical education, lack of regulation by medical council and rising expectations of the community, it is difficulty to ensure quality standards in Indian health care system. Given this situation health insurance systems will have to deal with this complex issue of quality of care in years to come.

9. Role of Regulators

The government has established Insurance Regulatory and Development Authority (IRDA) which is the statutory body for regulation of the whole insurance industry. They would be granting licenses to private companies and will regulate the insurance business. As the health insurance is in its very early phase, the role of IRDA will be very crucial. They have to ensure that the sector develops rapidly and the benefit of the insurance goes to the consumers. But it has to guard against the ill effects of private insurance. The main danger in the health insurance business we see is that the processed companies will cover the risk of middle class who can afford to pay high premiums. Unregulated reimbursement of medical costs by the insurance companies will push up the prices of private care. So large section of India's population who are not insured will be at a relative disadvantages as they will, in future, have to pay much more for the private care. Thus checking increase interests he costs of medical care will be very important role of the IRDA.

Secondly, IRDA will need to evolve mechanisms by which it puts some kind of statue in place that private insurance companies do not skim the market by focusing on rich and upper class clients and in the process neglect a major section of India's population. They must ensure that companies develop products for such poorer segments of the community and possibly build an element of cross-subsidy for them. Government companies can take the lead in this matter and catalyse new products for the poor and lower middle class as they have done in the past.

Thirdly, the regulators should also encourage NGOs, co-operatives and other collectives to enter into the health insurance business and develop products for the poor as well as for the middle class employed in the services sector such as education, transportation, retailing etc. and the self employed. This could be run as no-profit-no-loss basis similar to the scheme pioneered by Indian Medical Association for its members. Special licenses will have to be given to NGO for this purpose without insisting on the minimum capital norms, which are for commercial insurance companies.

10. Experience of Health Insurance in Other Countries: US and Germany

Various developed countries have differing insurance system to cover health risks. It is useful to contrast the American private health insurance system to German Social health insurance system. Table 3 gives this comparison.

It is evident that the German system is clearly superior to the American system. German system is social health insurance based on some key principles of solidarity, delegation and free choice, while American system is based on private market philosophy (Reinhard 1999, Stierle 2000). Thus the German system is much more suited to the needs of the developing countries. But some of the prerequisites of the German system are not present in India. For example, for social health insurance to work the work force has to be organised and working in formal sector so that their incomes are clear and there is a mechanism for payroll deduction of the contribution. It also needs a well-developed regulatory framework and culture of solidarity and self-regulation so that well off section of the community is willing to pay for the costs of sickness. Universal compulsory social health insurance is not possible in India at this stage but NGOs and workers in the formal sector can for organisations to try out such social health insurance in India. Experiences from other countries such as Malaysia and Philippines needs to be studied (Malaysia 1999, Philippines

Table 3: Health Insurance in USA and Germany

Key Features	American System	German System
Owners of health insurance	Private companies	Sickness funds composed of Members who are workers of one type - as in a co-operative
Coverage, and access to health care	70% of population covered, access to health care unequal	99.5% of population covered and access to every one is equal
Premium based on	Actuarial risk (age, sex, disease)	Income - % of pay roll. Shared equally by employer and employees
Selection and refusals	Do occur	Not allowed by law
Reimbursement to providers	Based on costs and per cases/procedure basis	Outpatient is on prospective per capita basis, in-patient per day, per case basis
Nature of subsidy (risk pooling)	From healthy to sick	Healthy to sick, high income to low income, young to old, small families to big families
Choice of providers	Yes - but being restricted in HMO system	Yes - wide choice
Coverage and co-payments	Limited to medical care and co-payment high	Coverage very wide and co-payment low
Nature of competition	Between companies	Not much - recently between sickness funds
Nature of regulation	Minimal by government, mostly by market forces	Self-regulation by autonomous bodies under overall framework of social legislation
Effect of medical costs	Highly inflationary - recently this effect is reduced due to various controls	Inflationary effect limited due to prospective per capita payment.

1999), so that we can develop a model based on good innovations from various countries while keeping the realities of Indian health system.

11. Conclusion

India has limited experience of health insurance. Given that government has liberalised the insurance industry, health insurance is going to develop rapidly in future. The challenge is to see that it benefits the poor and the weak in terms of better coverage and health services at lower costs without the negative aspects of cost increase and over use of procedures and technology in provision of health care. The experience from other places suggest that if health insurance is left to the private market it will only cover those which have substantial ability to pay leaving out the poor and making them more vulnerable. Hence India should proactively make efforts to develop Social Health Insurance patterned after the German model where there is universal coverage, equal access to all and cost controlling measures such as prospective per capita payment to providers. Given that India does not have large organised sector employment the only option for such social health insurance is to develop it through co-operatives, associations and unions. The existing health insurance programmes such as ESIS and Mediclaim also need substantial reforms to make them more efficient and socially useful. Government should catalyse and guide development of such social health insurance in India. Researchers and donors should support such development.

12

Agriculture Insurance: Status, Concerns and Challenges

D.C. Srivastava and Shashank Srivastava

Agriculture plays most dominant role in the development process of an economy, more so in developing economies. The history of development of industrialised economies indicates that during their initial stage of growth process there was sharp increase in agriculture productivity which helped in reducing the pressure of population from agriculture and induced growth in other sectors of the economy. As the economy developed, the share of agriculture in generation of national product declined and population dependent upon agriculture also fell down.

Presently in most of the developing economies of the world, agriculture constitutes sizeable proportion of gross domestic product, although it is gradually declining along with the process of development. Further, in most of these countries, more than half of the population is still living in rural areas and is dependent upon agriculture for income, employment and livelihood. Tables 1 and 2 indicate the above trend in some of the developing economies.

Agriculture and Economic Development

In economic literature, right from the classical economists, agriculture sector was conceived as one of the most important sectors contributing to the growth of all sectors of the economy and thereby to the welfare of the country as a whole. Ricardo in his 'Principles of Political Economy' identified the 'Law of Diminishing Returns' as one of the most important laws inhibiting the growth of the economy. He stated that a limitation in the growth of agriculture sets the upper limit on the growth of other sectors of the economy. Agriculture contributes to the process of economic development in several ways.

First, it supplies food stuff (wage - goods) to the growing population and labour force in other sectors of the economy and also

Table 1: Value Added in Agriculture as of GDP (1998)

Country	Percentage
Bangladesh	23
Cambodia	51
China	18
Ghana	37
India	25
Indonesia	16
Kenya	29
Malaysia	12
Nepal	40
Nigeria	32
Pakistan	25
Philippines	17
Sri Lanka	22
Tanzania	46
Thailand	11
Uganda	43
Vietnam	26

Source: *World Development Report, 1999-2000*, The World Bank

meets the increased demand for food emanating from rising levels of per capita income. In these countries, due to low level of existing food consumption, the income elasticity of demand for food is very high and a little increase in the per capita income, pushes up the demand for food quite sharply.

Second, agriculture contributes to the process of capital formation in the economy. The surplus from the agriculture sector has been able to finance investment in other sectors of the economy. However, generation of surplus from agriculture ultimately depends upon the increased productivity in the agriculture sector itself.

Third, agriculture provides raw material to a number of agro-based and processing industries such as jute, textile, sugar, edible oil etc.

Fourth, agriculture sector creates demand for industrial products

Table 2: Rural Population as Percentage of Total Population (1998)

Country	Percentage
Bangladesh	80
Cambodia	78
China	67
India	72
Indonesia	62
Kenya	69
Malaysia	44
Nepal	89
Nigeria	58
Pakistan	64
Philippines	43
Sri Lanka	77
Tanzania	74
Uganda	86
Vietnam	80

Source: *World Development Report, 1999-2000*, The World Bank

and services. A large segment of population lives in rural areas and increased income in rural sector resulting from enhanced agriculture productivity and 'marketable surplus', translates itself in boosting up demand for industrial products. Nurkse, the noted economist, has rightly stated that "The trouble is this: there is not a sufficient demand for manufactured goods in a country where peasants, farm labourers and their families, comprising typically two - thirds to four-fifths of population, are too poor to buy any factory products, or anything in addition to little they already buy. There is a lack of real purchasing power, reflecting the low productivity in agriculture". Fifth, the exports from agriculture sector of both primary and semi-processed products contribute substantially to foreign exchange earnings and ease the foreign exchange position in the country. The sector also relieves the pressure on foreign exchange through import substitution. Normally, sustained and stable growth of agriculture sector has produced stability in the economy, thereby creating congenial and conducive environment for accelerated investment and growth in other sectors of the economy. These countries have initiated several policy measures to improve agriculture productivity and income over a period of time. These include providing extension services, inducing farmers to adopt new technology, providing institutional credit, subsidies on inputs such as fertilisers etc., fixing minimum support prices for agriculture products, fiscal concessions etc. These measures have produced positive results and have led to gradual increase in agriculture productivity as reflected in Table 3.

Table 3: Agriculture Productivity: Agriculture Value-added Per Agricultural Worker (1995 dollars)

Country	1979-81	1995-97
Bangladesh	181	221
Cambodia	-	407
China	162	296
India	253	343
Indonesia	610	745
Malaysia	3,279	6,297
Mexico	1,482	1,690
Nigeria	370	541
Pakistan	392	585
Philippines	1,348	1,379
Sri Lanka	648	732
Thailand	630	928
Vietnam	-	226

Source: *World Development Report, 1999-2000,* The World Bank

Despite increase in agriculture productivity as is evident from the above table, the agriculture sector is still susceptible to vagaries of monsoon and natural calamities and catastrophes.

Insurance and Agriculture Development

There have been frequent fluctuations in the agricultural production and productivity caused by natural events and happenings.

Although the farmers in these countries have traditionally adopted various methods such as crop rotation and diversification, inter-cropping, use of hardy varieties, alternative sources of income such as dairying, cattle-rearing, handlooms etc., to minimise these risks but it has not been possible to completely eliminate them. The risks originating from natural calamities such as flood, drought, cyclones, windstorms, earthquake are common to all the farmers in the affected area and are not possible to be eliminated through individual measures. The agriculture insurance can play a very important role in meeting these risks and inject financial strength and stability to the farming community during such widespread disasters.

The growth of agriculture and its transformation from traditional to modernised and commercial sector is contributed by hosts of factors which may be both economic and non-economic in nature. The economic factors contributing to its growth are: use of hybrid seeds, application of fertilisers, insecticides and pesticides, deployment of tractors, use of threshing machine, increased irrigation through pump sets, canals, improved transport and communications, guaranteeing minimum support prices etc. The process of transformation is facilitated by package of these inputs, services, technology and information. The factors in isolation with others may not be able to achieve the desired results. In this package of services, adequate and timely availability of institutional credit plays a very crucial role. An examination of flow of institutional credit into different sectors of the economy in these countries indicate that financial institutions on their own have been reluctant to pump advance credit in the rural sector. In particular marginal and small farmers, artisans, landless agriculture workers and the segment of society lying below the poverty line have been deprived of the organised credit. There is a general perception amongst the providers of the organised credit that they may not get back the loan owing to poor credit worthiness of farmers and other vulnerable sections of rural society. They may also not be able to offer collateral to the financial institutions. It is a different story that the myth about defaults in repaying back loans by the poor sections of rural society has been exploded by the success story of Grameen Banks in Bangladesh which are successfully functioning under the leadership of Prof. Mohammad Yunus. Due to non-availability of institutional credit, the farmers have to resort to borrowing credit from moneylenders, traders and other unorganised sources at abnormally high and usurious interest rates.

In some countries such as Colombia, Philippines, Thailand including India, it is mandatory to earmark certain proportion of the credit to the agriculture sector. In India, agriculture has been placed under priority sector and banks are required to advance a certain minimum of their credit to the priority sector. Despite that, in 1999, only 11.6% of gross bank credit was deployed in the agriculture sector. There is a huge gap between and demand and supply of organised credit in the sector forcing the farmers to seek credit from unorganised sector to meet essential economic and social requirements. It seriously hinders adoption of new technology on the part of farmers, particularly by marginal and small farmers. Agriculture insurance can play extremely important and supporting role in increasing the flow of institutional credit to the agriculture sector. Agriculture insurance will largely solve the problem of collateral security requirement by banks while extending the loans. In case of crop failure, banks will receive the payment directly from the insurance companies. Agriculture insurance, thus, promotes flow of institutional credit to the agriculture sector which in turn induces farmers to adopt new technology.

Agriculture insurance also directly encourages the farmers to adopt the new technology. The transformation from traditional to modern structure of agriculture and adoption of new technology exposes farmers to new unknown risks and they are reluctant to bear these risks. Since new technology is normally capital- intensive, it also involves additional investment which may necessitate borrowings on the part of farmers. The apprehension about these risks prevents farmers to adopt new technology. Farmers may be induced to adopt new technology, if risks emanating from new technology are distributed through insurance coverage.

In some of the developing economies, savings in rural areas are held in the form of unproductive assets such as gold, jewellery etc. and are not invested in productive channels. These savings take the form of hoarding. The basic objective behind keeping these assets in such unproductive forms is to meet any unforeseen event in future as these assets are as liquid as cash. Insurance, particularly, life insurance, by indemnifying and covering these risks can play an important role in releasing these savings for productive investment.

Further, in most of the countries, government extends financial support to farmers, as a matter of national policy, in case of national calamities such as flood, cyclones, droughts, earthquakes etc. In case these risks are covered through insurance, the burden on government exchequer to that extent gets reduced. Insurance companies are also better equipped and possess requisite infrastructure to correctly assess the loss and distribute the compensation relating to their own liabilities as well as for the commitments made by the government for such natural disasters. One of the pre-requisites for transformation of agriculture sector from traditional stage to modern is the replacement of barter system of trade with monetisation and commercialisation of economic activities. Insurance services facilitate this process by promoting operation of agriculture activities through institutional channels.

Forms and Scope of Agriculture Insurance

Agriculture insurance is not restricted to crop insurance only, although it is one of the most important and major constituents of agriculture insurance. Agriculture insurance is much wider in scope and content and includes insurance of seed, cattle, horticulture, plantations, forestry, sericulture, aquaculture, poultry, viniculture and all such activities which are allied to agriculture. In its wider connotation, it should cover all operations commencing from sowing of seeds to marketing of final products which are connected to agriculture. It will also include all the capital equipments used during different stages of agricultural operations such as tractors, threshing machines, drought animals, pumpsets, processing plants etc. From this angle, agriculture insurance can be treated as synonymous with rural insurance.

The developing countries offer ample scope for agriculture insurance in their economies. These countries have been investing large sum of funds in agriculture to accelerate productivity in the sector. Every investment made in agriculture carries with itself certain risks and these risks can be undertaken by insurance companies. For instance, most of these countries have invested large amount of funds in developing hybrid seed, and promoting use of hybrid seed by farmers has been one of the major policy instruments to increase productivity in agriculture.

Insurance of seed crops is one of the areas offering ample opportunities to insurance companies. Similarly, another area of insurance could be indemnifying the risks emanating from professional liability of seed growers and merchants in case there is either complete failure or limited growth of crops on the farms using hybrid seed. Further, in some of the developing economies, particularly in African continent, the growth of economic activities in urban sector is either static or, at times, even declining. The scope for further penetration of insurance in this sector is, therefore, quite limited. The agriculture sector is still untapped and is also growing significantly owing to promotional policies initiated by the government in these countries. The trend to liberalisation is going to get momentum in future and with the conditionalities attached with WTO., the service sector will further be opened up and will be internationalised. It will intensify the competition in the urban sector and limit the scope for expansion of insurance in urban sector. The rural sector will offer wide scope for insurance companies particularly to local companies which have better knowledge of realties in rural marketing.

Constraints to Growth of Agriculture Insurance

However, despite such a wide scope of insurance in agriculture sector, by and large, insurance companies have been reluctant to enter the rural market. Several reasons account for the same. Broadly, insurance companies have not extended their activities to agriculture sector due to following reasons:

Scattered and Large Number of Holdings: In most of the developing economies, the total number of farmers and their landholdings is very large. These holdings are also scattered over a large and remote areas which, at times, are inaccessible by modern means of transport and communication. For instance, in India, the average size of holding is 1.5 hectare. These holdings are spread over in large areas comprising 28 states and union territories. Insuring such large number of units located in different agro-climatic zones is a serious constraint on the part of insurance companies.

Inadequate Expertise and Lack of Know-how: Most of the these companies do not possess requisite information and knowledge about the agriculture sector so as to enable them to extend their business activities over there. Their expertise at managerial and operational level to conduct business activities in rural areas may be limited. These companies may be required to engage the services of agriculture experts and scientists, veterinarians etc. for smooth running of business in rural sector. The nature of insurance in agriculture is quite different from that of insurance in urban sector and personnel handling business in urban sector may be incompetent to handle business in agriculture sector. The persons engaged to conduct exclusively agriculture insurance may have to be exposed to frequent training so as to upgrade their skill and apprise them of international practices.

Inadequate Infrastructure and Lack of Support Services: Most of insurance companies have built up infrastructure in urban sector and these may be inadequate or even non-existent in rural areas. These companies have not created functional infrastructure such as branch and divisional officers in rural areas to service agriculture sector. These areas also do not have loss assessors and surveyors to cater to the needs of agriculture sector.

Designing Products for Agriculture Sector: Most of these insurance companies lack expertise and skill to design products suited to the needs of the farming community. There will be need to innovate new products for agriculture sector and to modify and simplify the urban products if they are proposed to be introduced in agriculture sector. A large segment of rural population, particularly marginal and small farmers and landless agricultural workers, have very low per-capita income and their capacity to purchase insurance products may be limited. Products with small covers and low premium may have to be designed for them.

High Administrative Cost: The administrative cost of insurance business in rural areas is relatively higher compared to administrative cost involved in conducting insurance business in urban areas. The clientele in agriculture sector is spread over a large area warranting higher overhead cost in business operations. The premium per insured is quite low in agriculture sector. High administrative cost adversely affects the underwriting operations, reducing profitability of insurance companies in rural areas. It also accounts for hesitation on the part of insurance companies to enter rural market.

Illiteracy and Ignorance: The level of literacy in rural areas is quite low in most of these countries which translates itself into non-maintenance of records relating to per unit input cost, yield, etc. making it difficult for insurance companies to arrive at actuarial rates for insurance cover.

Moral Hazards: The insurance business is primarily based upon the principle of 'utmost good faith'. Due to non-maintenance of production, cost and loss records, the agriculture sector is more susceptible to anti-selection and moral hazards compared to the urban sector. It also acts as an inhibitive factor in the growth of insurance in agriculture sector.

Inadequate Capital Base and Limited Underwriting Capacity: The constraints to growth of insurance in agriculture sector emanate not only from external factors but they may also be internal in character. Most of the insurance companies may have limited capital base and their underwriting capacity may be limited so as to enable them to enter in agriculture sector. The nature of agriculture insurance is such that it requires large capital base and underwriting capacity since at times, the losses may be of very high dimension. Further, losses may also arise quite frequently.

Policy Package for Agriculture Insurance

The insurance companies which have confined their business operations to urban sector and plan to enter in agriculture sector may have to chalk out specific strategy and policy package for the same. The main elements of the strategy could be as under.

First, the insurance products designed for agriculture sector should be as simple as possible and in non-legal and non technical terminology. Most of the farmers are illiterate and ignorant and have not been exposed to insurance services. They have to be convinced about the benefits flowing from insurance covers. It may be difficult to market highly technical and complicated products in the agriculture sector. These covers should easily be understandable by the farmers. In order to gain a foothold in the agriculture sector, insurance companies may prefer to introduce some of the existing popular products with suitable modifications as to meet the requirements of rural sector. Once a beginning has been made and farmers get used to insurance services and are convinced about its benefits, technically strong products may be introduced. In the beginning companies may introduce non-crop products such as cattle insurance which can easily be administered and are also easily understood by rural population. Thereafter, products directly related with agriculture may be introduced.

Second, to the extent possible, package approach to insurance products may be adopted. In the agriculture sector, farmers are exposed to several risks and instead of designing several individual covers for these risks, it would be a good marketing strategy to formulate package covers, incorporating different risks in a single policy. It would enhance saleability of these products. However, these companies have to be careful to see that package covers are properly designed and not simply combination of individual policies so as to make them complicated and ambiguous.

Third, insurance companies should make all the efforts and initiate appropriate measures to bring down the administrative costs of agriculture insurance business. The delivery and servicing cost of insurance products in agriculture sector is quite high on the one hand, while premium per policy is low on the other. One of the policy measures may be to have a liaison with banking institutions which may have created infrastructure in rural sector and might be having efficient marketing network. A close co-operation with banking sector will help insurance companies to reduce and minimise their overhead cost. The co-operation may also be sought from local agencies such as Co-operatives, Panchayats, Marketing Boards etc. for marketing the products. These agencies could function as marketing agents for insurance companies and suitable agency commission and incentives may be devised for them. Similar to group life policies for industrial workers in urban sector which are purchased by the employer, in agriculture sector also, master policies may be designed and sold to some nodal agency who will be responsible for collection of premium from farmers, informing them about the coverage of their risks and also processing their claim papers. For controlling the cost, insurance companies instead of commencing their business simultaneously in all the areas of the country, may initially start operations in few selected areas based upon potentiality study. Based upon the experience and after establishing basic organisational infrastructure, these companies may gradually extend operations in other areas.

Risk Management

In modern times, risk management has become an integral part of insurance business. It implies identification, analysis and quantification of risks in physical terms in a manufacturing or trading firm. After these risks are identified, efforts are made to curtail or minimise or reduce them through corrective measures. The risks which can not be eliminated or cannot be minimised beyond a certain level have to be passed upon to a professional body like insurance company against a price to be paid in the shape of the premium. The management of the company has also to decide as to what extent and which risks have to be kept as self insurance and which have to be passed on to the insurance companies. Insurance companies assist the insuring firms in identifying the risks and also advise them on the measures required to be taken to minimise their risks. Although it may be argued that advising the insured to reduce their risks will be at the cost of their own business but in the long run insurance companies benefit from such risk reducing measures. Such risk management techniques assume paramount important in area of agriculture insurance. Insurance companies should be involved in identifying risks in agriculture sector and they should also advise the farmers on measures to minimise these risks.

Crop Insurance

Cultivation of land and growing of crops is the most important activity in the agriculture sector, which provides employment to majority of rural work force. Crop insurance, therefore, constitutes most important and major component of agriculture insurance. It is, therefore, worth examining various aspects of crop insurance as functional in different countries of world, particularly, in developing countries. The first and foremost issue relates to the number of crops which should be covered under the ambit of crop insurance. In a country, where the agriculture is confined to one or two crops, the choice is quite limited. The insurance coverage will be extended to only these crops. But the choice becomes difficult in a country where multiple crops are grown. Since in most of the countries crop insurance operates under government subsidy, government would encourage insurance of those crops which are important to the economy in the sense that they may either be the main cereals, or source of raw material to agro-based processing industries whose products are exported constituting main source of foreign exchange earning.

In case crop insurance is carried out by private insurance companies without government support and subsidy, they may opt for those crops in which methods of production are stable and standardised. With methods of production being modern and stable, the variations in output will be minimum except those caused by external factors such as cyclone, floods, hailstorm etc. For these crops it is easy for insurance companies to calculate the risks which may be caused by internal factors and help them in calculating actuarial rates for insurance covers.

Perils Covered

In most of the countries, the common perils to which agriculture is exposed to are covered under crop insurance. These include perils caused by fire, flood, hailstorm, malicious damage, earthquakes, landslides, damage by birds and animals, pests, insects, diseases etc. The perils owing to war are not covered under crop insurance. Similarly, normally losses sustained due to price fluctuations are not covered.

In most of the countries, loss of revenue to the farmers arising out of market uncertainties do not fall under the scope of crop insurance. The perils covered under crop insurance are production-oriented rather than market-oriented. In USA, policies covering loss to revenue arising out of fall in agricultural prices have been introduced.

Developing countries may plan to experiment such covers only after gaining sufficient experience in running schemes based upon production related covers. Further, in majority of these countries the policy of minimum support price takes care of instability in farmers' income which may have arisen due to violent fluctuations in market prices. Of course, only selected crops are normally covered under minimum support policy and large number of crops do not fall under the purview of the above policy. In India also, the minimum support policy has been in operation for quite a long time and has proved to be an effective tool in stabilising farmers' income.

Crop insurance has been offered either on single peril basis or on multi-peril basis. Under single peril basis, insurance is offered only against single or few selected perils, while under multi-peril basis, loss to the yield below a certain level which might have been caused by any peril, is compensated by insurance companies. Most of the countries in the world offer insurance on single or few selected peril basis. There has been difference of opinion as to whether the insurance companies should go for single peril crop insurance schemes or multi-peril schemes. Majority opinion goes against multi-peril insurance schemes in those countries where agriculture is practised on traditional lines. The reasons advanced are that these covers act as distinctive to farmers; have been cornered away by large farmers; have the premium rates at uneconomic level; have been guided by political considerations; have high administrative costs; and involve subsidisation by government since normally the scheme is run by parastatal bodies.

Level of Indemnity and Premium Rates

Broadly, the indemnity level followed by the insurance companies is of two types. The first principle followed is that the insurance companies compensate for the loss of yield caused by the perils already spelled out in policy cover. These perils could be either single peril or all risk multi-perils. The second principle followed is that the farmers will be compensated for the variable cost or input cost incurred by them till the time of occurrence of the peril. In the first case insurers have to wait till the crop has been harvested and the actual production /yield is known. Since the insurance companies have to wait till the crop is harvested, this method is more susceptible to moral hazards. In the second method, the input or production cost is calculated on the basis of the cost incurred on seed, tilling of land, sowing and plantation, fertiliser, insecticides and pesticides, labour input etc. At times, interest paid on loan taken till the occurrence of peril is also included in cost of production. Normally in developing countries the farmers do not maintain records on production cost and it becomes difficult for the insurance companies to arrive at actual amount incurred by the farmers till the occurrence of the peril. To meet this problem, some of the countries have devised a scale of progression of input costs to coincide with the crop cycle and losses are compensated as per the above scale. Some of the countries following the above scheme are: Indonesia, Thailand, China, Malaysia, Israel, Mexico, Argentina. In India, primarily the first method of yield loss is followed.

The fluctuations in yield are quite common and frequent and may occur on a yearly basis caused by one or other peril. It may administratively be difficult to calculate the loss of yield or input cost incurred till the occurrence of the peril. In order to reduce the administrative work involved in calculating large number of claims, in most of the countries the policy covers have been so designed that claims are payable only if the yield falls below certain threshold yield calculated on the basis of average of last few years. Such cut off points have also been laid down in respect of schemes based upon input cost. In India threshold yield represents moving average of past five years yield data. The levels of indemnity are at the levels of 60%, 80% and 90% specifying high, medium and low categories of risk.

The calculations of premium rates for crop insurance is extremely difficult and complicated exercise. It is relatively more difficult to arrive at the acturial rate in case of those crop insurance schemes which are based on input cost basis. While it is easier to have the data relating to yield for the previous years, such data in respect of input cost is not maintained by farmers in most of the developing countries. There is no fixed standard formula to arrive at actuarial premium rate and different countries have devised their own methodology to calculate the actuarial premium rate. The usual method to calculate premium rate involves making trend analysis of losses based upon the data for the past few years. The trend analysis will indicate as to whether losses are increasing or declining and accordingly, the projection for the future has to be made. Of course, the pattern of losses based upon trend analysis may have to be modified after taking into account the changes that have been taking place in the farming methods and technology. This exercise gives basic structure of the acturial premium rate for different crops. The premium rate so arrived at may have to be loaded to account for several factors such as those relating to risk and administrative expenses. Normally the risks which may necessitate loading of premium rates are those relating to moral hazards and anti-selection, climatic changes and fluctuations and impurities in agricultural data. The loading may also be necessary for building up reserves to meet losses arising out of national calamities. Further loading may be required to bridge the gap between the time of receipt of premium on the one hand and payment of claims on the other and for achieving the balance between premium and claim for an average of five to six years as it may not be possible to achieve such a balance on a yearly basis. After taking into account all these losses and loading them in premium rates, the administrative expenses incurred for running the scheme including expenditure on advertisement and publicity may have to be incorporated in the premium rate. Based upon the above factors, United Nations conference on Trade and Development (UNCTAD) in its report "Agricultural Insurance in Developing Countries" (UNCTAD/SDD/INS/1-1992) has devised the following formula for fixing premium for crop insurance :

$$\text{Gross Premium} = \frac{[E(L)+S]}{(I-X)}$$

Where $E(L)$ = expected losses
S = a loading factor for risk assumed
X = a loading factor for expenses.

Since crop insurance provides cover to the farmers, who have low income base, the loading factors should be kept at the modest level, otherwise the premium rate may work out to be so high as being unaffordable by these farmers. The accuracy of premium rate will also depend upon the authenticity of data on farm sector.

In so far as the assessment of loss is concerned, it has been either on 'individual approach' basis or on 'homogeneous area' basis. In 'individual approach' basis, based upon losses suffered by the farmers caused by perils covered under policy conditions, the claims are settled by insurance companies. It requires maintenance of accurate records and data relating to yield, production and cost of production by the farmers who have suffered losses. This approach is also prone to moral hazards. In 'homogenous area approach', all the insured farmers in an area are compensated for the losses caused by a common peril effecting the entire area. These areas are classified on agro-climatic basis and areas with identical features are classified into homogenous unit. In India, losses are assessed on 'area approach basis'. Majority of the countries in the world have followed individual approach for loss assessment.

Different Sectors in Agriculture

In most of the developing countries, the agriculture sector is very wide and simultaneously there may be co-existence of regions with different levels of development. In the same region also, there may be farmers using traditional methods of cultivation with low productivity on the one hand and farmers using latest technology with high productivity catering to the needs of other sectors of the economy on the other. UNCTAD study has classified agriculture in the following four sectors and each sector has its own unique features relating to crop insurance.
1. Traditional or subsistence agriculture.
2. Semi-commercial and emerging agriculture.
3. Commercial agriculture.
4. Specialised production systems.

This is a broad classification and it is quite possible that these sectors may overlap and may have certain common features.

1. Traditional Agriculture

This sector of agriculture is characterised by traditional methods of production, low productivity, production for subsistence, low or negligible marketable surplus, fragmented and small farms etc. The farmers in the sector are mostly marginal and small farmers and landless labourers. Their income base is very low. Since the paying capacity of farmers is extremely low, the crop insurance schemes in this sector are commercially unviable and have to be subsidised by the government. The crop insurance schemes are mostly implemented by parastatal bodies. Since the number of farmers is very large and they are also illiterate and dispersed, it becomes difficult to implement loss control measures. In most of the developing countries, this is the most dominant sector and crop insurance schemes are implemented basically as welfare measures rather than as insurance schemes.

While formulating insurance schemes for this sector, the services of other agencies such as financial institutions, farmer's representatives, panchayats etc. should also be utilised. For insurance in this sector and particularly for poor farmers, a view has been held that insurance cover may be made compulsory. In some countries the farmers taking loan from the banks are required to take compulsorily insurance and thus all the loanee farmers are automatically covered. Depending upon the response of the poor farmers to purchase insurance policies, policy of obligatory insurance may be framed.

2. Semi-commercial and Emerging Sector

The farmers in this sector are in stage of transition from traditional farming to technology-oriented farming and have better access to inputs, credit, irrigation facilities etc. A part of their produce also goes for marketing. It is relatively easier for insurance companies to enter in this sector as the level of awareness regarding risk and transferring them to insurer is more amongst these farmers. They also have better linkage with marketing and financial agencies. Insurance companies in this sector may commence their operations by covering few selected crops on restricted perils basis in selected areas and may extend their operations slowly to other crops and areas in a phased manner. Insurers may initially start group covers based upon some common features amongst the members of the group. The co-ordination with co-operatives already operating in rural areas for different purposes may be established for marketing the products.

3. Commercially-oriented Sector

The distinguishing feature of this sector is that production is not only for subsistence but for market also. The technology used is improved one and the farmers have better access to institutional credit. The farmers normally grow cash crops such as tea, coffee, oilseeds, jute on a large scale. Large poultry and dairy farms have also been established in this sector. The insurance schemes for this sector should be based on economic viability and actuarial rates should be charged. Normally the cash crops which are produced for industrial sector and exports offer better scope for insurance. Initially limited covers may be offered. The covers should be on individual basis and should be designed as per the needs of farmers. For popularising insurance schemes, insurance companies may like to take assistance and co-operation from banking institutions, input suppliers such as fertiliser units, agro-based industries such as sugar mills etc.

4. Specialised Production Systems

Farmers in this sector use capital intensive technology and production is primarily meant for exports. The sector is dominated by large farm houses, aquaculture, greenhouses, horticulture, rubber plantations. The production is carried out under strict quality control so as to meet international quality standards. The sector offers ample scope for commercially viable and profit-oriented crop insurance schemes. Normally insurance cover is given for the entire farm and is not confined to isolated crops grown in the farm.

Role of Government and Subsidies

As mentioned above, the farmers in the traditional sector are poor lying below the poverty line and are also illiterate and ignorant about benefits accruing from insurance schemes. Their paying capacity is also low. Crop insurance schemes in this sector are economically and commercially unviable. Insurance schemes in this sector cannot sustain on their own without government subsidy. However, from economic point of view, the benefits, both economic and social, from such subsidies should be compared to the benefits that may accrue to the farmers and society as a whole if the amount involved in subsidy had been given directly to the farmers in other forms. Based upon such calculations only, crop insurance subsidies should be continued. It is also necessary that the subsidies should be transparent and quantified. The actuarial premium rates should invariably be worked out and the extent to which premiums are subsidised should be known to the society, who is contributing to such subsidies. Further, the subsidy should be conceived as part of package programme of extending institutional credit to the farmers, encouraging them to use improved technology, hybrid seeds, fertilisers etc. It has also been pointed out that the implementing agency should be consulted before extending the subsidy and it should not be imposed upon them. They should be allowed to calculate the actuarial rates and then the subsidies may be extended, in whatever form, after mutual agreement between implementing agency and the government. The subsidy element should be known while formulating and implementing the crop insurance scheme rather than after the loss has occurred. As and when the crop insurance scheme is implemented with government subsidy, there should be continuous evaluation of the scheme and remedial measures to improve it may be taken, whenever necessary.

However, subsidy should not be construed as a permanent solution to the problems of poor farmers and the efforts should be made to phase it out over a period of time. It could only be a transitory short term measure. It has also been suggested that for poor farmers, crop insurance scheme covering national calamity of large magnitude may be formulated. The claim would be payable only when the losses are below certain stipulated level.

Experience Relating to Crop Insurance in Few Selected Countries of the World

It would be worth examining experience in area of crop insurance in some selected countries in the world particularly relating to their claim ratio. A brief about the experience of these countries is given as under:

Philippines

The crop insurance scheme in Philippines commenced in 1981.

Insurance covers losses arising out of natural calamities such as typhoons, floods, droughts, earthquakes and volcanic eruptions, plant diseases and pest infections. The losses out of avoidable risks attributable to the neglect of insured are not indemnified. The insurance cover is on the crop season basis and covers the period from direct seeding or transplanting up to harvesting. The insurance cover is only for standing crops; the harvested crop does not carry any insurance cover. The cover is extended to only two crops, paddy and corn. All the farmers obtaining credit from the lending institutions are covered under the scheme. However, the scheme is optional for self financing non-loanee farmers.

The scheme is operated on an individual basis and insurance cover is on the basis of input cost not on the yield basis. The farmers has the option to insure up to 125% of production loan ceiling. There was an overall ceiling on insurance cover of P.3750/- per hectare for rice crop and P. 6000/- per hectare for corn crop as at the end of 1987-88. Insurance premium has been fixed on actuarial basis, separately for rice and corn corps. The insurance premium are being shared by the farmers, the financing banks extending credit to the farmers and the government. For instance, for cover up to loan amount (production cost) in respect of rice crop and loanee farmers, the sharing was 2, 1.5 and 4.5 percent for farmers, lending institutions and government respectively (the total premium being 8%). For non-loanee farmers, it was 2 and 6 percent for farmers and government respectively. For corn crop, the sharing in respect of loanee farmers, it was 2.5, 1.5, and 9 percent for farmers, lending institutions and government respectively (the total being 13%). The scheme is implemented by the 'Philippines Crop Insurance Corporation', established by the government of Philippines with an authorised capital of P.750 million and paid up capital of P. 250 million.

The loss ratio was 166.3, 118.6,203.8,81.3 and 87.4 percent during the years, 1986,1987,1988,1989 and 1999 respectively.

Israel

In Israel, the crop insurance scheme covers the crop of fruits, cotton and vegetables. The perils covered are those arising from hail, frost storm and heat waves. By and large scheme is operated on multi perils basis. The cover is extended on group basis and de facto it is compulsory. The sum insured is on the cost of production basis. The reinsurance cover for crop insurance is up to 80% by the government and 20% by the private insurer. The scheme is operated by Insurance Fund for Natural Risks in Agriculture Ltd (IFNRA). The subsidy level is up to 50%. The premium rates range between 1.5. to 2%. The claim ratio amounted to 72, 148.4 and 52.4 per cent during 1988,1989 and 1990 respectively.

Mauritius

In Mauritius, sugar is the only crop covered under crop insurance scheme. The losses arising out of cyclone, drought, fire, excessive rain are covered and the scheme is operated on an individual basis. The sum assured is on the basis of value of output, and it is obligatory for the farmers to take the cover. The premium is on actual basis (8%) and reinsurance cover is extended by private insurers. The scheme is operated through 'Sugar Insurance Fund' (SIF). The claim ratio accounted for 8.8., 68.2,118.7 and 49.0 per cent during the years 1987,1988,1989 and 1999 respectively.

USA

In USA a large number of crops, almost more than 50, are being covered under crop insurance scheme. The losses caused by different perils such as flood, drought, hailstorm, cyclones, earthquakes, fire etc. are covered and scheme is operated on an individual basis. The scheme is optional for the farmers and sum insured is on yield basis. The actuarial premium (ranging between 5 to 7 percent) is charged and government acts as a reinsurer. The scheme is managed by 'Federal Crop Insurance Corporation, Commercial and Mutual Insurance, Companies and Managing General agencies. The claim ratios for the years 1986, 1987, 1988, 1989 and 1990, were 82.4, 55.1, 191.3, 107.9 and 58.3 percent respectively.

Australia

In Australia, crop insurance scheme covers all winter field crops accounting for about 95% of the total production. The scheme is operated on an individual basis and losses caused by fire, hail, and transport are covered. The sum insured is on yield basis and the premium rate ranges between 4 to 5% of sum insured. Reinsurance cover is taken from private companies and scheme is administered by National commercial Unions' without government support. During the years 1986,1987, 1988 and 1989 claim ratio amounted to 36.8, 150.8, 89.3 and 116.1 percent respectively.

Loss Ratio in Some Other Countries

The claim ratio (claims paid as percentage of premium) for some of the countries in respect of crop insurance is given in Table 4.

Table 4: Loss Ratio in Selected Countries

Country	Loss Ratio in Percentage	Years
Chile	41.47	1986-90
Cyprus	78.80	1986-90
Venezuela	56.33	1989-90
Windward Islands	72.24	1987-90
Zambia	67.28	1985-86
Zimbabwe	20.65	1986-90

Source: Crop Insurance Compendium, 1991 (Rome-1991) and UNCTAD - *Agriculture Insurance in Developing Countries.*

Reinsurance

Since claim ratio in crop insurance business is quite high, and the capacity to bear risk for insurance companies may be limited, one of the options could be to take reinsurance cover for this business. However, it may be difficult to obtain reinsurance cover for this class of business till such time the scheme is operated with uneconomical premium rate. Reinsurance companies may be interested in extending the cover only after the actuarial rates are charged and the scheme is operated on commercial lines.

Evaluation of Crop Insurance Scheme in India

The evaluation of crop insurance scheme in India could be traced as back as 1972-73, when it was introduced by general insurance wing of Life Insurance Corporation of India in respect of H-4 cotton. The scheme which was introduced on a limited basis continued up to 1978-79, covering 3110 farmers and settling claims worth Rs. 37.88 lakh against a premium of Rs. 4.54 lakh.

The scheme was succeeded by Pilot Crop Insurance Scheme (PCIS) in 1979. The scheme was introduced on area approach basis and covered millets, oilseeds,. cotton, potato and gram. Only loanee farmers were eligible under the scheme and that also on a voluntary basis. Initially sum insured was limited to 100% of crop loan which was subsequently increased to 150%. The sharing of risk was between the implementing agency (General Insurance Corporation of India) and the state government in the ratio of 2:1. The subsidy to the tune of 50% was extended to marginal and small farmers in respect of premium rate. Central and state governments shared the subsidy in the ratio of 50:50. The scheme was implemented on a pilot basis and continued up to 1984-85, covering 6.27 lakh farmers with claims amounting to Rs. 157.05 lakh against the premium of 196.95 lakh.

The first systematic crop insurance scheme implemented on a wider scheme known as Comprehensive Crop Insurance Scheme (CCIS) was introduced in 1985. CCIS was conceived as an instrument of risk management in agriculture, as a tool to provide relief to the farmers sustaining losses to the crops during natural catastrophe and calamities, and as an integral part of policy package for overall growth of agriculture and its productivity. It was also used as a tool to support and stimulate production of desired commodities such as food grains, pulses and oil seeds. The scheme covered the crops of rice, wheat, millets (including maize) oilseeds and pulses and covered all the farmers availing loan from financial institutions for raising the above crops. The scheme was voluntary in nature and it was left to the wisdom of state governments to opt for the scheme and the districts in which they wanted the scheme to operate. Insurance coverage was built in as a part of crop loan.

The premium rates were 2% of the sum insured for rice, wheat and millets and 1% for oilseeds and pulses. The sum insured was restricted to 100% of crop loan subject to the maximum of Rs. 10,000/- per farmer. The marginal and small farmers were subsidised to the extent of 50% of the premium, which was shared equally between Central and State Governments. The claims were shared between central and state governments in the ration of 2:1.

The scheme operated on 'area approach' basis. If the actual average yield of a defined area fell short of the threshold yield, all farmers in defined area deemed to have suffered loss in their yield were entitled to indemnity. The actual yield was determined on the basis of the 16 crop cutting experiments. The indemnity was calculated as under:

$$\frac{\text{Shortfall in yield}}{\text{Threshold yield}} \times \text{Sum insured}$$

Shortfall in yield was calculated by deducting the actual yield from the threshold yield, which was moving average of past 5 years yield data. The levels of indemnity were fixed at 60, 80 and 90 percent corresponding to high, medium and low risk areas. The variations in yield were fixed up to 15%, 16 to 30% and above 30% for low risk, medium risk and high risk crops respectively.

From the commencement of the scheme in 1985 till 1999, a total of 7.61 crore farmers and 12.75 hectares of land were covered under the scheme.

From 1985 to Kharif 1999, the total sum insured, the total premium and the total claims amounted to Rs. 24,922 crore, Rs. 402.83 crore and Rs. 2302.68 crore respectively. An analysis of claim ratio reveals that it was 5.74 for the country as a whole, highest being in Gujarat amounting to 16.60. The claim ratio was also quite high in Rajasthan (14.41), Orissa (6.32), Uttar Pradesh (5.85), Himachal Pradesh (4.75) and Andhra Pradesh (4.25). The details have been given in Annexure I. Year-wise details of claim ratio have been given in Annexure II.

The crop wise claim ratio reveals that it was maximum in groundnut crop (16.73) followed by bajra (7.54) in so far Kharif season in concerned. Table 5 gives crop wise details regarding claim ratio.

Table 5: Crop-wise Claims Ratio under CCIS (Cumulative between Kharif 1985 to Rabi 1997)

Crop	Claims ratio	Crop	Claims ratio
Kharif Season		**Rabi Season**	
Paddy	3.47	Paddy	1.63
Groundnut	16.73	Groundnut	2.95
Jowar	3.53	Jowar	3.16
Bajra	7.54	Bajra	1.08
Other Crops	3.73	Other Crops	1.89
Total	**6.77**	**Total**	**1.60**

Source: Compiled from Annual Reports of General Insurance Corporation of India (various years) and other sources.

Shortcomings

During the course of implementation of CCIS, several shortcomings of the scheme came to limelight. These were basically: coverage limited to loanee farmers: coverage of limited crops leaving several important commercial crops from its purview: sum insured limited to RS. 10,000, skewed selection of area notified by the participating states: indemnification being based on the unit area and compensation unrelated to actual loss: and non-participation of agriculturally advanced states like Punjab, Haryana etc.

Experimental Crop Insurance Scheme (ESIS)

During the course of implementation of CCIS, a new scheme, viz. Experimental crop Insurance scheme (ECIS) was introduced during rabi 1997-98 season for one year, subject to review after the first cropping season. ECIS covered all the marginal and small farmers, both loanee and non-loanee, growing wheat, paddy millets (including maize) oilseeds and pulses in 24 selected districts of 8 states. The entire amount of premium was borne by central and state governments. Share of central and state government for premium and claims was in the ratio of 4:1. Other features of the scheme were common with that of CCIS.

During rabi 1977-78, a total number of 4,54,555 farmers were covered under ECIS. The sum insured, premium received and claims paid amounted to Rs.168.11 crore, Rs. 2.84 crore and Rs. 37.80 crore respectively. The claim ratio worked out to be 1:13.30. ECIS was discontinued after rabi season.

National Agriculture Insurance Scheme (NAIS)

In order to make up for the deficiencies of CCIS, a new scheme called, National Agricultural Insurance Scheme (NAIS) was introduced from rabi 1999-2000, replacing CCIS.

The scheme covers all the farmers, loanee and non-loanee, including share-croppers and tenant farmers. The scheme is compulsory for loanee farmers and voluntary for non-loanee farmers. The scheme covered all food crops and oilseeds as well as annual horticultural/ commercial crops. During the first year of its operation, it will cover three annual horticultural/commercial crops, viz. cotton, sugarcane and potato, while during the second year four additional crops of chillies, onion, turmeric and ginger will be added. It is multi-peril scheme covering all natural and non- preventive risks. The sum insured could extend to the value of threshold yield of the insured crop at the option of insured farmers. However, a farmer may also insure his crop beyond value of threshold yield up to 150% of average yield of notified are on payment of premium at commercial rates. In case of loanee farmers, the sum insured would at least be equal to the a amount of crop loan advanced.

The premium rates are acturial for horticultural/ commercial crops and range between 1.5. to 3.5. per cent for food crops and oilseeds. In case the premium rates for food crops and oil seeds turn out to be lower than the actuarial rates, it has been proposed to shift to actuarial rates within a period of five years. Marginal and small farmers are eligible for 50% subsidy on premium rates, which will be phased out within a period of five years.

The losses covered are on "area-approach" basis, although it is proposed to pay the losses on individual basis for localised calamities such as hailstorm, landslide, flood, etc. on an experimental basis. Like CCIS, this scheme also functions on yield basis. If the actual falls short of threshold yield in the defined area, it is presumed that all farmers in that defined area have suffered the losses and are eligible for claim amount.

At the time of formulation of scheme, it was laid down that the implementing agency (General Insurance Corporate of India) will bear all claims up to 100% of premium for food crops and oilseeds, unless transition to acturial regime is made, and balance claims will be shared between central and state governments in the ratio of 1:1. In case of horticultural/commercial crops, implementing agency is supposed to bear all claims up to 150% of premium in the first 3 to 5 years and 200% of premium thereafter. It is a multi-agency scheme and is implemented through co-operation from Central Government, State Governments, financial institutions and insurance companies. At the state level, State Level Co-ordination Committee on Crop Insurance (SLCCI) has been constituted which notifies the crops and areas to be covered during the season.

All claims beyond the liability of the implementing agency are to be met by a corpus fund, with equal contribution from central and state governments. With GIC assuming the status of national reinsurer, the modalities for implementing the scheme are being worked out.

The scheme covered a total of 5,84,239 farmers during rabi 1999-2000. The sum insured amounted to Rs. 339 crore and premium collected and claims paid accounted for Rs. 5.25 crore and Rs. 3.34 crore respectively.

Non-crop Insurance Schemes

In additional to crop insurance scheme, several non-crop insurance schemes have also been introduced in the country. Some of the important non-crop insurance schemes are:
1. Pilot Scheme on Seed Crop Insurance (PSSCI).
2. Cattle Insurance.
3. Poultry/Duck/Quail insurance.
4. Horticulture/Plantation insurance.
5. Floriculture insurance.
6. Aqua-culture insurance.
7. Sericulture insurance.
8. Honey bee insurance.
9. Agriculture pump-set insurance.

10. Farmers package Policy.
11. Janta Personal Accident insurance.

The scheme on seed insurance (PSSCI) and cattle insurance merits alteration. PSSCI has been introduced from rabi 1999-2000. The cover is extended to breeder seeds, foundation seeds and certified seeds of all major crops in 10 states. The scheme covers seed crops of paddy, wheat, maize, jowar, bajra, gram, red gram, groundnut, soybean, sunflower and cotton. The scheme covers seed crop at field stage arising out of failure, rejection of seed crop, loss in expected raw seed yield and loss of seed crop after the harvest. It also covers germination losses at the certification stage. Most of the non-preventable natural risks such as flood, fire, storm, drought, excessive rain, incidence of pests and diseases etc. have been covered. The sum insured in equivalent to preceding three or five years average seed yield multiplied by procurement price/sale price of seed crop. The premium rates are 2% for wheat and groundnut, 2.5% for sunflower, 3% for paddy, 3.5% for jowar and 5% for gram, red gram, bajara, maize, soybean and cotton. Premium and claims up to 200% of premium will be met by government of India on sunset basis - first year - 100%, second year 50% and third year 25%.

Cattle insurance commenced in 1974 in the country. It covers cows, buffaloes, calves, bulls etc. The cattle have been classified under two categories - scheme and non-scheme. Scheme animals are those which are financed/subsidised under Central/State Government schemes. For scheme animals the premium rate is 2.25% for death cover and for non-scheme animals it is 4%. For exotic animals an extra premium rate of 2% is charged. For covering permanent total disability an extra premium of 0.85% and 1% is charged for scheme and non-scheme animals respectively. Group discounts for non-scheme animals between 2.5% to 15% and for long-term policies, discounts between 15% to 25% have been structured in the scheme. Presently about 1.5 crore animals are covered per year with a premium income of Rs. 115 crore. From 1977 onwards livestock covers extending to different types of animals such as camels, elephants, rabbits, horses, mules etc. have been introduced in the country.

Conclusion

Development of agriculture is most crucial for overall growth of the economy. It supplies food to the rising population, raw material to agro-based industrial units, creates demand for the industrial products and earns foreign exchange for the country. Agriculture insurance substantially contributes to the growth of agricultural sector. It facilitates flow of institutional credit in the rural sector, induces farmers to adopt new technology, converts hoarding into productive savings and provides financial stability and strength to the rural economy.

However, agriculture insurance if pursued isolately may not be able to produce desired results. It should be conceived as an integral part of rural development and poverty alleviation programmes. It has to be a part of comprehensive policy package. Crop insurance is one of the most important segments of agriculture insurance. Different countries have followed different methodologies for formulating and implementing crop insurance schemes. These schemes have been either on individual or on area approach basis and have functioned either on signal peril or multi-peril basis. There has been general reluctance amongst insurance companies to enter in the agriculture sector. Their expertise in conducting business in agriculture sector is limited. They have to enter in the agriculture sector with well-chalked out strategy.

Extending crop insurance to the traditional segment of the agriculture sector characterised by marginal and small farmers, fragmented and scattered small holdings, low income base, illiteracy and ignorance, is the most difficult task for the insurance companies. Since crop insurance schemes in this sector are commercially unviable, the support of the government in extending subsidy either through subsidising premium rate or through meeting a proportion of claim liability becomes imperative.

However, subsidies should not be conceived as a permanent solution to the insurance needs of the farming population. These subsidies are cost to the society. There is a need to work out cost-benefit analysis of these subsidies. An evaluation should also be made as to whether it would be beneficial to the interest of farmers, if the subsidies are extended indirectly through crop insurance or if they are given in other direct forms.

Crop insurance subsidies should be given only when it is established that they contribute to the welfare of the farmers more than if they had been given in some other form. Even after crop insurance schemes are subsidised, all the endeavours should be made to phase them out in the shortest period of time and operate these schemes on commercial lines. These schemes should ultimately become self-sustaining and commercially viable. As the agriculture development takes place and per capita income of average farmer rises and the level of awareness about insurance services and their utility increases, it should not be difficult for insurance companies to operate the schemes on actuarial premium rates.

Of course, these companies will have to design simple products catering to the needs of poor farmers and will have to take all the measures to minimise administrative costs in servicing these products. They may have to build up expertise and skill in their own organisation for innovating and marketing crop insurance products. The co-ordination from other agencies which have their existence in agriculture sector such as banks, co-operatives and panchayats may be solicited, particularly for marketing the products. It is relatively easier to operate crop insurance schemes in semi-commercialised and modern segments of agriculture sector on a self-sustained basis.

In so far as Indian economy is concerned, crop insurance schemes were introduced as early as in seventies. The claim ratio in CCIS which commenced in 1985 was extremely at a high level. It was heavily subsidised by the government. Its substitution by NAIS is a step in right direction as it is an effort to phase out subsidies gradually and operate the scheme on competitive lines. It has also been pleaded that the scheme should be made still wider as to cover perils not only associated with production processes but also those arising out of market uncertainties such as fluctuations in agricultural prices.

Insurance companies should also underwrite these risks so that farmers income and revenue are stabilised and are not exposed to frequent fluctuations in agricultural prices. The policy of 'minimum support price' of the government takes care of the problem to a large extent in respect of selected crops covered under the scheme. Of course, for other crops such insurance covers may be needed. However, in majority of the developing and developed economies losses caused by market fluctuations in agricultural prices have not been covered. Such covers have been experimented in USA. It is felt that the stage is yet not ripe for introducing such covers in Indian economy. The stage of development of agriculture sector as well as that of insurance industry in India is still not conducive for such marketing linked insurance covers.

Annexure I
Comprehensive Crop Insurance Scheme (CCIS)
Year-wise Premium and Claims from 1985- kharif 1999

Year	Premium (Rs. crore)	Claims (Rs. crore)	Claims ratio
1985-86	13.90	87.26	6.28
1986-87	19.51	173.96	8.92
1987-88	27.95	289.47	10.36
1988-89	11.94	33.06	2.77
1989-90	17.25	37.29	2.16
1990-91	11.16	85.60	7.67
1991-92	18.09	201.30	11.12
1992-93	22.92	50.96	2.22
1993-94	22.55	188.61	7.38
1994-95	29.71	58.02	1.95
1995-96	34.33	148.91	4.33
1996-97	38.06	167.61	4.40
1997-98	41.47	185.24	4.47
1998-99	46.35	127.55	2.75
Kharif 1999	43.29	461.29	10.65
Total	**401.48**	**2,296.13**	**5.71**

Source: Compiled from Annual Reports of General Insurance Corporation of India (various years) and other sources.

Annexure II
Comprehensive Crop Insurance Scheme (CCIS)
(Cumulative 1985 to Kharif 1999: State-wise)

States	Premium received (Rs. crore)	Claims paid	Claim Ratio
Andhra Pradesh	113.3	482.43	4.25
Assam	0.4	0.57	1.42
Bihar	18.74	47.69	2.54
Goa	0.03	0.04	1.33
Gujarat	65.42	1,086.21	16.60
Himachal Pradesh	0.08	0.38	4.75
Jammu & Kashmir	0.15	0.65	4.33
Karnataka	20.32	67.11	3.30
Kerala	4.10	9.60	2.34
Manipur	0.03	0.00	0.00
Madhya Pradesh	36.97	99.67	2.69
Maharastra	51.92	213.02	4.10
Meghalaya	0.07	0.10	1.42
Orissa	28.52	180.50	6.32
Rajasthan	1.59	22.92	14.41
Tamil Nadu	22.07	50.03	2.26
Tripura	0.12	0.06	0.50
Uttar Pradesh	8.52	49.90	5.85
West Bengal	30.01	35.06	1.16
Andaman & Nicobar	0.02	0.04	2.00
Delhi	0.05	0.00	0.00
Pondicherry	0.33	0.67	2.03
Total	**402.71**	**2,311.59**	**5.74**

Source: Compiled from Annual Reports of General Insurance Corporation of India (various years) and other sources.

13
Role of Insurance Intermediaries in the Emerging Market

Gaurav Garg

Insurance marketing has some unique features. It has to identify uncertainties in the operations of an economic system and create general awareness to cover these uncertainties by selling insurance products to the constituents of this economic system. The constituents of this system essentially the economic groups, if left to themselves, would rather carry their risks than buy insurance. The intangibility of this product and the contingent nature of its delivery further accentuate the problem. It is said, that world over insurance is always sold rather than bought. It is at this juncture that the insurance intermediary steps in. He is a facilitator in the whole process and has probably a more onerous marketing job than their counterparts in many other trades and services.

Intermediaries as They are Today

The four subsidiaries of GIC market their products through a three-tier marketing force consisting of: Agents, Development Officers and Officers in charge of sales at branch/divisional offices.

Insurance marketing will take a different direction with the liberalisation of the sector. Why do we need a new marketing model? With increased competition from the new market entrants it would become increasingly difficult to acquire new customers. Also with the change in consumer lifestyle and technology advancement, the demand would be for purchase convenience and speed of service. These factors would see the development of a wide array of distribution channels or intermediaries in this sunrise sector. This can be further strengthened if approached from the customer's angle:

Customers choice of a distribution channel is dictated by: Socio demographic factors, ease of access, complexity of product/service, need for advice.

Globally as a result many different channels have emerged:
- Bancassurance
- Direct Marketing
- Internet.
- Agents
- Brokers
- Company Employees

Of these in the existing scenario only the agents and the company employees are available as intermediaries in India. The introduction of these new channels and different kind of intermediaries would enable these new entities to use their knowledge of their clients to target products with a degree of precision. We will deal into these channels extensively.

The Agency Business as it is: A Brief Look Back

The Insurance Act permitted the appointment of 'principal agents'. In the year 1957 this system of 'Principal Agents' was discontinued. The Insurance Act prescribed 15% of premium as the maximum commission payable to agents which was reduced, in the case of marine insurance business to 10% by an amendment to the Act in 1950. Rates of commission were further reduced in 1968, on the introduction of social control on insurance business to 5% for fire and marine business, and to 10% for miscellaneous business. After nationalisation, the agency commission structure was reviewed by the general business for corporate clients whose paid up capital was Rs. 10 lakh or more, co-operative societies with capital of Rs. 5 lakh or more, business under the control of banks where bank advances exceeded Rs. 25,000, hire-purchased vehicles, and income tax exempted charitable trusts. In such cases the client was allowed a discount on the premium in lieu of the agency commission. Later in 1980, the rate of commission was reduced from 10% to 5% in the case of engineering insurance business and also for motor business in 1986. There are certain classes of insurance business like aviation hull and liability, marine hull (Ocean going vessels), and credit insurance, on which it has been the practice not to pay commission. Commission on several classes of business relating to rural areas, the economically deprived sections of the society and on many personal lines of business (Where the premium on individual policies is low) was increased from 10% to 15% to induce agents to market these classes of business.

With the nationalisation of the industry in 1968 the insurers had to depend on the field officers for business. The field officers numbers increased substantially. In some companies, they also performed some administrative functions related to marketing.

At the time of nationalisation of general insurance business there were field officers who were designated as Inspectors. A composite scheme relating to remuneration, incentives and other benefits to Inspectors – later re designated as development officers – has been in force since 1976. The scheme provided for premium-related incentives and benefits, as also disincentives including possible termination of service for persistent non performance. This scheme was revised in 1987 and in 1990, progressively raising remuneration and benefits and diluting the disincentives of development officers. Over the years, the number of development officers has increased substantially.

There is general agreement on the fact that the performance of agents and development officers has been generally unsatisfactory. It is widely believed that there are a large number of benami agents, showing up deficiencies in the process of appointment of agents. The institution of agents on the general insurance side has weakened considerably, essentially due to the progressive lowering of the rates of commission payable to them and exclusion of business of certain categories of clients for payment of agency commission. The existing structure of agency commission provided little scope for the emergence of professionals, much less of their becoming full time agents. The Insurance Act provides for issue of licence to individuals of at least 18 years of age to act as an insurance agent. The licence is issued on a declaration by the applicant in a prescribed form. There is a method of screening the genuineness of the applicant before the issue of licence but no follow up action is initiated to weed out those who are not serious in pursuing the profession.

Brokers

The institution of brokers which is well established in most insurance markets does not exist in India, except in the area of reinsurance.

Brokers are professionals who bring together the insured and insurers, carry out preparatory work for issuance of contracts, and where necessary, assist in the administration and performance of such contracts, in particular when claims arise. Brokers have a relatively more important role to play in free markets than in markets regulated partly or fully by tariffs. They are increasingly becoming professional risk managers. Unlike agents who are retained on behalf of insurers, the primary responsibility of brokers is towards the insured. They put across requirements of their clients before insurers and obtain from them appropriate insurance products. Whenever standard products are not adequate, they prepare a 'manuscript policy' and negotiate with the insurer to optimise satisfaction of their clients. As brokers negotiate with many insurance companies, they also act as catalysts of competition in the insurance market.

To sum up, the marketing apparatus consists of agents, development officers, and insurance officials. There is a need to promote and sustain professionalism among agents. To that end, there is an urgent need to upgrade the training and skills of the agency force. The commission structure for agents should be improved to attract and retain talent in the profession and to make it an effective instrument for procuring business and spreading specially, rural, personal and non-obligatory lines of business. In keeping with contemporary trends in insurance marketing, the system of brokers should be introduced.

Bancassurance: The New Mantra

Convergence is the new mantra. There is a change in consumer preference world-wide. This change coupled with the growth of electronic distribution and the impact of Internet has given growth to alternative channels of distribution like **bancassurance**.

Bancassurance is a French term referring to the selling of insurance through a bank's established distribution channels. The result is a bank that encompasses banking, insurance, lending and investment products to a bank's customers.

Bancassurance came into existence about fifteen years ago, with the introduction of Sorasaving, a simple interest-bearing annuity product underwritten by a life insurance company, Groupama, and distributed through branches of a French bank, Credit Agricole. Sales through the bank were very successful and eventually represented 80 percent of total sales. Groupma and Credit Agricole split after certain profit sharing issues arose. This led to Credit Agricole launching Predica. Through using the bank's distribution channel of 11,000 branches, coupled with a simple interest bearing retirement annuity type product with tax breaks, Predica came from nowhere to number two in the French life market in just two years, second only to French giant Caisse Nationale de Prevoyance (CNP).

Today bancassurance has rewritten the rules for the delivery of financial services products throughout Europe and is likely to do the same in India.

Bancassurance is already a reasonably well developed phenomenon in some European markets though, no one has achieved the success enjoyed by the French banking community. In Europe leading continental bancassurance groups derive between 20% and 30% of corporate profits from insurance-driven activities. In France, 60 percent of the banks have been selling general insurance products such as health, automobile, and housing insurance for more than five or six years. And their market is growing. In a year when the French market grew only 4 percent, the French bancassurance leader grew by almost 20 percent in 1999.

Bancassurance is only about 10 years old in the US and most banks haven't fully utilised their well-established distribution channel to sell insurance products to America's mass market. However, the action is picking up. Two years ago, in fact, two financial giants, Citibank and The Travelers, engineered a $37 billion merger to form Citigroup with the goal of integrating banking and insurance operations.

The Significance of Bancassurance

The reason that bancassurance has excited so much attention, is that it is being held up as the way in which financial firms will offer services in the future. Firstly the banks who have embraced bancassurance have demonstrated that a successful entry strategy offers significant profit potential for banks. Secondly, competitive pressure will be such that once other banks have entered insurance, those banks which have not done so are forced to emulate the moves of their competitors in order to prevent losing market share. A further reason for the interest in links between banks and insurance companies is that joint ventures have sometimes been used as a method of entering a new insurance market. Such alliances include Banco Bilbao Vizcaya and AXA in Spain, Credit Lyonnais and Allianz in France, Banco di Napoli and Zurich in Italy and the Bank of East Asia and Aetna in Hong Kong. We see a similar trend in India, with a number of nationalised and private sector banks being wooed by multinational insurance companies keen to enter the Indian market.

Reasons for Banks Entering Insurance

Banks have sought to enter insurance markets because of the following reasons:
- Bank managements have believed that such markets are potentially profitable.
- The value of a banking license is continuing to fall due to increased competition from non-bank banks, disintermediation and the internationalisation of the banking industry. Moreover, income earned by traditional bank activities has fallen. Banks have, therefore, been under great pressure to extend their business scope. This pressure has lead to systematic consideration of the possible use of the large branch banking networks for cross-selling non-banking financial products.
- Furthermore, banks possess significant, high quality information on the financial circumstances and requirements of customers. This offers the opportunity for highly targeted marketing of other financial services including insurance.

Dimensions of Bancassurance

Bancassurance encompasses all the sales of insurance products by banks. This includes business generated by banks simply acting as agents for wholly independent insurance companies. The main organisational forms taken by bancassurance are:

1. Distribution agreements where the bank acts as an agent for an independent insurance company.

2. Distribution agreements where the bank acts as an agent for an independent insurance company in which the relationship is strengthened by cross-shareholdings.

3. Distribution by the bank of insurance products supplied by a wholly owned subsidiary.

4. Distribution by the bank of products supplied by an insurer which is a member of the same integrated financial group.

5. Distribution by the bank of products supplied by an insurer which is a member of the same holding company, although the companies are not fully integrated.

6. Distribution by the bank of insurance products supplied by an insurer which it owns jointly with an independent insurance company.

The Distribution Strategy

The success of the bancassurance program begins with the correct delivery of the product to the targeted customer. One does not have to be an insurance expert to sell simple mass market products, success lies in designing simple products that can also be sold easily by bank tellers.

Also manufacturing and distribution costs must be as low as possible. The products don't need to be the cheapest, and the sales force doesn't need a great deal of training to market the product.

There are typically three product distribution concepts :

- **Stand Alone campaigns** – where the product is promoted and sold directly to the customer typically via direct marketing and/or face-to face sales methods.
- **Bundled** – where the product is promoted and sold as an appropriate adjunct to the bank product and is sold via cross selling at the time of the bank product sale.
- **Packaged** – where the product is an inherent feature of the bank product and is sold whenever the bank product is sold.

Bancassurance in India

Will it work in India? The industry believes that bancassurance will be a big thing here. Some foreign and Indian banks - Stanchart Grindlays, ABN Amro, Citibank, HSBC, American Express, IDBI Bank, Bank of Baroda (BoB) and State Bank of India (SBI) - are hoping to replicate the French success of this insurance-cum-banking model.

The mode of entry differs from bank to bank; a few banks are sticking to the strict definition of the term by actually setting up insurance joint ventures themselves. Alliances could be the way bancassurance evolves in India, at least in the initial years. ICICI Bank and HDFC Bank will be distributing the products of their parent company partnerships, namely ICICI Prudential and HDFC Standard Life.

Given their vast distribution reach and access to customer information, Indian banks are at a great advantage. For ultimately, *"Whoever controls the most customers will win, and that's where banks have a big advantage."*

Direct Marketing

With increased competition and new entrants it will increasingly become difficult to acquire new customers. Direct Marketing or DM as it is more popularly known will be one of the most frequently used delivery channels.

In the US 53% of the total media spend is on direct marketing, in comparison the spend on direct marketing in India is 14.7% only. There is still a lot of thrust on traditional channels rather than DM in India. This provides a great growth opportunity for DM as a channel in India, with companies realising the tremendous of this direct channel to the prospective customer DM will witness a tremendous boom in India.

Comparative Figures: Percentage of Media Spending by Channel

Medium	United States	India
Direct Mail	10.5%	1.6%
Telemarketing	44.4%	0.3%
Internet	0.2%	0.0%

Source: Lintas Direct.

Direct marketing as a channel for insurance sales has not been explored in India till now. This is a channel that has had tremendous success in the western world and is one of the most extensively used channels. In India DM as a channel is being extensively utilised by Banks and other financial institutions.

Typical Direct Marketing Channels: Above The Line: Television. Newspapers/Magazines. Radio. **Below The Line:** Telemarketing. Direct Mail. Internet. Inserts. Take ones. Kiosks.

E- insurance: An Emerging Field

As Companies rush to 'e-nable' their business, e- insurance is one of the growth areas in India.

Globally, insurance on the net has lagged behind other Financial services products, such as banking and brokerage. Of the total online users only 5% used insurance services online as depicted in Figure 1. This lag was and is due to a lack of relevant and adequate content. Traditional insurers, while leveraging on new information technologies, have been slow to utilise the Internet as an alternative distribution channel. Generally, the largest insurers have been focused on a static marketing presence online, encompassing product information, FAQ's and quotes. Only a few insurers have added the ability to submit applications on-line and none of the large insurers allow online changes to policies. This lack of participation in the e-business revolution is seen across lines.

Two factors are attributed by the insurance companies for the slow take off. First and foremost, insurance is a product that is sold and not bought. The internet is perceived to be a buyers medium, with online customers able to search quickly and easily for the most competitive prices and a variety of products.

Insurance is one product that cannot be commoditised easily. The more personal the selling process the greater the difficulty in using the net as a medium for selling. Insurance is one product, which involves personalised selling. The process of insurance sales requires a series of face to face interactions.

Figure 1: Online Users Of Financial Services

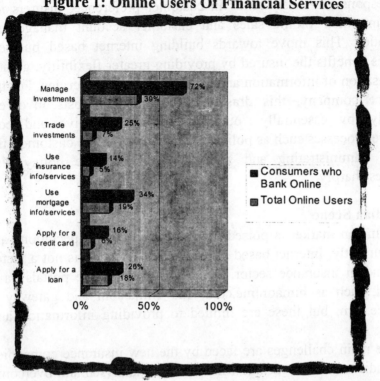

Source: Insurance Monitor-Price Waterhouse Coopers.

The convergence effect is being felt by this industry as well. In the US personal savings will be almost evenly distributed between banking, insurance, mutual fund and other financial institutions. The insurance industry is expected to lose market share to banking and other financial institutions.

Customers today expect enhanced levels of service due to increased competition. This customer demand will result in non-traditional access to specific information. The Gartner Group in a study conducted by them feels that, in 2001, 25% of all customers contacts and enquiries for enterprises will come via the Internet, e-mail, and online forms. Bancassurance customer service, which has been almost exclusively done via telephone (96% of all transactions), will become increasingly e-mail based in the next four years, decreasing telephone related service by 28%.

In response to these trends in customer preference, insurers are mobilising their online sales and customer account management capabilities. This move towards building internet based business solutions benefits the insured by providing greater flexibility, greater customisation of information and improved customer service. For the insurance company, this drastically reduces the costs involved. Similarly, by essentially "outsourcing" administrative and cost intensive processes such as policy administration to the customer, the cost of administrating and servicing the insurance policy also decreases sharply.

The Indian Scene

The Indian market is poised for growth and the expectations are high. Currently, Internet based selling and distribution is not a factor in the Indian insurance sector. Some Indian insurance portals have emerged, such as bimaonline.com, 123 Bima.com and gateway 2 insurance.com, but these are limited to providing information and FAQs.

Three main challenges are faced by the new insurance companies in the Indian scenario each of which must be analysed and overcome by using the internet. The first challenge is to develop products and services based on market positioning and brand value. As the number of competitors grows and brand differentiation becomes low, insurance products and services will increasingly by regarded as commodities. This results in low customer loyalty and high pricing pressures. As insurance products become commodities, product, service and process strategies also evolve on similar lines.

The second major challenge to face Indian insurers will be to design and develop strategies for delivering services to well-segmented customers.

The third challenge lies in developing the right combination of customer segments and applicable distribution channel strategies.

The e-insurance market will be governed by the same five major consideration of e banking.

Growth of the Net: It is estimated that India would have about 150 million net users by 2010. These figures represent a huge buying potential.

Competition Pressures: Insurance companies because of competitive pressures would be driven into internet rather than a clear ROI justification.

Customer: The availability of net-based services will be a huge factor for customer retention.

Cross sells: When linked with other financial products, a portfolio approach to investment, savings & risk coverage will increase cross sells and customer loyalty and retention.

Costs: In the beginning e-insurance will be a cost factor rather than a profit driver, but in the long run it will be a cost-reducing factor.

Agents as They Will be

It is expected that the agents operating in the market in India would essentially be of two kinds – tied and independent. The agents could be both individual as well as corporate. It has been the practice in India not to have agency business as a profession. It may not be practical to prohibit part-time agents at this point in time but the effort should be to encourage full time agents the reasons being:

Company has little control over agent activity and cannot influence sound/ethical work practices

Productivity levels are extremely low

Persistency is poor and adversely impacts company profitability

Agent turnover is high; that affects persistency and costs of recruitment and training of agents.

It may be possible, however, to mitigate the adverse impact of part time agents by introducing minimum annual business levels that would have to be attained in order to retain their licence as also the introduction of continuous training.

A professional, committed agency force would be a prerequisite to the growth of this channel.

Agency Structure

The insurance company needs to have an agency force that is controlled but can also provide for its own future growth. The key activities of recruiting, training and managing agents be performed by people with direct exposure to the agency business. Accordingly an agency force can end up with layers of agents, with each layer reporting to its recruiters. Interaction between the layers is a key determinant of success, with control and transfer of knowledge being the principal issues. Compensation for one layer on the activities of the layers below should follow the level of interaction and influence between those layers.

It is felt that meaningful interaction would happen only up to two layers apart – that is an agent will be influenced and managed by the layer immediately above, and to a much lesser extent, the layer immediately above, and to a much lesser extent, the layer above that. Compensation should therefore be limited to the agent, his manager and the manager's manager.

Agency Functions

The various functions that the agent should be expected to perform could include: Client identification. Marketing. Investor education and counseling. Market expansion and quality control of front-line agents. Collection of premium on behalf of the insurance company where specifically authorised to do so by the insurer. Issuance of cover notes where authorised. It should, however, be the individual companies responsibility to ensure that the processes comply with regulatory requirements.

Agency Recruitment and Licencing

This is an important part of the control mechanism to ensure the development of professionalism in the agency force. However, it is also a potential bottleneck in the development of the agency forces of the new companies, if the process is not sufficiently streamlined.

The example that is often quoted is that of China, where the regular set of agents, trained and marked the agents' exam. The examinations were set only twice a year, with long lead times for submission of agents particulars and the process curtailed the recruitment activity, and therefore growth of their agency forces.

Agency Training

The lack of an adequately trained agency force often implies lack of professionalism resulting in clients being sold the products that

carry the highest commission. The agents should demonstrate proficiency in: Product Knowledge. Sales skills. Designing solutions/best advice. Tax implications. Profitability assessment of business (for non-life insurance)
- In the international markets training is a very costly activity involving the intermediaries in a considerable amount of course attendance, self-study, and field accompaniment.
- It may be useful, however, to guard against the UK trend which has emphasised product technical awareness rather than a skill based bias thus depersonalizing the agent client relationship.
- Pre-licensing insurance education and training and continuing education are both necessary in the Indian context.

The training requirements should be the responsibility of the insurers with the regulator laying down the requirements and playing a monitoring role.

Agency Remuneration

Commission is the most popular mode of remuneration in the international markets. The aim of the method of remuneration should be to: Reward agents for above average performance in key areas; Encourage career advancement; Penalise unsatisfactory practices; Offer agents an adequate income attracting quality people to the professionalism.

Brokers

The nature of the activities of the broker and the market they operate in should be the basis for categorization of brokers. The brokers should be divided into two categories. Reinsurance brokers. Other insurance brokers (Both life and non-life)

In most developed markets the insurance brokers are regulated with respect to:
Registration,
Experience, training and qualification,
Solvency requirements,
Professional indemnity.

The regulations, requirements for each should be separately laid down.

The opening up of the insurance market to the brokers would allow them to operate in the life, non-life and re-insurance markets
- Non-life insurance as well as group life and group mortgage insurance is the domain of brokers in many markets.
- The salient functions of the brokers are expected to be:

Pre-sales and after sales service to the customers.

Provision of relevant information to the underwriters to assess risks and decide premium.

Design covers that meet the client requirements.

Recommend risk improvement and loss minimisation measures.

Assist clients in negotiating claims.

Provide risk management and insurance education.

Collection of premium.

The needs of the individual insurers would determine, to a large extent, the functions that the brokers perform

Currently, in view of s.64VB and the non-acceptance of third party premia by the insurers the brokers role would be curtailed to advisory.

Internationally there are trends of brokers moving to fees rather than commission incomes.
- The remuneration for the brokers should be sufficient to take care of the staffing and infrastructure and their role and function.
- In the international markets the average level of remuneration to the insurance broker is 15-20% of the gross premium quoted to the client; this norm could apply in the form of a cap on commission in India.
- The commission for reinsurance brokers should not be capped and allowed to be governed by the international market practices
- There should be a distinction between the first year and renewal commissions for brokers.

Some niche areas may, however, demand higher remuneration based on the effort.

The various duties imposed on brokers in international markets include:

Duty of disclosure.

Duty of utmost good faith.

Duty of submitting a business report.

Duty to abide by prohibited activities.

One of the salient supervision requirements is that of ensuring independence of the broker by requiring disclosure of the spread of business

A professional indemnity coverage should be made compulsory.

A code of conduct for brokers needs to be devised and put in place by the regulators.

A protection fund with contributions from the brokers needs to be created for the benefit of the consumers.

Levels of professional qualifications for each director and employee dealing with customers should be fixed.

Conclusion

The role of the intermediary has never been so fully conspicuous than now with the deregulation of the sector. We hope to see an entirely new face of insurance marketing in India, which would consciously move from a brand driven one to a pure commodity product based marketing strategy. The intermediary in its various forms would evolve and play a vital role in the development of this entire industry. This article clearly aims to highlight the importance of this crucial link. The final outcome of all this would be an industry that would be extremely customer focussed. All this points to one adage, i.e. customer is the king.

Part III

Editorial Note

Part III covers the issues relating to tariff system, reinsurance, risk management and risk financing, alternate risk transfer techniques, and information technology in insurance industry.

Chapter 14 attempts to examine the present functions of TAC and the role it is expected to play in a competitive environment. The paper has traced the evolution of the formation of TAC right from the time when General Insurance Council was formed in 1950. The paper points out that in a liberalised scenario, the role and functions of TAC will have to be redefined.

Chapter 15 analyses the concept of reinsurance, its evolution over a period of time, methods of reinsurance, and existing arrangements in respect of Indian insurance industry. The paper has reviewed existing reinsurance programmes of Indian industry and has examined the role of reinsurer in the liberalised economic environment.

Chapter 16 covers issues relating to risk management and risk financing techniques. The paper defines risk and risk management as proactive management process which seeks to identify the key critical functions of an organisation, its business and markets etc.

Chapter 17 defines risk management and describes its various classifications. The paper discusses in detail the alternate risk transfer techniques and its consequences.

Chapter 18 examines alternate risk transfer techniques in the context of Indian insurance industry.

Chapter 19 deals with the need for information technology in insurance industry. The paper discusses database management systems, data warehousing, decision support systems, group linking software, imaging and workflow technologies, mapping, call centre technology, video linking, cat models, intronet extronet and internet and electronic commerce which are all important for insurance companies. The paper has also analysed the challenges that insurance companies may have to face while conducting business through e-commerce.

Chapter 20 on information technology in general insurance traces out the growth of information technology in general insurance industry over a period of time.

14

Tariff Advisory Committee: Redefined Role in the Liberalised Scenario

R. Beri

1. Historical Background Leading to Formation of TAC

The Tariff Advisory Committee has been in existence in one form or other over a period of 127 years. It was first formed as a voluntary organisation in 1872 in Bombay and called the Underwriters Association. The TAC has continued to be in existence from then onwards to fulfill the insurers' need for uniform rules and regulations which were considered essential for smooth functioning of the industry.

A. Era of Voluntary Regulation: In 1858, with the formation of the Fire Offices Committee (FOC) in London, the British market moved towards uniformity in rating. Some of the tariff insurers of the Indian market followed these rates but the non-tariff insurers who formed the majority followed their own rates, and even had widely different rates of agency commission. Competition and rivalry among the brokers worsened the situation. The chaotic situation was due to many problems arising from incorrect stamp duty rates, the need for local rating, new legislative measures and the absence of regulations on storage and transportation of hazardous goods. All these demanded close co-operation from the insurers and required a common platform for joint action.

The response of the Indian market to this situation was the formation of a voluntary organisation in the year 1872 by the name of Underwriters Association at Bombay. This organisation had committee members elected from among the various insurers. These members worked in close conjunction with the Fire Offices Committee (FOC) and the Accident Offices Association (Overseas) both based in London. The practices followed by this Underwriters Association were by and large continued till the nationalisation of the general insurance business in India.

This was followed by the formation of Bombay Association of Fire Insurance Agents in 1882, Calcutta Fire Insurance Agents Association in 1888 and Madras Fire Insurance Agents Association in 1896. The aims and objectives of these associations were similar and related to facilitating discussions and settlement of problems arising out of insurance transactions, application of tariff rules, establishing uniform use of custom, securing common interpretation, keeping a watch on any legislation relating to the industry, analysing origin and cause of frauds, establishing libraries and also collection and publication of statistics in specific areas like losses due to fire along with their causes as well as estimates of expected losses.

Despite the marvelous efforts made by these associations, by the beginning of 1905, competition threatened to oust cooperation out of the market such that many of the tariff offices withdrew from their existing associations. Emanating from this situation, it was clear that without an apex organisation, insurance business could not survive and in response, on May 31, 1905, in succession to these various organisations, a body by the name of Fire Insurance Association, was formed, which united all the local offices.

In early 1928, realising the efficacy of unity in protecting the interests of the Indian underwriters, prominent businessmen in Bombay met and formed Indian Insurance Companies Association. This group began to organise conferences to educate the public on the benefits of insurance to focus attention on the drain on national wealth through *invisible exports*, as well as to arouse public interest in favour of Indian insurance. A similar organisation was almost simultaneously formed for life insurance also.

B. Era of Governmental Regulation: During the period between the two World Wars the newly established Indian insurance companies had to face competition from foreign insurers who had vast experience, technical knowledge, better management expertise and a glut of funds. Also, at this time exchange banks failed to settle claims of Indian insurers outside India. These two were the major problems faced by Indian insurers. In 1935, the Government of India appointed Mr. Sushil K. Sen to investigate and report on insurance reforms in India. Mr. Sen recommended the British concept of minimum control by Government with maximum public awareness.

The Government convened an Advisory Committee of leading insurance men, elicited their suggestions and submitted a Bill to the Legislative Assembly in 1937 which was passed as Insurance Act, 1938.

However, this Act failed to create efficient legislative measures to control and regulate the rates, advantages, terms and conditions for insurance transactions in India. The Government of India in 1945 appointed a committee under Mr. Cowasjee Jahangir to investigate the problems faced by the insurance industry in India. The recommendations of the Cowasjee Jahangir Committee were largely accepted in the amendment of the Insurance Act, 1950. Accordingly, the General Insurance Council was constituted. Under its supervision, the Tariff Committee was formed and vested with powers to control and regulate the rates, advantages, terms and conditions that may be offered by its member insurers and associate member insurers in respect of general insurance business. The Tariff Committee was an all-India body controlling and exercising powers over all Regional Councils. However the rates, advantages, terms and conditions were fixed by the Rating Committees of the Regional Councils.

The Insurance Act of 1938 was drastically amended in 1968 by the introduction of social control measures which provided for more effective supervision and control over insurers doing general insurance business in India. This amendment, further provided for increased amount of deposit from insurers as well as increased powers for the Controller of Insurance to inspect and issue directions to the insurers on all matters including appointment and removal of their directors. By the same amendment, the Tariff Committee was replaced by the Tariff Advisory Committee as a body corporate having perpetual succession. The amendment made the Controller of Insurance as the Chairman of the Tariff Advisory Committee and he was authorised to appoint the Secretary of the Committee.

C. Nationalisation and After: On May 13, 1971, an ordinance was promulgated by the President of India to take over the management of the general insurance companies by the Government of India. In 1972, the General Insurance Business (Nationalisation) Act, 1972 was passed and the General Insurance Corporation of India was established with effect from January 1, 1973. Almost simultaneously, vide a Gazette Notification dated December 29, 1972, various sections of the Insurance Amendment Act which had brought Government control over insurance (under the earlier social control measures), were made inapplicable in relation to the General Insurance Corporation of India and its subsidiaries.

The Nationalisation Act of 1972 strengthened the Tariff Advisory Committee and it was given vast powers to control, regulate, fix, amend or modify the rates, terms, advantages and conditions in respect of general insurance business.

By amending section 64VA of the Act the composition of the Tariff Advisory Committee was changed so that the Chairman of the General Insurance Corporation of India or a Member of the Advisory Committee nominated by him would be the Chairman of the Tariff Advisory Committee.

By another Gazette Notification dated June 19, 1974 it was decided that the Secretary of the Tariff Advisory Committee would be an officer of the General Insurance Corporation of India nominated by the Chairman of the Tariff Advisory Committee. The Tariff Advisory Committee, thus, as a fully Governmental body, started having full powers over the nationalised insurance business of India with powers to control, regulate, fix, amend or modify the rates etc. from time to time and to the extent it deemed expedient. The Committee's decisions became binding on the industry and breaches of tariff were to be investigated by it and reported to the Controller for taking punitive action on the erring company.

As regards its financial status, Tariff Advisory Committee is authorised under the Act to collect from all the insurance companies a levy of up to 1% of the gross direct premium income underwritten in India.

The Tariff Advisory Committee brought the major areas of insurance such as fire insurance, marine hull insurance, marine cargo insurance, tea crop insurance, business interruption insurance, engineering insurance, personal accident insurance, workmen's compensation insurance, motor insurance, industrial all risks insurance etc. under the tariff regime. Other branches of insurance such as aviation hull insurance, satellite insurance, product liability insurance, professional liability insurance, crop insurance, cattle insurance, poultry insurance, health insurance, fidelity guarantee insurance etc. were left as non-tariff areas. By later amendments Marine Cargo Insurance (1.4.1994) and Personal Accident Insurance (1.4.1994) were detariffed.

D. Malhotra Committee: Indian economy is changing from being a controlled economy with *commanding heights for the public sector* to a *market driven one* inviting participation of private investors, both foreign and Indian, in a big way, under the various programmes of reforms by the Government of India. India, being member of World Trade Organisation (WTO), is also committed to integrate the Indian economy with that of the other member nations in a phased manner.

In this background, the Government set up in April 1993, a high-powered committee headed by late Shri R. N. Malhotra, former Governor, Reserve Bank of India to examine the structure of the insurance industry and recommend changes to make it more efficient and competitive, keeping in view the structural changes in other parts of the financial system of the economy. The Committee interacted with the insurance companies, their staff unions, various chambers of commerce, trade bodies and a cross section of the country's public and analysed the present Indian insurance industry. The Committee, which submitted its report on January 7, 1994, felt that the insurance regulatory apparatus should be activated even in the nationalised insurance sector, and recommended inter-alia, the establishment of a strong and effective Insurance Regulatory Authority (IRA), in the form of a statutory autonomous board on the lines of Securities and Exchange Board of India (SEBI).

2. Regulatory Functioning of TAC in India

Upon formation of interim body of IRA, the functions of controller of insurance were transferred to the chairman, IRA. As a result, the chairmanship of TAC was transferred to the chairman of IRA. This came into effect from 22.7.1998 through a Gazettee Notification of the Government of India.

Tariff Advisory Committee (TAC) is a statutory body under the Insurance Act, 1938. Section 64U of the Act defines its as a body that controls and regulates the rates, terms and advantages of general insurance business in India. The Committee w.e.f. 1.12.1998 consists of an apex body with the Chairman, IRDA as Chairman and 15 members drawn from the Central and State Governments, the Insurance Regulatory Authority, the insurance industry and from professional bodies representing trade and industry. The organisation is headed by the Chairman and under him the Secretary of TAC functions at the Head Office situated at Mumbai. Under the Secretary there are five Regional Offices situated at Ahmedabad, Calcutta, Chennai, Delhi and Mumbai and two Divisional Offices at Bangalore and Lucknow.

Under the Tariff Advisory Committee a few groups/committees like Technical Assistance Group (marine insurance), Technical Assistance Group (tea insurance), Technical Assistance Group (petrochemical insurance), Fire Sub-committee, Engineering Sub-committee etc. are appointed. These committees comprise specialists from a particular branch of insurance who periodically meet and analyse the various matters referred to them and submit their recommendations to the TAC. The Secretary of the TAC presides over the meetings of these various sub-groups.

As per section 64U of the Insurance Act, 1938 (and subsequent amendments), the Tariff Advisory Committee was established "to control and regulate the rates, advantages, terms and conditions that may be offered by insurers in respect of general insurance business." The purposes served by the existence of the TAC as revealed in the Insurance Act and Insurance Rules can be briefly summarised as follows:-

A. Market Stability and Correct Pricing: The insurance policies have to be priced correctly to ensure on the one hand that the insureds do not end up paying more, and on the other hand that the insurers have sufficient funds with them to pay the claims of the insured when the need arises. Correct pricing ensures stability in the insurance market, which in turn bolsters the confidence of the insuring public.

B. Standardisation: The terms and conditions of the insurance offer required are to be standard, uniform and clear enough so that the insureds are not confused by rosy looking promises, the meanings of which they are unable to evaluate. In short the insureds' interests are protected by such standardisation of products.

C. Ensuring Equity amongst Insured: It has to be ensured that there is no unfair discrimination between two similarly placed risks. Also, care should be taken so that the individual characteristics, whether merits or demerits are taken into account in evaluating a risk.

D. Ensuring Equity amongst Insurers: A level playing ground has to be provided for the insurers so that competition is equitable and based on uniform rates, terms and conditions. This emphasises on providing better services for the insureds.

E. Collection of Information: Section 64UC of the Insurance Act, gives TAC powers to collect statistics from the Insurance companies, to send its people to collect data, audit or verify the accuracy of the information submitted.

3. Need for Change in a Liberalised Scenario

The Insurance Regulatory and Development Authority Act, 1999 along with the resultant modifications to the Insurance Act have reconfirmed the regulatory role of Tariff Advisory Committee.

The Tariff Advisory Committee felt that its role and functions need to be redefined to meet with the requirements of the emerging markets once the insurance sector opens up. For this purpose a Vision 2000 Committee was set up which was to look into all matters relating to insurance regulation for both public and private players. This Vision 2000 Committee felt that to ensure healthy growth of the market by ensuring fair and equitable rates, terms and conditions, to serve the interest of the consumers and simultaneously ensure that financial health of the insurer is not put in jeopardy through rate cutting, Tariff Advisory Committee has to devise necessary regulations. The Vision 2000 Committee expected that gradually the Indian market would have to move from a tariff regime to a non tariff regime after six to eight years, so as to ensure competition amongst the insurers on pricing, improve management of losses and facilitate smoother integration of the domestic rates with international rates and trends.

The Vision 2000 Committee also felt that the scenario after six to eight years would be congenial for a non-tariff regime, that would integrate and ensure better risk management practices and scientific underwriting, as rating of risk would be done strictly on merits. With this long-term end in mind, the Vision 2000 Committee recommended that Tariff Advisory Committee should endeavour to facilitate a smooth changeover from the existing tariff regime to a responsible non tariff regime.

The recommendations of the Vision 2000 Committee as regards functions of TAC can be briefly summarised as follows:

- to evolve and encourage best technical and professional underwriting standards and practices,
- to evolve standards of safety devices, equipment and protection systems,
- to provide a forum for exchange of ideas on technical aspects of insurance business between the consumers and underwriters,
- to evolve and recommend loss minimisation measures to the consumers and underwriters,
- to serve us a store house of vital information and industries data as regards law, statistics, potential hazards of specific industries etc. and
- to evolve, continuously update and issue guidelines for drafting of insurance policies so as to make them user-friendly.

In order to fit into this new role, Tariff Advisory Committee will have to change its functioning so that minimum benchmark guide rates for insurers can be fixed, data can be collected and processed as well as relevant information from other markets collected and disseminated to the underwriters and insurance consumers. Publication of technical journals and providing facilities for testing of safety appliances, studying individual industry profiles and assisting insurers in developing technical expertise also would be part of Tariff Advisory Committee's work in the new scenario. Also, the Tariff Advisory Committee would have to conduct technical audit of the companies and give its recommendations/observations for improving underwriting standards. Tariff Advisory Committee would have to also develop customer focus.

Tariff Advisory Committee: Redefined Role

The Committee also visualised that in the year 2000 and beyond, TAC would have to deal with a large number of insurance companies, a larger population of insured, as also a larger number of mega size risks. Hence, a certain measure of flexibility would have to be given to the insurance companies to design their products and meet with the requirements of the customers. In case of larger risks, tailor made policies would be required. The group felt that in view of the multi-dimensional role of Tariff Advisory Committee in the new environment, it would be desirable that the Tariff Advisory Committee be renamed as Indian Insurers Council to signify its unique character.

Internally, the Tariff Advisory Committee is gearing up to fit into the newer and more challenging role. It has committed itself to a new set of organisational objectives which may be summarised as follows:

1. Tariff system should be made sensitive to the market requirements and should undergo changes in a phased manner to adequately protect public interest while bringing out the best benefits of competition. The tariffs should be simplified to make them better understood, easier to comply with, i.e. more customer friendly.

2. Tariff Advisory Committee would ensure a level playing ground for all concerned by providing tariff that can be used as an underwriting tool so that a minimum base level rate is available to break-even.

3. Tariff Advisory Committee would undergo an internal liberalisation to eliminate delays in decision making.

4. It should serve as a store house of vital information like loss statistics, hazard potential of specific industries etc.

5. It should have its own R and D facilities to create bench marks for new products and pricing them appropriately.

6. Codes of Practices for achieving minimum safety level need to be prescribed for specific industries. The safety standards would require to be updated periodically. All these would be in line with Loss Prevention Council (UK).

7. A continuous interface would be maintained with international bodies like Loss Prevention Council, NFPA, FM etc.

8. Through regular training and interactions, Tariff Advisory Committee can impart its rich and varied experience gained over

decades through risk inspections to the technical staff of insurance companies.

9. Tariff Advisory Committee can also be associated with companies' technical personnel in carrying out exercises like PML assessment in a professional manner.

10. Developing software packages for insurance rating of specific industries.

11. Assisting IRDA on technical matters as and when required.

With the winds of change blowing over the insurance industry in India, the Tariff Advisory Committee is gearing itself towards a greater customer focus by making the tariffs user friendly. Fire tariff having been simplified w.e.f. 1.5.2000.

We realise that India remains one of the very few tariff markets in the insurance world. This in fact puts a greater responsibility on the committee to make the tariffs contemporary, easy-to-read and comprehend while, at the same time, based on the latest technology available to the insurance sector all over the world.

As the Indian insurance market braces itself to see real competition ahead, with the users of insurance covers clamoring for more and more alternate products at reasonable cost, Tariff Advisory Committee plans to revise the tariffs every 2-3 years so that there is a balance between the interests of the insurers and the insureds.

15

Reinsurance in Indian Perspective

E.K. Dastur

The Concept

Any insurance company portfolio is characterised by a number of policies. Each policy is a physical risk or exposure, which the insurance company writes against fortuity. These risks vary in nature and size and the claims experience is unpredictable. The claims experience is normally influenced by major losses (accumulation losses) arising from one event, where each major loss being made up of many individual losses,

- the high frequency of many small losses,
- changes in the structure of any risk owing to changes in
   economic, political, technology and social environment.

Unless appropriate measures are taken a portfolio will therefore be unbalanced. A direct consequence of lack of balance is that results fluctuate. Depending on their size, fluctuations in the course of results will affect values which are vital to the company, such as solvency, liquidity and the continuity and/or stability of results. One of the corporate goals of an insurance company is to restrict fluctuations in the results to within certain parameters. There are generally three ways of achieving this, viz. self-retention, coinsurance and reinsurance.

Self-retention

For the portfolio to absorb the fluctuations, the direct insurers must set their acceptance limits at a correspondingly low level, writing only small shares in order to achieve a portfolio which is as homogeneous as possible. The possibilities for acquiring business are restricted as a result. However, the direct insurers also thereby limit their opportunities for growth in markets with competition, since their competitors can write business with higher acceptance limits. Insurers who opt for self-retention will be stunted in growth.

Coinsurance

Insurers opting for the coinsurance route must come to an agreement with selected competitors and also divulge information about their customers. In addition, insurers organised in a coinsurance arrangement must take special care to ensure that the assumption of risk arranged in this way does not result in any disadvantages for their insureds. In practice, the principle of coinsurance is chosen above all for special and/or very large risks.

Reinsurance

Where insurers opt for the third method, they are said to purchase reinsurance cover. Insurers may use reinsurance cover for different purposes, for instance to reduce their commitment to a single major risk, to cover catastrophe risks like those arising from the natural hazards of earthquake or flood, for example, or to protect themselves against major variations in the loss experience of entire portfolios. Insurers and reinsurers agree between themselves the reinsurance solution which meets the insurers' specific needs, with account also being taken of the insurers' market opportunities. Their position in the market should be strong and outwardly independent, without insureds being aware of the reinsurers.

It is an established norm that the fundamental concept of insurance is spreading of risks based on law of large numbers. Thus, the purpose of reinsurance is purely extension of the aforesaid concept. It is a means which an insurance company uses to reduce the possible losses, of the perils it has accepted and thereby stabilise the results.

The fundamental principles of reinsurance are similar as those of the insurance, viz. principle of indemnity and principle of utmost good faith.

The reinsurer operates on the premise that in the absence of detailed underwriting information about the risk on which he is committed, control of his underwriting destiny must rest upon his knowledge of the professional status and integrity of the insurer and the underwriting skill and qualifications of the underwriter who is committing him on the portfolio underwritten, without detailed selection on the part of the reinsurer.

Need of Reinsurance

As mentioned above, the need for reinsurance would also follow the same business and financial considerations as an original insured would require to insure with any insurance company.

The insurance companies by insuring property, persons or liability representing great values at risk and for large sum insureds, often wish to be able to accept the whole or substantial part of the risk for their own account. However, the financial strengths of each insurance company constraints it from doing so, as it would not be prudent for any organisation to trade on its capital for more than its own worth, or for that matter keep every single risk for its net account. This makes it imperative to reinsure a single risk or its portfolio. Thus, reinsurance gives protection against eventualities and supplements the need of insurance companies by limiting their loss from any single incident or accumulation of losses arising out of any event.

It is also desirable that the affairs of the insurance company are regulated to avoid widespread fluctuation from year to year. Due to financial constraints mentioned above, an insurance company cannot retain full volume of business for its net, as major fluctuation in claims cost, resulting out of inadequate spread of risks can seriously undermine the financial strengths.

Apart from the above, the practical considerations of protecting the solvency margins also leads to reinsurance. The local regulation for any insurance company may limit the retained premium income in relation to capital and free resources, thereby necessitating to offload the surplus risks by means of reinsurance. Apart from the above, considerations like inflationary trend, composition of insurance portfolio, also play an important role in the decision of buying reinsurance protections. Reinsurance also can be a means or tool of profit gearing or expense sharing for any new and start-up insurance company to bring stability to its results and at the same time protect it's balance sheet.

Evolution

Reinsurance has its origin much after the concept of insurance was established in the early sixteenth century. Need for protecting large risks naturally led to the form of co-insurance, which subsequently was still found to inadequate. Therefore, to spread the risks further, it was necessary to protect it with markets beyond the existing local markets.

What was initially reinsured as individual risk on facultative basis gradually developed into a portfolio protection for each class. Facultative reinsurance was the most common form of reinsurance in the initial years whereby risks were reinsured on individual basis. Subsequently, for the purpose of bringing stability to the portfolio of the insurance companies, it was designed to give protection for the whole portfolio of any particular class. Such protection of portfolio was on the concept of partnership and ceded proportionately in form of treaties. Subsequently, Lloyds introduced the concept of excess of loss reinsurance, whereby for an agreed premium the reinsurer accepts liability for any loss exceeding an agreed figure. This new pattern of reinsurance was useful to protect portfolios against catastrophe hazards like earthquakes, windstorms etc.

Methods of Reinsurance

The specific needs of insurers are as varied as the reinsurance solutions. There are three broad types of reinsurance covers available to display the requirements of each insurer.

Facultative Reinsurance

Where the subject matter involves reinsuring an individual risk, this is known as *facultative reinsurance*. The insurer cedes part of the risk to one or more reinsurers and is, therefore, known as the *cedent*. As the word *facultative* implies, the cedent may offer the risk, or part of it, for reinsurance, i.e. it may offer the business if it wishes. The reinsurers, for their part, are at liberty to accept or reject the offer.

Reinsurance Treaty

A treaty is arranged for the reinsurance of a specific portfolio, with risks being ceded automatically for the entire portfolio within the terms of the treaty. Cedents do not have to decide whether or not to cede each individual risks but undertake to cede the entire portfolio. Nor do the reinsurers have to go through an individual acceptance procedure, since they are contractually bound to accept the entire portfolio.

Thus, for the reinsurance of individual risks, facultative treaties are arranged, while for the reinsurance of entire portfolio, treaties are arranged. Treaties are again segregated into two types, viz. proportional and non-proportional (excess of loss).

Proportional Treaty

The proportion is the central feature of proportional treaty reinsurance. What is specifically involved here is the proportion which the treaty limit of the relevant reinsurance cover bears to the individual original risk ceded. The terms used here is *proportionality principle*. In fire insurance, liability is defined as the total sum insured (maximum liability based on the full value) or as the highest estimated loss (i.e. estimated maximum loss or maximum possible loss). In the third party liability business the liability is determined to be the limit of compensation required to rectify a loss. This corresponds total value. Besides the proportionality principle, the product proportional treaty *reinsurance* is associated with another feature, viz. the direct insurers cede the risks at the original conditions agreed between them and the policyholders. The reinsurers are, therefore, involved in the risk under the same terms and conditions as the direct insurers.

Quota Share Treaty

In a quota share treaty, the proportion is defined as a fixed, invariable percentage which is generally applied to the entire portfolio of risks as the quota share ceded to reinsurance. The exceptions are risks which exceed the amount of the quota share limit. An absolute quota share limit of this kind is agreed because the quota share reinsurance could otherwise be too unbalanced, and the reinsurers would no longer know their maximum liability per risk. With risks for which the quota share limit is not high enough, the percentage is reduced in the ratio, quota share limit to the original risk. The cedent's liability on any one risk is, therefore, reduced by the define percentage as the quota share ceded.

Surplus Treaty

This treaty allows variable percentages for the retention and for business ceded to reinsurance, depending on the size of the individual risk. As can be seen below, compared to quota share reinsurance, the system of surplus reinsurance is more complex.

The liability in the cedent's retention is defined as a fixed amount. Risks within this amount are retained by the reinsurer in full for its own account. Only risks on which the cedent's liability exceeds the amount of the retention are ceded to reinsurance, cession being effected on the basis of the ratio, portion of liability over and above the retention to overall liability. The percentage for cession varies depending on the size of the overall liability.

The surplus reinsurance eliminates the peaks in the portfolio for the insurer, thus providing its portfolio with certain homogeneity and also automatic capacity.

Non-proportional Treaty

Unlike proportional reinsurance, which is based on original liability and proportional cession, with non-proportional reinsurance it is the amount of loss and the cover, which is limited in amount, which are considered. This is also termed as excess of loss reinsurance. The essentials of an excess of loss treaty are:
- one or more classes of business from which losses are reinsured;
- a fixed limit – the deductible or excess point, up to the amount of which insurers bear all losses for their own account;
- a limit of cover, termed as layers, up to the amount of which the reinsurer pays portions of claims above the deductible.

Non-proportional reinsurance offers insurers another way of cutting probable claim peaks back to the level of retention they find acceptable. The fact that the distribution of claims and the distribution of liabilities in an insurance portfolio differ is of relevance here. The occurrence and amount of a loss are fortuitous, with varying degrees of probability. As far as the period of time is concerned, basically only the losses occurring during the agreed period of the contract are covered. In reinsurance terminology this is referred as years of occurrence. Unlike proportional reinsurance, non-proportional reinsurance cover is separate from the original portfolio and, therefore, from the terms of the original policies and from the original premiums.

Excess of loss treaties primarily can be broad based on:
- Protection against losses for any one risk with the per risk excess of loss cover (generally termed as working XL).
- Protection against losses for any one accumulation event with the per event catastrophe excess of loss cover (Catastrophe XL).
- Limitation of the claims burden from the retention for any one year with the aggregate excess (stop loss) reinsurance cover (for Balance Sheet protection).

Reinsurance in the Context of the Indian Market

Existing Arrangements: Prior to nationalisation in 1973, there was very little reinsurance prevalent in the local market. The branches of the foreign companies operating in India were protecting their portfolio within their parent company's global programme, overseas. Similarly, most domestic companies did not have to purchase huge reinsurance protections as their portfolios consisted of mainly householders and small to medium commercial and industrial risks.

For the purpose providing reinsurance capacity in a limited way there existed an Indian Insurance Pool whereby the local companies were members. The purpose of the Pool was to share the business underwritten by each company and thus try to stabilise the result of the market as a whole, in a limited way. Apart from the Pool, obligatory cessions were made for 10% each to India Re, a local reinsurance company owned by the Government and Indian Guarantee, a subsidiary of Oriental Fire and Marine Insurance Company Limited. The purpose of forming the above was to retain premiums domestically to the extent possible.

Subsequent to nationalisation, the aforesaid companies were merged into the statutory entity, viz. General Insurance Corporation of India (GIC). Post nationalisation, the erstwhile companies were merged into four regional companies, which in turn were made wholly owned subsidiaries of the GIC. Thus, GIC became the parent body to oversee the affairs of the general insurance industry. As such, a common agenda was followed in conducting business including reinsurance.

By virtue of the merger of the aforesaid India Re and Indian Guarantee, GIC continued to receive the obligatory cessions for 20%. Apart from receiving these cessions, the role of being the local reinsurer was thrust upon GIC. Thus, the onus of arranging reinsurance protections for the insurance companies, was upon GIC. Keeping in mind Government's agenda to create maximum retention capacity within the local market and thus retain premiums locally, a common integrated reinsurance programme for the whole market was embarked upon. The composite financial strength assisted in gradually increasing the retention levels of the market as a whole. Coupled with the aforesaid, the tariff structure operating in most classes has assisted in reflecting good underwriting results, thereby strengthening the financial results of all the companies.

This in turn has resulted in more and more retentions especially for classes which have achieved a greater degree of homogeneity in the portfolio as well as volumes. At the present time less than 10% of the gross direct premium is ceded as reinsurance premiums. Reinsurance is now primarily purchased for peak and/or non-homogenous/special risks like Air India, Indian Airlines, ONGC etc. or for new classes such as directors and officers liability, errors and omissions cover, liquidated damages cover, kidnap and ransom cover, performance bonds etc. for which there is not sufficient volumes and spread of business.

The above explains how pivotal a role the prevalent reinsurance programme had played in the development of the local market in terms of risk retention capacity, developing automatic reinsurance capacity and thereby retaining more premiums, creating investible surplus and strengthening the balance sheets. The existing companies have become strong financial entities to be classified as Financial Institutions and are well geared to face competition in the newly liberalised set up. At the macro level this has boosted investments in industrial and infrastructural sectors assisting in the growth in the economy at large.

Review of the Existing Reinsurance Programme: The existing reinsurance structure is integrated programmes for the whole market that each company commonly adopts, irrespective of their financial capabilities, profitability etc. In this context, it is insensitive to true net retention of each company.

Reviewing the features of the integrated reinsurance programme, comparison has to be made between the levels of the market retention for each class against the reinsurance cessions to examine how much profit is retained and thereby establish whether the current levels of retentions are as profitable as they can be. Thus, optimum retention and not the maximum retention is the primary focus around which the whole programme is structured.

Empirically, the retention for any one risk should be between 1% to 2% of the shareholders funds (share capital and free reserves). Applying this yard stick will reveal that the composite financial strength of the Insurance companies is capable of retaining at much higher levels than the current maximum retentions fixed for various classes.

The retention levels, amongst other considerations like premium volumes, risk profile, growth portfolio, be viewed from the angle of diminishing utility of retained exposure equating in less and less monetary benefits, beyond the optimum level of retention for a particular portfolio. Under the prevalent programme it may be noted that the current level of retention is lower than what could be retained by the market on a composite basis. Due care has also been exercised though to a lesser degree, to lend sensitivity to financial strengths of each company in isolation, because all the companies do not have identical net worth.

Apart from the above aspect, considerations have also been given for additional financial exposure arising out large catastrophe events. In India's fast growing economy most private and public entities require various forms of insurance. Thus, GIC and the subsidiaries interact with all levels of the society as being the sole provider of insurance for every single policyholder. This puts GIC and its subsidiaries in a position of not just strength but also vulnerability. Strengths are derived as being a sole provider and vulnerability comes from responsibility to underwrite every single policy, thus the lack of selectivity. The strengths and vulnerabilities increase rapidly as the economy continues to grow.

Thus, strategically the retention levels are pegged to address the above issues.

As a case study, the fire portfolio is reviewed in detail. This would be the true reflection of how reinsurance programmes are structured in India as,
- the fire portfolio is largest amongst all classes
- has the highest *per risk* sum insured for any class
- the existing reinsurance programme maximises the full retention capacity of the market and has full automatic capacity without requiring to approach the international market for facultative terms. Thus obviating the need of being influenced by the market cycles of the international reinsurance market. Also requires less vertical capacity.
- Fire portfolio is fully tariffed and thus insensitive to market competition in terms of rating.

The cessions pattern and the retention of each company is based on quantitative definitions of the risks. Within the fire portfolio the risks are divided in three segments based on Probable Maximum Loss (PML) limits, viz.

1. Small risks up to sum insured of Rs. 50 million
2. Medium-sized risks ranging between sum insured of Rs. 50 million and PML of Rs. 250 million
3. Listed Risks–PML exceeding Rs. 250 million. There are approximately 600 risks currently within this category.

Each of the reinsurance arrangement is explained in detail below.

1. Net Retained Account
(a) Obligatory cessions

20% of the small risks and medium sized risks are currently ceded to GIC.

Listed risks are also ceded for 20% subject to a maximum monetary limit of Rs. 50 crore.

GIC's maximum retention is capped at Rs. 50 crore PML basis.
- Based on study of the profile of top 30 risks on October 1, 2000 the above retention equates to only 2.1% of the top risk
- This is protected by the *Per Risk* and *Catastrophe* excess of loss programmes further reducing it to Rs. 6 crore on absolute net basis.

(b) Market pool

GIC is the manager of the pool. Currently 30% of each risk is ceded to the pool and retroceded back which is fully retained by the companies, subject to a monetary limit of Rs. 750 crore PML.

This is protected by the *Per Risk* and *Catastrophe* Excess of Loss Programmes further reducing to Rs. 9 crore on Absolute Net Basis for all companies combined.

(c) Net retention of each company

Comparative Analysis of Maximum Net Retention and Absolute Net Retention for Each Company for the Fire Portfolio

Maximum net retention for each company is Rs. 125 crore PML.
Absolute net retention for each company is Rs. 15 crore.
Based on the capital and reserves as on March 31, 2000 of each company the retentions are as follows:

Company	Maximum Net Retention	Absolute Net Retention
National	6.60%	0.79%
New India	2.91%	0.35%
Oriental	6.99%	0.84%
United India	5.77%	0.69%

Currently GIC purchases excess of loss cover up to Rs. 300 crore PML for *per risk* and Rs. 600 crore PML for *per event* (catastrophe) for the net retained amount. The cost of purchasing the above programmes is 2.14% of the gross direct premium (retained) which is competitive considering the large limits of indemnity which GIC is purchasing.

The programme has been of utility over the years and have responded adequately in terms of claims recovery for events of high severity such as Gujarat cyclone (1998) and Orissa cyclone (1999).

The absolute net retention level of each company should be based on its financial strengths and will vary from company to company. However, the current programme being market driven, the amount retained per company is uniform and thus is insensitive to this aspect.

The net retained portion each of the obligatory cessions, cessions to market fire pool and the net retention of each company is on combined basis protected by net account excess of loss protection on *per risk* and *catastrophe* basis separately.

2. Surplus Treaties

The surplus treaty of each company under the existing programme mirrors identical in terms of cession limits and the portfolio ceded. Cessions to the company's surplus treaty currently start at a much higher level, above Rs. 2,500 million PML and are mere capacity providers. Cessions to these treaties are geared on line basis. Currently the capacity of each treaty is Rs. 7.50 crore PML, equating in a total capacity of Rs. 30 crore PML. The Surplus treaties are utilised to fill up capacity and thereby achieve as much automatic capacity as possible.

3. Market Surplus Treaty

The market surplus treaty over the period of time has worked as a second surplus and functioned as a capacity provider. Cessions to this treaty are made after full capacity of the underlying treaties is exhausted. Currently risks in excess of Rs. 280 crore PML are ceded to this treaty.

4. Facultative

Currently all risks which fall above the limits of the market surplus property are ceded to GIC on facultative basis. GIC writes the full facultative requirements of the market. This is possible as they are fully backed by an facultative excess of loss protection which can absorb risks up to any limit. Cessions to this programme are on proportional basis. However, the programme operates on excess of loss basis, with a small second retention of Rs. 5 crore PML and indemnity split into different layers. Each risk is ceded in the same percentage to the second retention and the indemnity of the programme. Therefore, the premium paid for this protection is much lower than the premium received by GIC.

GIC derives benefit from this facultative excess of loss programme which has been in existence since many years. This facility has utility of writing domestic facultative business for unlimited capacity. On the backing of this reinsurance facility all facultative business of the Indian market are absorbed within the automatic capacity.

To summarise, the above capacities are stacked one above the other as shown in the Schematic Diagram, providing unlimited vertical capacity. This is achieved successfully because of the integrated approach, whereby the risks could be absorbed horizontally such as utilising all the companies retention capacity as well as utilising the capacity of the companies surplus treaties.

The volumes have also helped to drive the programme in achieving the unlimited automatic capacity.

For other classes like marine (hull and cargo), engineering and miscellaneous accident the structure of the programme is similar to the fire programme with minor changes, depending upon the type and feature of risks for each class.

For classes like energy, aviation, liability etc. which are not driven by volumes, the propensity is to keep low retention for the net account and reinsure the balance amount by the facultative method.

Reinsurance in the Liberalised Market

Role of the National Reinsurer: Following the liberation of the insurance industry and the with delinking of the existing subsidiaries, GIC's role will be solely to function as a national reinsurer. Therefore, the existing market reinsurance programme would disintegrate and that capacity would now be defrayed amongst existing and new entrants who would be arranging their own reinsurance programmes.

The national reinsurer may have no control for arranging the insurance companies reinsurance programmes but will be looked upon to provide reinsurance capacities. Therefore, it should endeavour and absorb as much of the reinsurance offered by the domestic insurance companies in order to maintain its position as a leading reinsurer in the Indian market.

Objectives of the National Reinsurer

- Receive statutory cessions.
- Provide maximum reinsurance capacity in the domestic market for other than statutory cessions and thereby retain maximum premium within the local market.
- Play a pivotal and influential role as a pro-active reinsurer for the domestic insurance companies and assist to develop their portfolio for writing large and complex risks.

The disintegration of the existing composite programme for the market poses fresh challenges and thus GIC has to design for a fresh programme which would be solely for its protection. This leads to rather anomalous situation at a crucial juncture when its role is most important for the market, because at one end the financial strength of GIC will be reviewed in isolation from its existing subsidiary companies, resulting into reduced retention and acceptance levels. At the same time the need of this market will require more and more local reinsurance capacity.

Furthermore, GIC will still continue to interact with all segments of the general insurance business because in its new role of a statutory reinsurer it will still continue to be the sole provider for insurance for every single policy underwritten.

The above makes an interesting challenge for GIC to respond to its new role and quickly establish leadership with much smaller resources than in the past.

Domestic Market Considerations
- Liberalisation of the local market bringing in new entrants from the private sector.
- Autonomy of local subsidiaries.
- Future growth in the industry following economic reforms.
- Demand for more flexible and comprehensive products.
- Reduction in the tariff.

Outlook for the Domestic Market for the Future
- India is an expanding market and, therefore, there will be increase in demand for insurance vertically and horizontally.
- Greater requirement for new insurance products.
- Further competition following liberalisation.
- Dismantling if the tariff structure at a later date.

How to Achieve the Objectives ?

Meeting the challenges of reduced financial structure and the need for increasing capacity can be achieved in the following manner:

- Provide maximum reinsurance capacity to the domestic insurance companies and thus assist to develop and grow the direct portfolio.
- Design and structure reinsurance programmes for the domestic insurance companies especially for the net account and thereby play an important role as a partner for developing direct business

and to a lesser extent even influence the rating for non-tariff business.
- GIC to arrange their own reinsurance programme to meet with the above requirements.

GIC's reinsurance programme will be a blend of XL protections, proportional treaties and automatic capacity like facultative XL programmes, line slips etc. Pursuant to the new set up and following the possible disintegration of the current programme there will be need for more vertical capacity as perhaps companies underwriting business will not be compulsorily required to utilise the available capacity of other insurance companies.

As the insurance companies will have to necessarily utilise the available market capacities before approaching international markets for purchasing reinsurance, thus GIC will have to provide more capacity for the peak risks. This is achievable by utilising the exist automatic reinsurance facilities like the facultative excess of loss programmes for fire portfolio or lineslips for engineering and so on.

To address the above situation retention levels will have to be revised from the existing levels wherever possible. Fortunately, the current net worth of approximately Rs. 2,200 crore shall enable GIC to achieve this end. Increased retentions will facilitate to achieve more capacity for the surplus treaties as they are geared on line basis. The volumes arising due to receipt of statutory cession will also drive their own reinsurance capacities.

The challenges will be more for providing capacity for classes which do not have spread of risks or the volumes of premium. For such risks it would be desirable to cede these classes along with the more established classes and thereby trade on profitable business.

For the insurance companies, especially the new entrants designing reinsurance programmes will be interesting. The relatively smaller net worth will make it difficult to maintain high retentions and thereby create vertical capacities. Also, arranging such reinsurance programme will be expensive in terms of high cost for the net account as also low commissions which will be achieved if the proportional treaties are too unbalanced. Thus, the companies will seek more support from the domestic reinsurer during the formative years till such time their portfolio and results stabilise.

16

Risk Management and Financial Planning

S.S. Shekhar

This article covers aspects and issues relating to risk management and the risk financing techniques available. Risk management- traditionally considered synonymous with insurance has evolved with the business complexity and has taken into its fold business risks so as to provide a platform for an organisation's decision making process. The later part of the article covers various methods of risk financing available for the CFO of an organisation.

Definitions of Risk Management have been traditionally synonymous with buying insurance. This has been specially true in the Indian environment and the corporate Risk Manager has the sole responsibility of negotiating insurance contracts. In a recent research program (conducted internationally) to understand the future market for Risk Management and Risk Finance services - most respondents interviewed, while having commendable definitions of risk management had little by way of explanations of how in practice they operationalise their grander risk management ambitions. Risk Financing for many is the annual budget for insurance premiums. Others held that Risk Financing was synonymous with 'financial Risks' and essentially comprised such instruments as hedging and options.

The rapidly changing and increasingly complex competitive environment has created an array of risks to be managed - global competition, shifts in consumption patterns, e-business, political and social risks, environmental consciousness, growing liability consciousness, etc. The success or the failure of an organisation will largely depend on its ability to assume such risks and not their avoidance. This calls for a paradigm shift in the way risks are managed and financed.

Risks and Risk management are difficult concepts to define. Most definitions have tended to focus on the negative consequences of risk assumption - something, which necessarily signifies danger, a loss potential, and to be avoided, if possible. The word 'risk' is derived from 'riskcare' - Italian for 'to dare'. And in this sense risk is a choice, a conscious decision rather than fate. It is impossible to avoid risks - since all choices and actions contain risk. Our challenge is, therefore, to carefully select the risks we assume, quantify them and ensure that the rewards attendant with the assumption are greater than the loss potential. This is easier said than done and in practice such quantification of the reward/loss potential is extremely difficult - due to the presence of a plethora of variables beyond control of the organisation, the dynamic nature of the market place, the rapid technological changes and the difficulty in obtaining vital and reliable information in support of the risk assumption decisions. Hence the definition of business risks and processes to manage them must recognise the 'imperfectness of the art', the 'flexibility' and 'continuity' that must accompany such definitions and process.

A broad definition of Risk and Risk management could be:

"Risk management is an ongoing, proactive management process which seeks to,
- Identify the key critical functions of an organisation, its business and market;
- Monitor and assess events that can have a bearing on their operations and
- Evaluate such events for their business impact due to an organisation's action or inaction in response to them
- Assess such risks qualitatively and quantitatively so as to provide input for top management to make its decisions relative to innovation, expansion and protection of stakeholder value,
- Develop plans and procedures to manage such risks and ensure business continuity".

The strength of the above definition stems from its consideration on the possible 'upside' of risks and the maximising of stakeholder wealth as the Risk Management objectives. This brings us to the question - what are these risks and what are their sources?

Risks have been traditionally divided into 'pure risks' and "speculative risks'. Historically, the practice had confined itself to the management of 'pure risks' - which have been insurable - risk of fire, earthquakes, wind, legal liability etc., Occurrence of such risks which are likely only to cause a loss to the organisation, with no possibility of a gain. Solutions to these risks were primarily protection from the perils and purchase of insurance with focus on the extent of coverage, adequacy of limits and the cost of risk transfer. The risk management concepts evolved further to add new areas arising out of the changes in the internal and external environment. Thus the concepts of risk management were applied to the organisation's so called 'speculative risks', covering all aspects of marketing, finance, operational and reputation risks.

The risks in the two categories are shown in Table 1. The sources of risks are both internal to an organisation as well as external.

The organisation's external risks are beyond its control. These risks are a part of the complex and dynamic environment that is changing rapidly. The risks in this category include political risks, economic, rapid technological changes, financial markets etc. The risk management process would essentially require:

1. The key to an organisation's success in managing and indeed benefiting from such changes is in identification of such risks. This requires creating an ongoing process for the systematic collection and evaluation of information relating to the external risks. This involves a proactive monitoring of the environment for changes - typically obtained from disparate information sources - e.g. primary research, secondary data, etc.

2. Quantify and evaluate the impact of such changes on the organisation's strategic and operations plans.

3. Develop a strategic response and create a framework for its implementation.

4. Implement and marshal resources to the opportunities presented.

5. Measure performance.

Internal risks would be largely controllable and offer substantial opportunity for management and shareholder value protection/enhancement. They are subject to qualification and can often be unilaterally managed by the corporation. The risks may be resident and isolated in a particular process or function. But normally and more frequently risks do not operate in soils but transcend processes and impact on a variety of areas within the organisation.

Table 1: Risk and Uncertainty in Business

Business Risks	Pure Risks
Technological: includes risks of obsolescence, efficiency, time changes in the expected cost of inputs, invention of substitutes etc.	Technical: This includes risks from hazardous processes, machinery breakdown, failure of safety devices, etc.
Political : Regulatory changes, restrictions on repatriation of profits, taxes, nationalisation, political unrest, war, trade restrictions etc.	Physical Effects of nature: Windstorms, floods, earthquakes, etc.
Economic: Changes in the level of economic, activity, inflation, monetary and fiscal policy changes, etc.	Social deviations: Theft, fraud, riots, negligence, etc.
Social: Changes in the consumption pattern, tastes, labour unrest etc.	Personnel: Loss of key staff.
Financial: Availability of capital, cost of credit, bad debts, forex rates, interest rates etc.	Environment and Legal: liabilities arising from pollution to the environment, product liability, liability arising from accidents caused to the employees and society from the activities of the company.
Market: errors in forecasting, globalisation e-business, competition, substitutes, changes in need, loss of market shares etc.	
Production : Limitation in technical ability, snags in new processes, changes in expected costs, non-availability of quality raw material.	

Thus an accidental malfunction of a valve can release harmful chemicals into the environment. The environmental impact of such releases may invite public liability litigation and the image and reputation of the organisation will suffer, thus impacting its market share. The risks would typically include:

Operational Risks: such as product/service quality, cost effectiveness, environmental impact of operations, product development, product liability and recall costs, human resources, raw material availability and costs, natural catastrophe, legal and regulatory compliance, etc.

Financial Risks: these would include credit risks-both received and given, currency risks, interest rate fluctuation, economic factors, liquidity, cash flows, etc.

Technological Risks: obsolescence, implementation, selection gaps, etc.

These risks while providing risk management challenges also provide the largest benefits, if managed properly. A corporate risk policy and guidelines need to be formulated-defining the organisational risk appetite. The policy document would typically identify the sources of the risks and the limits of the responsibilities and provide consistency in managing risks. The policy document would also establish a framework for the establishment of management processes for managing the risks and would typically include implementation of Business Continuity management (BCM) process, an Environment Management System, a Quality Management system, Safety Management process, Information Security Management process etc.

The business continuity management process establishes mechanisms to continuously monitor and evaluate organisational risks. Establish mechanisms for their reductions and control. Assess their business impacts, develop alternative continuity strategies, establish procedures and plans for emergency response, develop and implement continuity plans, provide for training and awareness campaigns and maintain and exercise the plans.

With the evolution of risk management, the array of risk financing tools available has also expanded. For the large corporates risk transfer through insurance has been replaced by more effective and

Risk Management and Financial Planning

flexible solutions. Risk Management practices helped corporates understand their risks and increase their ability to retain a large composition of risks. From globalisation and competition grew requirements for alternative risk transfer mechanisms - which were provided by the financial markets.

How a firm decides to handle its risks depends upon its corporate objectives, attitude to risks as also on its financial situation. Essentially, risk financing is concerned with the selecting the cheapest method, commensurate with the degree of financial security desired. A necessary objective is also to spread the cost of losses more evenly over time in order to avoid a sudden and crippling loss. Typically the decision options in risk financing would include:

- Risk Retention
  Charging losses to the current operating costs
  Making ex ante provisions for the losses through a contingency fund
  Captives- single parent captives and group captives
- Risk Transfer
  Transfer of the risky activity
  Insurance
- Alternative Risk Transfer and Finite risk transfer
- Hedging, Derivatives

Various methods of financing risks internally - Risk Retention - include charging losses to the operating costs, setting up contingency funds and the use of captives.

Charging losses against operating costs requires the absorption of such losses within the operating cash flow. The practice may be adopted for those risks that are small and regular in occurrence. The ability to do so largely depends on positive cash flows throughout the year. Obviously the size of losses that can be absorbed will depend on the size of such cash flow surpluses. The practice is not applied to an organisation with irregular cash flows or where the risks are random and the magnitude of the losses high.

For managing random and large loss risks, internal contingency funds can be set up. The fund could be typically created by the transfer of periodic contributions into the fund. As the contingency fund has to be in a readily realisable form and the money will need to be invested in liquid assets, hence such contingency reserves are not available for the organisation's investment requirements. Large diversified multi-location organisations can create a central fund. The issues which, however, need to be considered include the non-availability of tax deduction from such funds, overseas country regulations on such repatriation of funds and exchange controls.

Captives are a natural progression of the internal funding by organisations and could be single parent captive or multi-parent captives. Single parent captive insurance companies were founded when corporations perceived an opportunity to simultaneously take advantage of self funding manageable levels of risks while benefiting from tax deduction permitted for premium paid. Multi-parent captives are formed by a pool of organisations with similar risk management standards and whose interests are in similar fields.

Risk Transfer is either by way of outsourcing a hazardous business process or by the transfer of the financial losses to an insurer. Alternate Risk Transfer (ART) and Finance solutions would include the following.

ART is a method of obtaining reinsurance capacity from capital markets. This was a repackaging of insurance and reinsurance products into financial instruments such as bonds, options and other derivative products. The investors included mutual funds, hedge funds, banks as well as investment departments of insurance companies. Products included:

Event Linked Bonds: These are floating rate notes and are sold to investors. If the insured catastrophic event does not occur during the bond period the investors receive principal and interest. In case of the occurrence of the catastrophe event the investors lose some or all of the principal due.

Industrial Loss Warranty: These are essentially bonds. These are double trigger reinsurance policies. Here the event is defined by the occurrence of two triggers viz. loss to the company and loss to the insurance industry.

CAT Swaps: Exchange of CAT exposures based on the concept of spreading risks.

CAT Options: CAT options are traded in exchanges e.g. the CBOT. An industry loss index is used as a benchmark for qualifying the trigger point of the option.

Weather Derivatives: Typically used by utilities e.g. energy companies wishing to smoothen their cash flows which may be affected due to weather conditions e.g. an unusually warm winter.

Equity: The companies could sell their equity in return for money to finance their cash requirements in the catastrophe aftermath.

Contingent Surplus Notes: Here investors are obliged to purchase surplus notes (debt instruments) on an occurrence of a catastrophe. Cash is used to settle claims. Here the insured is required to repay the investors overtime. Hence the investors lose no money, however, they carry the risk of insurer's default.

Finite Risk Transfer insurance is an alternative to Retention and pure risk transfer. This type of risk financing provides insurance coverage tailored to the requirements of the insured company. The insurance costs reflect the insured's own experience rather than the overall experience of a pool of similar insured. The insurance contracts would typically feature multi-year, multi-line covers and profit sharing from investment income.

Derivatives were designed to enable market participants to eliminate risks. For example, a farmer growing cotton can fix a price for his crop even prior to it being planted thus eliminating price risks.

In conclusion, today's risk managers need to look beyond managing insurable risks. The process of risk management has to be an enabling tool for top management's decision making process. The complexity of the processes and the requirement of specialised knowledge in areas as diverse as operations, finance and technology has demanded that the risk management be a line function - much like a quality management process. Risk management decisions need to be taken with active involvement of all levels of the organisation from the CEO to the operation manager and financial head. To support uniformity in the process, the management has to set in place Risk Policies and guidelines and support implementation of management systems. What cannot be managed or retained has to be secured from loss - through appropriate risk finance options.

17

Risk Management and Insurance Industry

Devesh Srivastava

Risk means the chance or probability of loss occurring. Risk is defined as a state of knowledge in which each alternative leads to a specific outcome, each outcome occurring with a probability that is known to the decision maker. Risk is calculable. Risk can be measured by way of standard deviation between expected result and the actual result.

As opposed to risk, uncertainty is a subjective phenomenon where the probability or outcome of the event is not calculable. Consequently, whereas risk is insurable, uncertainty is not.

Risks can be classified into the following:

Pure vs. Speculative Risks: If the occurrence of an event results in either no change in the situation or a loss with no possibility of a gain, this risk is termed as a "pure risk" (e.g. fire, storm, etc.). Where the outcome may be either a loss or profit, the risk is called a speculative risk (all business risks). Most pure risks can be dealt with by insurance but speculative risks are generally uninsurable.

Dynamic vs. Static Risks: Dynamic risks arise from the changes that take place in society like economically, socially, technologically, environmentally or politically. Static risks are those that would exist in the absence of such changes. Dynamic risks closely resemble speculative risks and pure risks are example of static risks.

Fundamental vs. Particular Risks: Fundamental risks are those which affect the whole society. They are impersonal in both cause and effect. Particular risks affect mainly the individual or the firm and arise from factors over which he may exert some control.

Classification by Size of Loss: Risks can be classified according to potential loss severity as under:

Class I – Those losses, which do not disturb a firm's finances.

Class II – Those losses, which would necessitate borrowing for additional finance.

Class III – Large losses, which may bankrupt a firm.

Class I & II risks can be handled by the firm internally whilst Class III risks are usually transferred to an insurer.

Both pure and speculative risks can be handled by:

Avoidance: It is either ceasing to undertake the activity which creates the risk or performing it in another way or at some place else. For example, the risk of flooding may be avoided by moving to a site well above recorded flood levels.

Reduction: Reduction or loss prevention covers all methods employed to reduce the probability of loss- producing events occurring or the potential size of losses that do occur. Examples are (i) provision of safety devices, (ii) contingency planning to minimise the extent of losses and (iii) training people to meet emergencies and to carry out salvaging operations.

Retention: Means to pay for small losses from own resources or possibly set aside a contingency fund to meet larger losses. Retention of risks may be either a deliberate decision or an inadvertent omission.

Combination: works on the principle of the law of large numbers. By combining a large number of independent exposure units in one portfolio, large diversified organisations can reduce the variations of its aggregate actual losses from the expected losses for any one year. Insurance companies do precisely the same thing.

Transfer : (a) by transferring the activity which creates the risk, say by subcontracting; (b) by contractual agreements like indemnity clauses in contracts of sale. The most important form of risk transfer is insurance.

Hedging: Hedging is normally done through forward contracts like an importer may hedge against exchange rate fluctuations by entering into forward contracts.

Research: Research is to get more information on the events so as to help reduce risk. For example a firm may conduct a market research before launching a product so as to reduce uncertainty. But such research cannot guarantee that actual outcomes will match the expected.

Logically the risk management process follows the following sequence: (a) Risk analysis (b) Risk control and (c) Risk financing.

Risk Analysis

Risk analysis arguably is the most essential step in Risk Management because no exposure can be rationally managed unless and until it's properly analysed. Identifying loss exposures typically begins with the study of specific items of value which an organisation may lose, the property it owns or uses, the net income it earns from its operations, its freedom from liability to others and the services of its key personnel whose talents cannot be readily replaced. All the accidental events with which a risk manager deals with involve loss of one or more or all of these four basic losses type.

The Role of an effective risk manager can be drawn up as under :

1. Primary responsibility of risk Manager is the identification of the risk- perceive the nature of the risk and also determine the probable cause, that can lead to the risk exposure and its probable effects. Provide operating line management with the tools of research to determine systematically risk exposure within their own spheres of operation. Seek co-operation from the local experts in the field .

2. Advising the top management on the techniques to be used for the evaluation, control and financing of the risks- compatible with corporate objectives

3. Administering insurance programs. Risk manager has no direct execution responsibility for implementing physical risk control policy-but it is necessary that he should be aware of the happenings. Involvement of technical people along with risk managers is necessary when finalisation of FEA drawings takes place.

4. Communication and co-operation with colleagues throughout the organisation.

5. Motivating the management in the advantages of risk management.

6. Educating the management through preparation of Risk and Insurance Manuals.

7. Record keeping and the reporting of the activities of Risk Management Department.

8. Periodic review of the risk management programmes.

Risk Control

Having identified and analysed the probable losses, the next logical step is to contain and reduce the probable losses. This can be done by avoidance; reduction, retention, combination, transfer, hedging and researching already detailed earlier. Hereafter for residual risks, risk financing remains the only viable option.

A firm may be exposed to various types of risks:

Product on Risks: Failure to produce desired output e.g. breakdown of key machine may lead to stoppage of work. New products may not farewell. Abandon a project mid-way. Rise in cost of Raw Materials.

Marketing and Distribution Risks: Sale goes down leading to more stocks on shelf. Competitors. Changing fashion/tastes of consumers. Lower export sales due to change in political strategies. Economic conditions at home.

Financial risks: Increase in cost of borrowing due to hike in rate of interest. Non availability of credit. Debtors failure to pay. High capital gearing ratio i.e. Loan capital higher than equity capital.

Personnel risks: Loss of key employees. Employees shifting to competitors. Dishonesty, embezzlement, infidelity etc.

Risk Financing

The main risk financing options are: transfer of the risk or financial responsibility for the risk to a third party; retain financial responsibility for the risk; transfer financial responsibility for the risk to an insurer; a combination of insurance transfer and retention

The role of risk financing is to ensure the economic provision of funds to finance the recovery of the organisation from property damage, liability damages, business interruption and personal losses.

Thus it involves:

- evaluation of total values at risk from each class of exposure;
- estimation of total costs of loss within a specified time period together with the maximum severity of any one loss;
- identification of appropriate sources of funding in advance of the loss;
- appraisal of the economic viability of the replacement or repair of assets subject to loss;
- arrangements for securement of these funds in event of loss, and
- direction and control of the use of the funds upon the occurrence

of the loss.

Risk Financing devices include insurance; the use of internal cash resources or reserves; credit facilities such as lines of credit; and captive insurance companies.

Traditional Risk Financing Techniques

Risk management practice normally divides traditional risk financing techniques into the following categories: (a) transfer to a non-insurer, (b) retention and (c) insurance.

Transfer to a Non-Insurer: This is usually arranged as part of a contractual agreement transferring either the activity giving rise to the risk or the financial responsibility for the losses arising out of the risk.

Retention: An organisation may decide to retain its losses as insurance may not be the most appropriate method of financing loss or it may not be possible or desirable to place some or all of risk with an insurer. In certain circumstances it may be cost effective to retain potential loss than to place it with an insurer. Insurers recognise this point and offer concessions in the form of premium discounts for the retention of some of the potential risk by the insured. Other factors, which would lead to retention, include: Exposures not legally possible to insure. Exposures which are not insurable such as hidden cost of losses, or Exposures which are insurable but for which cover is either not available or is not available on terms acceptable to the insure

The most popular device is the deductible under which the insured is responsible the first part of each and every loss to a pre-determined level. The motivation for retention will have a number of facets:

There may be an economic advantage in retaining the funds that would be paid immediately to an insurer. The financial ability of the organisation to bear the risk. The loss characteristics of the exposure.

The desire of the management to undertake the additional risk and administrative responsibilities. The options which the organisation has are: Pay losses as they arise from cash flow. Create an internal reserve fund to which funds are allocated in anticipation of the loss; and Create an external reserve fund either in conjunction with an insurer or insurance subsidiary, or as a separately incorporated insurance subsidiary.

Self-Insurance: Self Insurance means that the cost of losses arising from the pure risks are borne directly by the organisation and not transferred to a third party. The result of this is that the organisation suffers a reduction in net worth through either a reduction in assets or an increase in liabilities as a direct result of the loss.

Financing of Self-Insurance: Non-replacement. In this case the firm does not replace the damaged asset. This is advantageous if replacement was not necessary to maintain continuity of production and services and the asset has been running at a loss. Non replacement would increase the profitability as the drain on cash low would be reduced by more than the fall in cash in flow.

On the other side the organisations networth in balance sheet terms would be reduced by the historical cost of the asset less depreciation.

Current Expense: This approach charges losses arising from certain exposures as they occur as operating expenses against cash flow. The essential features are: A conscious decision not to insure the exposure; losses classify as operating expenses; cost can be charged against monthly and annual budgets.

It is most suited to financing losses with relatively high frequencies and low severity's which constitute an avoidable regular expense to a business.

Contingency Reserve: A contingency reserve is an accounting devise to segregate a portion of the surplus arising from the trading operations each year which is equal to the expected value of retained losses during the period.

The advantages are that funds are not held specifically to meet this cause and can therefore be used elsewhere in the organisation until required. The disadvantages that as the funds may be committed to a project they many not be available to finance the loss.

Internal Risk Funding: It is a separate fund maintained with the sole intention of providing liquidity to meet pure losses as they arise. It may be operated: On a year to year basis or as a means to spread losses over a number of years. The first option creates a fund out of operating expenses and charging losses against the fund. It is appropriate for smaller and more frequent losses.

The second option is designed to smooth the cost of loses by spreading these over more than a single accounting period. It caters for losses with low frequency and high severity.

The benefits include, Pooling of organisation risk; Savings in premium; Retention of a higher level of risk than would be possible for individual operating units. The major disadvantages is that the fund will be exhausted by losses either before it has become fully operational or once it has been established because losses have been under estimated.

Captive Insurance Company: As early as the 1950s industrial and commercial groups began setting up in-house insurance companies to insure some or all of their risks.

Originally, captives were mainly established to take advantage of the tax deductibility of insurance premiums saving the purpose of self insurance and to benefit from lower captive costs compared to traditional insurance (e.g. lower operating costs and no acquisition costs).

The benefits are: (a) Savings in insurance costs, (b) Selection of risks, (c) Risk control, (d) Supplement to conventional market cover, (e) Access to reinsurance markets, (f) Taxation, (g) Benefits of offshore insurance locations, (h) Implementation of global risk financing strategy and (i) Development as a profit centre.

The main problems of a captive insurance company are: (i) Narrowness of the portfolio of exposure, (ii) costs of establishment and operation, (iii) co-operation with the direct insurance market, (iv) local insurance regulations, (v) government controls over insurance companies , (vi) internal management pressures, (vii) sensitivity to poor loss experience and (viii) management costs.

Insurance

Insurance is the transfer of financial responsibility for the risk at the point of occurrence, and conventionally involves the insurer in a commitment to pay. Provided the terms and conditions of the policy are met, payment of the premium secures a source of funds in the event of loss. The insured is thus exchanging the uncertain cost of retained losses for the certain and known cost of the premium. The costs arising from pure losses during the period of cover are then fixed for the insured. The stabilisation of loss costs means that earnings are less susceptible to the effects of pure loss than when these are retained.

Insurance however does not always fully compensate the insured for losses suffered. This may be the result of limitation of the liability accepted by the insurer, poor management of insurance by the insured leading to gaps in cover or uninsurable losses.

The Management of Insurance

The following problems have arisen in the management of insurance's
- uninsured losses due to failure
- to identify potential loss
- to arrange cover for new property acquired
- to confirm to requirement of insuring arrangements
- under insurance
- over insurance due to
- exposure insured wise
- overlapping covers
- insurance of non-existent exposure
- uneconomic insurances

The Performance of Insurers

Poor satisfaction with insurers is often directed at
- Poor quality of service
- the cost of premium relative to the companies on loss experience
- the volatility of premium cost

The thumb rules for taking an insurance for a specific exposure or loss are:(a) A large number of homogenous units (people, companies, entities, etc.) with a similar potential for loss or exposure must be available for insurance. "The law of large numbers", (b) Losses must be definite and discreet in time and place, (c) Losses must be fortuitous, accidental in nature, unexpected and beyond control of the insured, (d) Losses must be large enough to cause financial burden, (e) Losses must be measurable or calculable, a monetary amount must be determined for the loss, (f) Past experience or a history of the specific losses must exist to provide a guide for actuaries to estimate frequency, severity, costs and determine fair rates, (g) The cost of insurance must be affordable and should be a fraction of the value of the insured item, and (h) Individual or aggregate losses which may cause the downfall of the insurer must not exist.

The decision matrix would be as under :

Type of loss	Frequency	Severity	Predictability	Impact	Decision
Trivial	Very High	Very Low	Very High	Negligible	Non Insurance
Small	High	Low	Reasonable within 1 year	Insignificant	Self Insurance
Medium	Low	Medium	Reasonable within 10 years	Serious	Mix of retention and transfer
Large	Rare	High	Low	Catastrophic	Insure

Modern Risk Financing Techniques

The meaning of Alternative Risk Transfer (ART) has changed substantially over time. In the 1980s and early 1990s, ART primarily characterised non-traditional forms of commercial insurance (e.g. the establishment of captives owned by the insured). Major drivers of demand were the shortage of traditional (re) insurance coverage and skyrocketing prices.

In the late 1990s, ART is reflected in innovative products and tailor made solutions for (major) non-insurance clients and primary insurers.

Basically, the ART spectrum consists of
- alternative solutions and products (such as finite covers based on the time value of money or holistic solutions adopting a more comprehensive approach to risk management)
- alternative risk absorbers (such as capital market investors purchasing catastrophe bonds) and
- alternative sales channels (such as captive insurers).

Against this backdrop, the basis for traditional insurance and reinsurance - the law of large number - will increasingly be supplemented with techniques based on redistributing risk to a larger investor base (e.g. via securitisation), intertemporal diversification (e.g. via finite covers) and diversification across the (re) insured's individual portfolio.

A well-established ART variation in finite reinsurance. This reflects one of the concept's key characteristics: the reliance on intertemporal diversification rather than diversification based on the law of large numbers.

The spread-loss treaty is one of the simplest examples of finite reinsurance. The basic aim being to smooth the fluctuations in loss experience over several years.

Dual-trigger contracts are particularly attractive to clients who are well able to absorb a certain insurable loss and an uninsurable loss on a stand-alone basis but not in the event of both occurring in the same fiscal period. The pricing advantage of dual-triggers is obvious.

Another innovation heralding the convergence of capital markets and (re) insurance is contingent capital. Such solutions provide a company with post-event capital - either as debt or as equity- so as to protect its balance sheet against major catastrophic losses.

Contingent debt transactions frequently involve the establishment of a Contingent Surplus Notes (CSN) trust. An insurer may issue surplus notes, which are sold to investors via a CSN trust. The CSN trust places investors' funds in appropriately liquid investments. For an agreed period of time the insurer has the option of exchanging the trust's investments for surplus notes. As they provide standby funds investors enjoy a return higher than that available from the trust's investments. This difference is the CSN arrangement's cost to the insurer. From the insurer's point of view CSN's major appeal is that they make funds available when they are needed- at a predetermined interest rate.

For publicly traded companies, Contingent Equity Puts (CEP) entitle the company to sell its equity (e.g. non-voting preferred shares) at a pre-negotiated price in the event of a catastrophic loss. CEP could step in, for instance, when traditional (re) insurance cover is exhausted. The buyer of CEP benefits from balance sheet protection for catastrophic losses. Further-more, rating agencies are likely to react favourable to the arrangement of post-event equity.

One of the most exciting developments of recent years is the tapping of capital markets as ultimate absorbers of risk. This involves either securitising risks or creating insurance derivatives.

Future contracts can be described as agreements to buy or sell something at a particular price on a specified future date. With catastrophe futures, buyers and sellers agree on a future price of an index, which is determined by insured catastrophe losses in a certain area over a specified period of time. If there is a major insurance loss the index rises and the buyer of the insurance future contract (e.g. a primary insurer) benefits from a rising contract value and can offset a part of the insured losses.

A second approach involves investors- up to now primarily institutional investors - directly participating in certain (catastrophe) risks by buying bonds whose interest payments or even repayment are contingent upon insurance losses or events. Insurers or reinsurers issue those bonds to investors who are prepared to accept reduced interest payments or even losses on the principal in the event of an earthquake for example. Securitisation is widely regarded as a major market of the future. Primary insurers require more capacity to offset (catastrophe) risks than traditional reinsurance can offer.

Structuring an Effective Risk Management Framework

Many stakeholders are interested in risk management but want to know more about how it would work and the roles stakeholders would play. Risk management offers insurers and industry two benefits. The first is assigning the greatest costs to the greatest risks. The second is managing resources more efficiently. Companies will be able to decide how much risk management they want to use. Applications will range from a particular segment to the whole system.

Cost effectiveness is an important risk management goal. The issues are: 1. What safety level will the risk management programmes have to reach? 2. Can operators equal or exceed current safety levels and save resources too? 3. Will insurers try to dictate how safety resources are allocated?

Some of the key insights are:
- Risk management programmes can help operators: better

understand facility risks, identify and reduce risks not recognised before, have a traceable and defensible basis for making decisions, improve safety, and make operations more cost-effective.
- Risk management helps insurance companies take a more active approach by searching for the most likely and highest consequence failure events, locations, and causes, besides preventing accidents.

Top management commitment and support is vital to successful implementation of a risk management strategy.
- Corporate business and field operations must work together to ensure that risk-based decisions are reflected in preventative maintenance, capital and major maintenance, and design decisions.
- Performances monitoring, including process and results metrics, are important to understand program success.
- Data must be available. Data collection is difficult and risk conditions are continually changing.
- Risk management and supporting sensitivity analyses can help focus data collection.
- Field workers must accept headquarters decisions to use risk management.
- Cultural inertia can hinder efforts to try risk management. Short-term, tangible successes important to field safety personnel and headquarters are important to build support.

Care must be taken in how to synthesise and present risk management analyses, results, and conclusions. It is possible to overwhelm management with numbers and miss the key conclusions.

Many of the inputs on and results of risk management are subjective, but subjective does not mean technically unsound. Risk management is a structured, disciplined approach that experienced insurers take to identify the best information. The engineers use their judgement and experience rather than complying with the current one-size-fits-all regulations. Cross-functional teams add to technical quality and sound, practical decisions.

A phased development approach, building applications gradually as needed, is recommended.

It is important to have early and clear agreement on the risks to be managed, their importance, and how they will be measured.

Risk management programs take time, money, and hard work. Risk management programs don't have to find and reduce many risks to pay for themselves.

The traditional models of involving the public in making decisions are changing. Affected parties are playing a much more active role in determining what risks are examined and acceptable.

Informed consent is now a condition of doing business. Risks must be disclosed to and be acceptable to a broad range of stakeholders, who have many means of recourse if their concerns are not satisfied. Many members of the public expect zero risk - an unreachable goal. A legitimate goal of risk communications should be to educate people about risk and its nature, management, and measurement.

Public interest issues are often under represented or missing from risk assessment and risk management efforts. The resulting gap or disconnect can be costly. The insurance industry should not: believe that the public is a monolith, think that risk management is none of the public's business, or dismiss the public's right to know based on the belief that the public is not technically competent to judge risks.

One should not just communicate the results of our risk management programmes to the public but should get the public's perception of risks. Public perception is a critical part of a risk management program that has dynamic relationships between risk assessment and risk communications. Risk communications is only as persuasive as the facts permit. Safety performance will drive safety perception.

Changing from a compliance-based safety program to a risk management program will hinge on educating all affected stakeholders. Unfortunately, public interest in safety is not high, until an accident happens. But the more you work with stakeholders before an accident, the easier it is to respond to an accident.

Direct links exist between the new risk management and shareholder value. An organization's share value is primarily driven by four factors: growth, earnings, and consistency of performance and perceived quality of management. Of these, consistency- or the management of volatility – often receives less attention that it deserves.

Some observers argue that investors do not put a premium on an insurer's attempts to manage volatility, because investors can presumably achieve this result more efficiently by diversifying the holdings in their own portfolios. These observers further argue that investors do no appreciate, and do not reward, the company that spends resources on risk management to smooth results on their behalf.

Research into the linkage between performance consistency and market valuation, however, indicates otherwise. It suggests that consistency of financial performance explains a remarkably high degree of the difference in share value (specifically, "market value added") among financial services companies (indeed, among companies in virtually any industry). This is true even after controlling for such other influences as growth and return. Investors do, in fact, assign a higher value to organisations with more consistent performance than their peers do.

Done properly, risk management can enhance all the key drivers of share value: growth, earnings, and consistency of performance and perceived quality of management. The new risk management identifies and manages the serious threats to growth and earnings, and focuses on those risks that actually represent opportunities to exploit for above-average growth and earnings. Achieving consistency of result is, of course, a central goal of the new risk management. And institutional investors are increasingly defining quality of management to include enterprise-wide risk stewardship.

New Corporate Governance Guidelines. In recent years, many equity markets around the world have embraced new corporate governance guidelines aimed at attracting additional investment by providing shareholders the right to information and protection from the companies they invest in. Many guidelines now require that a corporation have a system in place to manage all the risks of the business and to report on the adequacy of this system in its annual report.

Implementing Risk Management Programs. The drivers of change have caused leading organisations to develop a set of principles to guide the implementation of a strategic risk management

programme. These principles include.
- Linking business and risk strategies
- Allocating capital to reflect business risks
- Integrating capital management and risk management
- Measuring performance on a risk-adjusted basis
- Managing risk/return through relationship and product plans
- Optimising overall risk/return on a portfolio basis
- Building risk management explicitly into the business planning process.

The actual implementation of the new risk management follows a four-part process that puts these principles into practice:
- **Risk Assessment** : identifying prioritising and classifying all the risks facing the business
- **Risk Shaping** : quantifying risks, mitigating risk factors and financing risks
- **Risk Exploitation:** identifying risks that represent more opportunity than threat and developing and implementing a plan to take advantage of them.
- **Risk Monitoring:** tracking risk, environment and corporate capabilities to stay ahead.

Meeting the Challenge: Risk Management has become a more complex and demanding profession. Risk mangers have greater responsibilities than ever before. Increasingly, they are being asked to manage both risks and opportunities with an eye on improving shareholder value.

Risk Managers at Insurance companies must develop the strategic vision to see their job as focused on enhancing shareholder value. Many Insurance executives and Board members are looking to their risk managers to be full, strategic partners. Those who are up to the challenge will provide a new source of competitive advantage to their organisations.

18

Alternate Risk Transfer Techniques via Finite Risk Insurance

E.K. Dastur and K.R. Makhania

The Present Risk Environment

Insurance allows individuals to transfer risks to insurance companies for consideration of a premium. Expected cost of insurance is the difference between the premium and the present value of expected losses. The decision to purchase insurances is justified if the insurance company has comparative advantage over the policyholder in combating the risk. Such advantage accrues to an insurance company from the following sources:

1. Reduction of risk accomplished by volumes of a large portfolio achieving homogeneity and reinsuring the same by traditional means.
2. Better access of capital markets.

It is imperative that an insurance company should hedge its risks by arranging alternative risk transfer techniques or innovative financial instruments, otherwise it may be exposed to serious liquidity risks.

The deregulation of the Indian insurance industry has happened. It is expected that with the opening up of the industry, the non-life insurance segment would get a major boost. India had experienced many serious catastrophes due to earthquake, hurricane and cyclones in different parts of the country. Of course, some parts are more prone to this threat. These calamities not only take human lives but also caused heavy damages to properties. Consider a scenario in an urban Indian town where a devastating earthquake destroys many valuable and insured prime properties. The sudden spurt of claims can cause severe drain on an insurance company's liquid assets and, therefore, may face a serious threat of default risk.

Unless the insurer anticipates such scenarios and protect it from possible default situation, it may remain vulnerable. Insurance companies in the west, primarily in the USA have found alternative ways to combat default risks, through introduction of innovative financial instruments or non-conventional insurance techniques. The response of such reinsurance techniques can support the insurers in the event of such catastrophes and thus protect the balance-sheet in an increasingly volatile environment.

The economic, social and legal environments present new challenges to the insurance industry on the threshold of the new millennium. The impact of natural and manmade catastrophes has increased significantly. The social and legal environment has also shifted the financial responsibility to those who can afford such consequences.

Market Forces

Competition has intensified in the insurance industry. Real-time access to information is a major contributory factor. Global financial institutions are extending their product range into traditional insurance businesses. New participants are buying their way into still profitable niche markets. Simultaneously, insurance buyers are demanding a broader approach to risk. As a consequence, traditional reinsurance products alone are no longer sufficient to meet an insurer's needs.

Risk Awareness

Reinsurance is purchased as a strategic tool to efficiently protect and manage an insurer's balance sheet. Integrity to the balance sheet is essential in maintaining an insurer's franchise with its policyholders, and with its shareholders and potential investors, who provide the company's capital base. Balance sheet integrity is also the main focus of the rating agencies.

Alternate risk transfer techniques distinguished it from providing traditional line by line reinsurance products and focuses solely on the insurers key balance sheet figures and ratios. The coverage is designed tailor-made to suit the insurance company's requirement and achieve the broader objectives. Priorities have shifted to solutions which protect the entire balance sheet. Whether clients refer to them as funding, financial, finite, blended or non-traditional reinsurance, they are but the same by going beyond conventional reinsurance.

Alternate Risk Transfer Techniques

Alternate risk transfer techniques are more cash sensitive. In addition they offer alternate capital resources to support current and future growth. They include not only insurance to extend to financial risks which can negatively effect an insurance company's balance sheet. Despite their diverse utility to various insurers, they are customised solutions, each one unique to the specific demands of individual clients.

Alternate risk transfer techniques can be purely financial driven transactions or blended with small measure of risk transfer. Alternative risk transfer solutions are designed with profit and loss potential predictable for both sides which primarily spreads risk over a period of time and thus have a stabilising effect on the ceding company's balance sheet.

Practically this means that eventually the ceding company pays most of its losses, but the reinsurer ensures that such burden on the ceding company's liquidity is evenly spread over a period of time. This approach does not really differ from traditional reinsurance except that the contractual terms manifests the intent.

More and more finite products are being combined with traditional reinsurance solutions in blended covers. This trend can be attributed to two things: first, to the fact that in certain countries auditors, supervisory bodies and tax authorities refuse to recognise finite solutions as reinsurance unless they involve a substantial transfer of underwriting risk. Second, and presumably more important, are the manifold advantages which primary insurers can derive from combining traditional and finite risk reinsurance.

In a *single* reinsurance programme, insurers can arrange a price for each specific type of risk, and that not only for a period of several years, but also and increasingly for risks from a number of different lines of business. Primary insurers utilising such covers profit accordingly from reduced transaction costs for risk protection. Moreover, blended covers can be written to include risks which have traditionally been considered uninsurable, for example political and financial market risks.

Utility of Alternate Risk Transfer Techniques

- make provisions for unexpected loss or other event and/or to

- spread the financial impact of single event over a period of time;
- provide additional underwriting capacity;
- insure, uninsurable risks;
- remove the impact of adverse development of (discontinued) lines of business;
- stabilise annual results;
- improve predictability of earnings, surplus, investment return and loss ratios;
- stabilise and improve company ratings;
- get relief from temporary strain on earnings due to severe catastrophe claim;
- absorb the impact of changes in the regulatory environment;
- manage critical balance sheet ratios.

The need for finite risk solutions for reinsurance was felt during the last reinsurance cycle following Hurricane Andrew in 1992. The dimension of catastrophe risk such as Cat 90-A, Hurricane Andrew, Northridge earthquake highlighted the insurance industry's exposure to series of unprecedented catastrophe losses within a short span. With the advanced computer modelling techniques of potential catastrophes, has shown that the industry and society face huge risks of hurricane, earthquake that could cause billions of dollars in insured property losses. Lot of empirical research has been carried out in the USA and Europe to simulate and estimate the possible impact of catastrophic events.

Modelling of catastrophic risk involves estimating return period of the event and the corresponding non-occurrence probability. Demographic projections indicate that, because of population growth in areas exposed to natural calamities, insurers' exposure to catastrophe losses will continue to increase. The catastrophe risk models developed by research bodies initially generate the events (simulated), then overlay them geographically onto the insurer's book of business, and determine losses based on various parameters such as quality of construction etc. and insurance policy specifies.

From the insurer's angle, estimating the possibility of occurrence of catastrophe in a given year and the probable estimated loss in value terms are both important. A study in 1995 has shown that a magnitude of 8.5 in Richter scale of earthquake in the New Madrid area of the central USA could have caused more than $ 115 billion in insured property losses.

The Indian insurance industry has also suffered its fair share of majority catastrophic events, more recently like the Gujarat cyclone in 1998, Orissa cyclone in 1999 and in between Gujarat and Maharashtra floods in 1998 followed by the Andhra Pradesh/Tamil Nadu cyclone,1999. The current financial year has also seen a series of catastrophic events such as the Andhra Pradesh floods, the Calcutta floods and Andhra Pradesh/Tamil Nadu cyclone. India being a country with large geographical spread is always at risks from catastrophe perils like floods and cyclones, not to mention the occasional earthquake event that may happen.

How the Alternate Risk Transfer (ART) Proposal Operates?

Due to the diversity of the products available, it is difficult to find a generally accepted definition. It is, however, an undisputed fact that finite risk reinsurance represents a combination of risk transfer and risk financing which emphasises the time value of money. Instead of searching for a straightforward definition, it is more expedient to identify some features which are shared by most finite solutions.

Assumption of Limited Risk by the Reinsurer

One essential characteristic is the assumption of limited (finite) risk by the reinsurer. In finite risk contracts, the primary insurer (cedent) transfers two things: first, the risk of unexpectedly rapid settlement of losses and commensurately reduced investment income from the relevant loss reserves, and second, a limited, yet significant underwriting risk. The latter is the risk that the losses actually paid over the term of the finite contract may turn out to be greater than expected.

Multi-Year Contact Term

Another characteristic feature is a contractual period of several years, which contrasts with those of most traditional reinsurance contracts. Cedents can reckon with long-term cover under reliable conditions, and finite risk reinsurers with a continual flow of premiums. This not only provides both parties with considerably greater latitude for negotiating prices and conditions, but also gives them a basis for establishing a long-term partnership. As a rule, the risk spread is effected on a per-contract basis over time.

Sharing of Result With the Cedent

Profits accruing over a multi-year period are paid back to the cedent to a substantial extent, so that there is a close connection between the cedent's own loss experience and the actual cost of reinsurance. In this way, the cedent receives compensation for the limitation of the risk assumed by the finite risk reinsurer.

Future Investment Income as a Pricing Component

Expected investment income is explicitly defined as a factor in the premium calculation. The consideration of the time value of money has an effect especially in certain types of liability business where settlement may take decades.

A sample structure would be as follows:
- In the ART proposal the Insurer may opt for a limit of indemnity as per its requirements. The reinsurer will then provide capacity (indemnify) for consideration of the premium.
- Such premium will be calculated based on the severity and frequency of losses in the recent past, to formulate the pay back.
- The contract can be on an annual basis or for long term over a period of three to five years.
- The premium for each year is fixed upfront and thus insensitive to fluctuations at renewal, arising out of claims.
- In the event of a claim free year, there is a built in mechanism to refund large portion of the premium as a *no claim bonus*.
- The reinsurer will keep small portion as a consideration of lending its capital.
- In the event of claims the reinsurer will pay the claims up to maximum of indemnity limit.

The insurer will then repay the reinsurer this claim amount funded over a stipulated period of time in equal instalments, manifested in the contract. This will ease the sudden spurt of liquidity drain on the insurer.

ART is normally preferred over traditional reinsurer in situations mentioned aforesaid such as non-availability of capacity, high reinsurance cost and traditional covers or for the top end protections whereby the claim activity is rare, but can be very severe if it happens. Thus ART can be achieved alternative to traditional reinsurance and is significant to protecting the balance sheet.

Indian insurance companies should be allowed to protect themselves against huge catastrophe risks through ART mechanism. Although ART may not be a true risk transfer, the Central Government through supervisory and regulatory bodies like Institute of Chartered Accountant, IRDA and CBPT have to take cognisance of its value and allow insurance companies to book the cost of reinsurance purchased on ART route. As there is not much empirical studies conducted out in India to stimulate and forecast catastrophe loss situations, making it more imperative to hedge such risks through ART than traditional reinsurance as it is a cost effective mechanism.

19

Information Technology and Insurance

S.D. Totade

There has never been a time when the effective use of IT has been more crucial to the success of the insurance industry. The insurance markets are being revolutionised by technology at a high speed pace. IT and software solutions, allowing cross-border trade to become electronic and paperless, are increasingly on offer to importers, exporters, shipping companies and financial institutions.

1. Information Technology

The computing technology, networking technology and advanced electronics together make today's I.T The convergence of electronics and telecommunications created by devices like fax, telex which the business world-wide has been using extensively over last three decades. The convergence of computers and telecommunication has generated various computer network making the business data transfer feasible. The computers with advanced electronics has provided the multimedia facilities i.e. apart from the data in electronic format the voice (audio) and image (video) also can be a controlling input to and output from a computing device.

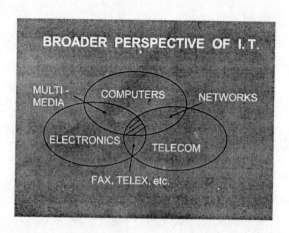

1.1 Hardware: Developments in Information Technology have been characterised by miniaturisation and reducing cost with improved performance and better reliability combined with shortened product development cycles, due to advances in chip technology.

The early use of huge computers during World War II was for military purpose. The computer technology went hand in hand with the advances in electronics. The computers for commercial use in 1960s, made use of transistors instead of vacuum tubes in the earlier computers. The integrated circuit (IC) technology of 1970s forms the backbone of latest computers. With the feasibility of circuits having large scale integration (LSI) and very large scale integration (VLSI) powerful computers came to the table tops (Micro computers) and then to laptops and now to palmtops.

1.2 Software: Like the hardware, the computer languages (software) have also undergone change. The software transitions from very hard to use machine level language (MLL) through Symbolic / Assembly Level Language (ALL), High Level Language (HLL like Cobol, Basic etc.), fourth generation (4GLs like relational databases) have today reached to expert systems. This has brought the computer closer to business managers who may not be necessarily computer professionals. With complicated operating systems for mainframes and mini computers the personal computers came handy with operating systems like DOS, UNIX. This changed the concept of huge data processing centre into decentralised data processing units. The recent additions of user friendly interfaces like Windows brought menu driven, user friendly computing to the society.

Word processing and spreadsheets made processes more efficient and one could edit documents or do calculations faster. But there was no sharing of information.

1.3 Computer Interface and Storage Devices: The dialogue with computer which is through input and output devices has changed its form and medium. The first interface with computer was the punched card (Holerith Card). Today the typewriter like keyboard or pointing and clicking device like mouse are in common use. Digitisers have introduced the flexibility of translating maps and figures to computer memory. Scanners have added image capture facility to computers. The touch screen add-ons and touch panels would accept finger touches as if they were mouse clicks.

The storage devices have changed from bulky and sequential access magnetic disks and tapes to handy and flexible floppy disks, hard disks. Optical disks offer mass storage capabilities. Today's compact disks with high storage capacity of 600 MB onwards are replacing concepts of publication of books/manuals and encyclopaedia or any other business information with relatively less cost.

1.4 Data Distribution and Networking: Advancements in IT has provided connectivity amongst computers for electronic data interchange. This enabled the organisations and individuals to spread messages within and outside the organisations at a very low price on electronic mail. Electronic data transmission enables information sharing within specific sites on Local Area Networks (LAN) using coaxial or unshielded twisted pair (UTP) cables. Operating offices of a business house can be connected through leased telephone lines to form a Metro Area Network (MAN) allowing data transfer within different offices of a city. Electronic data transmission over long distances using satellite communication links or fibre optic cables forms WANs. The new client-server technology has provided an open systems environment with broad interoperability across diverse hardware platforms and connectivity between offices. The client-server computing also made distributed data possible, had workflow and office automation support as well as graphics user interface leading to customer-oriented information systems. Digital telephone lines (ISDN) provides for transmission of text, picture, film and sound to any remote place.

2. Information Technology for Insurance

2.1 Database Management Systems: The principles of tracking and measuring responses can pay off for the insurance industry. To find more clients, we need to consider many factors, including : lapsation, cash value, premium and competition. But the need to record and study the characteristics of persistency – the length of time we retain policies, customers and agents is most important for insurance companies.

A database with five to ten years history of households or clients, products and agents can help you follow the most profitable combinations of the three. Such historical retention was prohibitively expensive in the past. But clear advantages of new PC (Personal Computer) and RISC (Reduced Instruction Set Computing) technology gives companies power to keep tens of millions of policies on a device with thousands of bytes of data per policy/client/agent. Now such 10 year database analysis are cost effective. By reviewing the database one can see how many clients have actually migrated not just how many policies have lapsed or surrendered. Using database technology, companies can get a comprehensive view of their business and analyse the effects of competition, performance, loyalty and lost opportunity.

The insurance industry needs to provide a consistent, long term, systematic support of the processes that identify customer needs and desires. Database measurement and research can lead to fulfilment with a combination of winning products and services marketed by a well trained distribution force.

2.2 Data Warehousing: Data warehousing technology is based on integrating a number of information systems into a 'one stop shopping' database to achieve vision of making company national in scope, but regional in focus. Traditionally the sales and the claims side have been separated. Data warehousing will allow managing by profit levels with an integrated approach rather than by limiting losses. A data warehouse basically is a depository that stores information in one database that had been stored in many sources. By housing the information in one database, information can be accessed more easily, efficiently and inexpensively for comparison and analysis.

The concept of make and sell is out. Insurers need to sense and respond. Dataware can be a source to analyse the customers and historical data, such as number of policies written, number of new policies, retention, premiums and losses. The data warehouse as a centerpiece of an information delivery system is going to be critical to insurer's ability to effectively manage profitability and to achieve both growth and a level of operational excellence.

Data Mining [1] is the cornerstone of Customer Relationship Management. The Financial Services Industry has only begun to fully

316 Indian Insurance Industry: Transition and Prospects

realise the potential of Data Mining as a means to control costs and increase revenue. The earnings are enormous for companies that utilise Data Mining effectively. Data Mining is the most effective means to acquire substantial competitive leads. This rapidly evolving field makes updating your knowledge of trends, developments and competitive intelligence more than a necessity, it is an absolute must.

2.3 Decision Support Systems: The path of Business applications of computers encompasses many stages which are demonstrated in the figure above. The Computer Based Information Systems (CBIS) path shows the very early applications like Transactions Processing Systems (TPS) followed by the Management Information Systems(MIS). The computer applications like Decision Support Systems (DSS), Expert Systems (ES) and Executive Information Systems (EIS) are still awaited in insurance business. Office Automation (OAS) happens to be a continuously ongoing, dynamic process for any business.

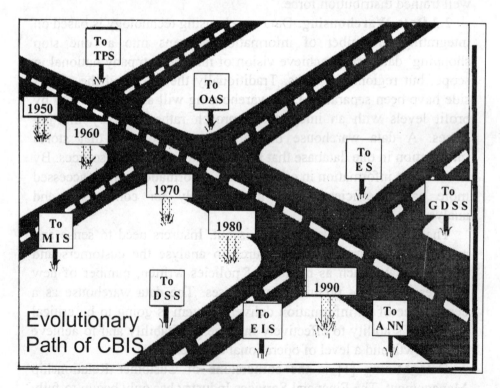

The Evolutionary Path of CBIS (*Source : Kroeber and Watson [1988]; modified*)

Insurance companies need to think differently about information and technology. Insurers historically have been heavy users of technology but mainly for making administrative functions more efficient. They also had large quantities of data, but very little useful information. New opportunities are emerging as technology advances make the capture, access and management of information easier. Simultaneously the general ability to use information is becoming competitive weapon in delivering high quality, efficient service.

The comments in the Chapter on IT and insurance in Report of the Committee on Reforms in the Insurance Sector include [2],

"Computers are still being used for limited data processing - important though that is and indeed needs further extension- and not as instruments for developing Decision Support Systems."

Companies need to utilise decision support systems by implementing data warehouses that pull information from existing legacy systems into a customer information database. Such decision support systems will equip the insurance managers with ability to allow for customised products and services that are more in line with what customers want.

Any need to analyse historical and demographic data quickly and easily to improve business profits warrants the need for a Decision Support System. The earlier databases were designed and built based on products and not customers. Before the recent advancements in decision support system tools, a product approach to storing data made it difficult and costly to obtain a horizontal view of vital customer information.

2.4 Group Linking Software: Group linking software enables sharing of information and particularly suits document heavy insurance business. Tracking of policy application shows how information that is input and accessed from a number of locations can increase efficiency.

An application for coverage is entered into the groupware system from a forms generation package. Keyfields in the form are already linked to this software allowing a user to click on a field and view information regarding that area e.g. cost of coverage for similar risks. The user clicks again and taps into research information regarding such risks, underwriting guidelines or other documentation. If underwriting guidelines have been updated the changes are highlighted in red and marked with a start.

Users from other locations can view any information as soon as it is added to the file. As each user completes work on the file it is moved to the next station. The basic promise behind the groupware is to allow an unlimited number of users to collaborate on a project at any time, in real time, and to track the location and progress of the project. The ability to replicate information and to synchronise databases or applications no matter where you are in the world is what made group linking software a breakthrough technology. Some of the group linking software are Lotus notes, exchange, first class.

2.5 Imaging and Workflow Technologies: The proposal forms may be scanned into an imaging system, data may be extracted for update to computer and for automated underwriting workflow may be implemented. It is estimated that imaging and workflow enabled underwriting could reduce the time taken to issue a policy as much as 60%. Under the imaging system, every document – be it correspondence, forms, photocopies of cheques, faxes etc. are all maintained in a shareable electronic folder – neatly indexed, updated, and available simultaneously to all concerned.

The recent report of metlife insurance indicated the performance improvement attributed to imaging and workflow technology to the extent of 50,000 claims document – clearance in 8 hours in case of dental claims of health insurance services [3].

2.6 Mapping: Mapping technology can be used by insurers to meet different needs, such as identifying loss prone areas or geographic claim analysis. It helps the insurer to analyse the extent of its network i.e. the insurer can determine whether it has too many or too few agency force in a particular area. Mapping is a very convenient way to layer disparate information from various databases to create pictures.

Maps can illustrate how many buildings are located in a flood plain, or whether two buildings covered by the same insurer's fire policies are close by each other and thus present a potential double loss if fire breaks out in one of them.

2.7 Call Centre Technology: Good customer service is a crucial element in gaining, maintaining and retaining profitable customer.

Call Centre concept based on Interactive Voice Response Service (IVRS) is gaining importance in this aspect. The primitive concept of Call Centre was based on an enquiry system providing information services to customers through telephone line answered by employee/s. The totally automated Call Centre concept provides better service through automated computerised exchange but lacks in flexibility i.e. only predefined queries are serviced.

The insurance companies world-wide are accepting the auto manual Call Centres as one of the important strategies for Customer Relationship Management.

2.8 Video Linking: A video linking facility between two remote units of an insurance company or between an insurer and a broker allows underwriters at one place and brokers at other unit to discuss risk face to face. The video link helps maintain the personal relationships between underwriters and brokers which is very valued for insurance business and in turn would help to draw business it would not have seen if people use telephone or fax alone for contacting.

2.9 Cat Models: Catastrophic models use data from the recent spate of natural disasters which helps develop more predictions of insurers property exposures in future disasters. Using this data curious "What-if" scenarios of probable maximum loss (PML) using the best estimate available at an insurer's exposures are tested. Finally an underwriting policy that limits the company's exposure to catastrophic losses is implemented. Other information such as where the faults are, construction specifications, soil type, amount of ground motion likely to occur at a given site is also used in the models.

This new technology is helping insurance companies to better understand their exposure to mother nature's perils with more accurate computer models providing precise information on catastrophic exposures. This helps insurers and reinsurers to better access their catastrophic exposures and as a result, raise rates in certain areas. Insurers will be in a position to better price and spread the risk. This could mean that fewer insurance companies would be seriously hurt or driven out of the market by a single catastrophic event and the buyer will benefit from a stronger insurance industry. The technology may show insurers that a given type of property or a specific area is so susceptible to catastrophes that they will refuse to underwrite such risks at all.

2.10 Intranet, Extranet, Internet: Intranet is the network connecting different offices of the same business to permit the internal data transfer within the business.

Extranet is a network allowing the business to communicate with business partners like suppliers, vendors, banners, regulations etc. on the electronic channel.

Internet is a global network of many computer networks. Any user who would like to exchange some information with other user at a remote location, can log into the computer of internet provider via modem or an Internet Access CPU (IAC). All IACs have a registered address at a central computer station in US. IAC will look up for the address of the target computer and establishes a link using other computers as transmission stations. The linking process lasts only a few seconds.

The internet and online service providers are providing opportunities to create new forums which can be utilised by everyone world-wide. Insurers can browse through many useful sites on the internet.

Risk Web site provides an electronic discussion list of risk and insurance issues. Captive.com site offers business-to-business risk and insurance exchanges, answers to frequently asked questions. Some other sites provide information and statistics on occupational safety and health administration, weather & weather related events, disasters and catastrophes to make educated and timely decisions about mitigating risks.

2.11 Insurance and Electronic Commerce: Enormous opportunities are being created by the Internet's new connectivity such as improving customer service, reducing cycle time, becoming more cost effective, and selling goods, services, or information to an expanded global customer base. As entire industries are being reshaped and the rules for competition are changing, enterprises need to re-think the strategic fundamentals of their businesses in order to be successful. E-business is first about business, rather than technology. Technology, while important, is the less difficult part. The difficult part is managing the changes in business strategies and institutional processes that are needed for enterprises to take advantage of e-business, or to avoid losing out to competitors who do so.

2.11.1 E-Insurance Benefits: E-Insurance will derive multiple benefits to the insurer like,
- Information collection will be better and cheaper
- Speed of Response: Issuance of Policy and settlement of claims will be faster
- New Ways of doing Business in a competitive market
- Flexible Pricing and Customised Service
- Global Accessibility i.e. Lapse of Physical Boundaries
- Increased Sales without additional sales force
- Immediate Premium Collection and Funds Transfer
- Reduced cost per transaction
- 24*7 Availability
- Improved Service
- Real Time Knowledge Base Building

2.11.2 E-Insurance Challenges: Electronic Insurance will not only provide many benefits but will also pose business and technological challenges.

2.11.2.1 E-Insurance Business Challenges: The following points have been detailed in a study on insurance and e-commerce done by Grace, Klein and Straub of the Centre for Risk Management and Insurance Research, Georgia State University [4].

Disintermediation Increases Business: The study has shown that the cost of distribution decreases with the increased value of connection. Products with relatively high fixed costs and low value (such as travel, credit, or burial insurance) are relatively expensive to produce. Customers pay a high price per dollar of coverage for these products. The Internet allows the disintermediation of this relatively high overhead for these low face-value products. This means that prices can be lowered and more insurance sold by reducing the transactions cost of the exchange. Increased

Reorganisation of Companies-Virtual Companies: Many insurers will be prompted by the opportunities presented by E-commerce to restructure the packaging of insurance services. Insurance companies using E-commerce may reengineer, outsource, and/or streamline their management functions, or marketing and distribution arms. To more efficiently deliver their services, some insurers will be able to reduce their significant investments in physical facilities and certain personnel. E-commerce will enable independent agency insurers to more easily adapt their distribution mechanisms to market competition and expedite their transactions with intermediaries.

As the study notes: "Virtual companies may emerge which rely heavily on information technology for many line functions while other insurers will use it to significantly increase the productivity of their human and physical resources. E-commerce could offer significant efficiencies and new market outlets for both large and small companies. Insurers will significantly utilise information service providers to facilitate their efficient application of this technology.

Insurance Customers: What do They Want? Customers could get different and better service though the Internet. It is possible to obtain quotes from a number of companies. In some cases, the Internet provides rating agencies' evaluations of insurers. The Internet and outsourcing can provide additional cost savings to the consumer. Technology can bring the customer closer to the insurance contract, by removing layers of inefficiencies.

Consumers will also obtain price comparisons for relatively generic contracts, such as life insurance and rates for a standard set of auto insurance coverage for given vehicle and driver characteristics.

Consumers also could have access to internal records to see where their claims are in terms of payment, when their next annuity payment is due, and how their mutual fund is performing. This can be done without calling a burdensome voice-mail system, being put on hold, or finding a person who can give them the desired information efficiently.

ebix.com is an electronics insurance auction market permitting auction of risks to be insured. This covers the auto property and term life insurance i.e. catex.com is a electronics reinsurance market.

The Death of the Insurance Agent? One of the reasons why insurers have been slow to use electronic commerce could be the fear of swallowing up the agent's business. The Internet does not necessarily imply the death of the agent. Many insurers are examining their agent's role in the process and are also developing direct contacts with the insured through their Web presence. Agents could enhance their advisory role to consumers as their paper and money-processing functions diminish."

2.11.2.2 Technological Challenges: One of the most prominent challenges of e-commerce is Security. It is very evident that many users are reluctant to do business on the Internet due to security reasons. Issues of transmission security, host server security, confidentiality, authenticity and ways to counter these challenges are covered, in the following topics.

Security

Database Security: The business database security is utmost important. This has to be monitored by security of the web server and web access.

Web Server Security: Security policies should be defined like- who is allowed access, nature of the access and who authorises such access? who is responsible for security? what kinds of material are allowed on server pages?

Password Sniffing: The most significant security risk on the Internet today is the use of plain text, reusable passwords that are sent over the internal and external networks. User names and passwords are the most common way of authenticating users on the Internet today. They are widely used by many Internet protocols, including remote log in, file transfer, remote e-mail reading, and web access. Protection against password sniffing is to avoid using plain text user names and reusable passwords.

Network Scanning Programmes: Automated tools should be used to scan your network. These tools check for well-known security-related bugs in network programs such as send mail and ftpd. Computer are certainly being scanned by crackers interested in breaking into the systems, therefore, network scanning programs should be regularly run.

Physical Security: One can ensure physical security by having an alarm system that calls the police, having a key-lock on the computer power supply. There should be adequate protection against fire, smoke, explosions, humidity and dust.

Web Access Security: Organisations run web servers because they are an easy way to distribute information to people on the Internet. But sometimes this information is not required to be distributed to everybody. Host-based restrictions can be implemented using a firewall to block incoming HTTP connections to a particular web server [5].

Transmission Security: Encryption is a key technology to ensure transaction security. Various types of encryption technologies are: -

Single key cryptography/Symmetric or Private Key encryption: A private key is generated and is sent to receiver through a secret channel. Every message is encrypted at the sending end and transmitted over the network. The receiver applies the private key to decrypt the message.

Public key cryptography: A key pair, public key and a private key is generated. Sender sends the message using public key for encryption. The receiver who is the only person having private key can receive the message.

VPN-Virtual Private Networks: The current firewall technology includes VPNs, a way to enable secures communication across Internet. VPN is a less expensive alternative and an interoperable standard. A VPN link is very flexible and works with any applications that uses TCP/IP, unlike SSL [6].

2.12 Privacy: Privacy is likely to be a growing concern as Internet-based communications and commerce increase. Designers and operators of web sites who disregard the privacy of users do so at their own peril. Users who feel that their privacy has been violated may leave the web. Thus it is important to protect personal privacy on the Web. Every time a web browser views a page on the web, a record is kept in that web server's log files.

Legislation : Online businesses know a lot about their customers and they can learn a lot more. As with any business online service providers know the names, addresses, and frequently the credit card numbers of their subscribers. Internet service providers can learn a lot more about customers, because all information that an Internet user sees must first pass through the provider's computers. Legislation can be passed to prevent the Internet service providers from parting with personal information of the clients. Whether or not such legislation passes in the future, web surfers should be aware that information about their activities may be collected by service providers, vendors, site administrators, and others on the electronic superhighway.

Proxy Server: One approach to privacy is to use an anonymizing Web server. These are servers that are designed to act as proxies for users concerned with privacy. Using an anonymizer requires that you place faith in the person or organisation that is running the service, that's because the anonymizer knows who has connected to it and what pages they have seen.

Authenticity: Digital Signatures and Digital Certificates can be used to establish identity and assure the authenticity of information that is delivered over the web.

Digital Signatures: Each user of a Digital Signature system creates a pair of keys: A private key used for signing one's signature to a block of data, such as an HTML document, an email message, or a photograph. A public key used for verifying a signature after it has been signed.

Server Certificates: Every Secure Socket Layer (SSL) server must have an SSL server certificate. When a browser connects to a web server using the SSL protocol, the server sends the browser its public key in an X.509 v3 certificate. The certificate is used to authenticate the identity of the server and to distribute the server's public key, which is used to encrypt the initial information that is sent to the server by the client [7].

Client Certificates: Every client certificate is a digital certificate that is designed to certify the identity of an individual. As with certificates for web sites, client certificates bind a particular name to a particular secret key. Certification authorities issue them. Microsoft's Internet Explorer, Netscape navigator and other SSL applications support client-side digital certificates.

Specialised Protocols: Specialised protocols are used for sending information and payment card details over the Internet.

Secure Sockets Layer (SSL): SSL is Secure Sockets Layer, a general-purpose protocol for sending encrypted information over the Internet. SSL is a layer that exists between the raw TCP/IP protocol and the application layer. While the standard TCP/IP protocol simply send an anonymous error-free stream of information between two

computers, SSL adds numerous features to that stream including:
- Authentication and nonrepudiation of the server, using digital certificates
- Authentication and nonrepudiation of the client, using digital signatures
- Data confidentiality through the use of encryption
- Data integrity through the use of message authentication codes.

Secure Electronic Transaction (SET): SET is the Secure Electronic Transaction protocol for sending payment card information over the Internet. SET was designed for encrypting specific kinds of payment-related messages. SET uses encryption to provide for the confidentiality of communications and uses digital signatures for authentication. Under SET, merchants are required to have digital certificates, issued by their acquiring banks. Consumers may optionally have digital certificates, issued by their banks [8].

3. Conclusion

The supporting technology requirements will be a real time, rather than batch; longitudinal rather than episodic; will require connectivity rather than be self contained; will be interactive; will rely on large relational databases.

Today's consumers don't like to wait. Insurance companies that are unable to react to their customers demands will lose market share to their competitors that can. The question now facing insurance companies is no longer if they should take advantage of the Internet, but how should they do it. Should you adapt your existing products or create Internet specific insurance products and brands? Do you focus your efforts on distribution or service [9] ?

Notes

1. Data Mining and Warehousing for Financial Services. Website : http://www.ibc.uk.com

2. Report of the committee on Reforms In The Insurance Sector, pp. 80.

3. Insurance Technology – January 2000.

4. Study Report on "*E-Commerce in the Insurance Industry : Issues and Opportunities*" by Martin F. Grace, Robert W. Klein, Detmar Straub, Centre for Risk Management and Insurance Research, Georgia State University.

5. Web Security and Commerce by Simson Garfinkel with Gene Spafford.

6. PC Magazine, September 1, 1999.

7. Web Security and Commerce by Simson Garfinkel with Gene Spafford.

8. Web Security and Commerce by Simson Garfinkel with Gene Spafford.

9. E-Business Strategies for the Insurance Marketplace.

20

Information Technology in General Insurance

Prince Azariah

Early Days of Computerisation

In the late 1950s, when the benefits of commercial data processing were being realised, the insurance industry was one of the first to take to business automation. At that time, the objective was still to automise boring, repetitive and labour intensive accounting tasks in the back office. With the introduction of large mainframes like to IBM/360 and the IBM/370 in the early 1960's, much of the data entry of accounting information and the production of massive reports were computerised. Third part vendors developed software for the insurance companies and this included MIS as well as back office automation of accounting. It was not till very much later in the 1970s and 1980s that the printing of policy papers and claims cheques were automated. Even then, most of these were done on IBM systems like the 43XX, 3XXX, AS/400 and later on the System/390.

In India too the insurance companies were among the first to adopt computerisation in the early 1960s. Here too much of the automation was in the area of accounting. Owing to the general lack of computing infrastructure, insurance companies got their data processing done through data processing centres like Mafatlal Computing Centre, Tata Computer Centre and such newly formed data centres. These centres initially had unit record machines (URMs) till they obtained computers like the IBM 1401, and the British ICL 1900 series of computers.

When the insurance companies were nationalised, computerisation received a serious setback as the trade unions took the same approach as their counterparts in the nationalised banks who discouraged computerisation, as they felt it was against the working class, and would affect the growth of jobs in the financial sector. Hence, there was virtually, no computerisation in the insurance companies all through the 1970s and the 1980s except what back office data processing which was given out to be done by the data processing centres.

LIC started earlier than GIC, and in the early 1980s procured its first mainframe computer, the ICL 1900 series computer in 1982. The choice of the ICL computer looked it in for further replacement by the ICL 2900 series, and till early 1990, LIC continued with the use of the ICL range of computers, which by then had become obsolete. Software was being developed mostly by the hardware vendors themselves as part of the implementation of hardware.

Back Office Computerisation in Insurance Companies

In the mid-1980s the banks in India commenced computerisation under the Rangarajan Committee recommendations for automation in banking. This gave an impetus for the insurance companies to go in for computerisation. In 1986, NIIT was appointed as the consultant, and specialists were recruited from the open market to play the role of system analyst, and systems engineers. These specialists were employed at GIC as well as the four subsidiaries. Core teams were set up and assigned the task of developing software in the areas of underwriting, claims and accounting. The hardware platforms were similar to what was adapted by the nationalised banks. These were UNIX systems and the development software was Unify RDBMS, C and COBOL.

These were mostly referred to as DO (Divisional Office) and RO (Regional Office) system. Branch offices were not computerised. Branch documents were sent to their respective Divisional Offices were they were entered into their DO system.

Computer Staff

Because of union restrictions, only back office computerisation was permitted. Two cadres of staff were created: the programmer, and the data-entry operator. The programmer was wrongly named, and he was the only cadre who was allowed to start-up and shut-down the computer, take printouts, take backups, and assign log-in rights to various data-entry operators. The data-entry operators were the only cadre who would actually sit on the terminals, call up the screens and enter data into the system from policy documents, claims registers and various other accounting documents. Front Office computerisation was not allowed.

Progress of Back Office Computerisation

The Head Offices monitored the progress of implementation of the computer systems on a monthly basis. Very soon the progress of implementation was failing well behind schedule, and the backlog of data-entry was pilling up at every Divisional and Branch Office. An attempt was made in 1992 to outsource the data-entry of back logs, but this did not work, as no computer company was prepared to accept data from locations other than the metros.

Reinsurance System

It may be recalled that in 1986, core groups were formed to develop the DO and RO systems. In addition to this, some very specific software was also developed by the teams in the subsidiaries. United India team developed a fairly robust accounting software, but this was implemented only at United India. Similarly, Oriental Insurance developed a fairly robust reinsurance system, but in the interest of rapid implementation, it removed several checks and balances that would have ensured that all necessary data was captured. The software eventually was implemented, but it could not capture critical operations data and hence was of little use by the reinsurance underwriters. Only accounting information was available. This serious loss of opportunity was partly rectified when the SWIFT operations were centralised into GIC in 1991.

The reinsurance software was taken from Oriental and rewritten to suit the SWIFT operations at GIC. The platform for rewriting this software was FoxPro. This software, though cumbersome and not totally complete, served as the backbone of SWIFT operations in GIC for most of the decade.

In 1998, this software was completely written program by program on Oracle for two reasons. The GIC Management Services Division (MSD) officers had recently trained in the Oracle platform and needed a live system to test out their Oracle skills. The second reason was that it was decided to completely rewrite the SWIFT software in Oracle to make it Y2k compliant.

Computerisation in the 1990s

The Malhotra Committee Report devoted one full chapter to computerisation in insurance. The senior management was by now aware that in order to meet the new challenges of globalisation, it would have to embark upon a massive computerisation plan. A plan was mooted in 1994 to form a separate IT company as a joint venture with a strong computer hardware company. This joint venture company would supply computer hardware, networking components and application software for the insurance industry. It would also absorb all the IT officers from the corporation, who by now were leaving for greener pastures. Digital Equipment Corporation, the hardware company with whom the joint venture was being discussed, meanwhile got into serious financial difficulty and was eventually bought out by Compaq. The joint venture to form an IT company fell through. It the next 6 years, the concept of forming a joint venture IT company kept coming up, but was never really accepted by management.

Systems Studies and Office Computerisation

In 1994, it was decided that the subsidiary companies should develop their own computerisation plans. Each of the subsidiaries appointed a computer consultant to advise them on their IT plans. United India as the first to start the ball rolling. It appointed Tata Consultancy services (TCS) to prepare the IT Plan. However, its recommendations were not taken seriously. Oriental was the next company, which asked CMC to make the study. It also asked them to develop its front office software. This software was developed in Microsoft Access, and even before it was fully tested, Oriental Insurance started rolling out the software at its branches.

Although the choice of MC Access as the development tool was to be questioned repeatedly for the next 6 years, but Oriental steadily went ahead with its rollouts till most of the branches were covered by the software. Since it was the first to start (in 1994), it also suffered from having the oldest hardware, which resulted in the software not performing optimally.

National also chose CMC to do its systems study. The only result of this is that it rushed ahead and bought large quantities of hardware and deployed them in every branch, but it did not have the necessary software. Hence, the MSD of National developed software in-house, but developed the software in the only language their officers were trained in: FoxPro.

New India was the last to get its Systems study done, from TCS. By now TCS had benefited by the experience of three previous studies. It also drew upon its overseas experience and the study that emerged was clearly the best of the lot. New India had also developed a front office software using Oracle which did not quite take off. It later employed Mafatlal Consultancy Services to develop an integrated software which covered both the front office and the back office modules. This was the first serious effort by any company to develop an integrated software.

A Common Approach

By now all the subsidiaries were in different software platforms and were finding it difficult to integrate their front office software to the back office software. Around this time, in 1995, the Corporation had decided to take on a Head of the Information Technology Management Group (Head-ITMG) on contract from the market. However, not much progress was made in this direction.

Investment Software

As investment is one of the most essential activities in the insurance business and is basically responsible for making up for the losses suffered in underwriting business, it was essential to develop computerised system for investment operations.

Starting with this document, the development and implementation of software for Investment operations was outsourced to Mafatlal Consultancy Services. It was developed within a time span of about five and a half years. The software was improved for GIC and its subsidiaries. This was also the first time software was actually shared between GIC and the subsidiaries. The attendant advantage was that investment operations within the industry was streamlined.

Connectivity Within the Industry

In 1996, another project was initiated which changed the way the industry carried out its communications. A VSAT-base network was set up which connected the Head Offices of GIC, the four subsidiaries, and TAC. This service was provided by the National Informatics Centre (NIC). Internet access was made available at the Head Offices through this service. Local Area Network was implemented at the Head Offices of GIC and the subsidiaries. E-mail was given to the executives and officers at the head offices. Thus every senior executive had a unique e-mail address which he had printed on his visiting cards. GIC and the subsidiaries set up their own web sites within the "nic in" domain.

Communication became very speedy not only within the industry, but also between major customers and business partners within the country and around the world. All this happened within the year of Internet services becoming popular in the country. The services were not very good but in those days it was as good or as bad as available elsewhere in the country. The project hence never moved on to the next phase of connecting up to the Regional Office level. However, regions could connect to the Head Offices through a dial up connection.

Reinsurance Software Package

It was realised as early as 1995 that there was urgent need for software for reinsurance operations. However, no progress was made in this field.

Integrated Software for Underwriting and Claims

The most important application software for the industry would naturally be the application that would interface with the customer, and that was the software for underwriting and claims management. Every company had its own project for the same, but they could not be very productive because they always attempted to integrate their front office software to their ageing back office software.

All the subsidiaries made concerted efforts to develop the integrated software for underwriting and claim but nothing substantial was achieved in this area.

Y2K Remediation

Much of 1999 went in Y2k remediation. This took up lots of time and money, but at least ensured that a lot of very old computers were replaced. GIC and subsidiaries also took up plenty of time and energy in formulating a strategy for the exclusion of Y2k related claims. Road shows were conducted repeatedly in major cities to educate the branch managers and key customers about the Y2k exclusions. Y2k audit also took up considerable effort, as these were monitored at the level of a national Y2k task force consisting of all leading ministries.

What Will IT be Like in the Coming Years ?

The Malhotra committee had recommended that Information Technology should be used as the enabler to give the insurance industry its cutting edge over competition. It would help in reducing administrative costs and these savings could be used to build on its customer service and brand building. This can be done most effectively through the use of efficient IT infrastructure. It can be argued that much of the Internet related technologies developed only in the last four years, and were not fully available to the nationalised insurance companies. It is also true that with all the problems of working in a public sector environment, several quality projects like networking, implementation of investment management software and the implementation of the integrated software for underwriting and claims management brought the IT preparedness of the industry to a fairly decent level. Rugged use of IT in the year 2001 will tell whether at all the nationalised insurance companies will give competition a run for their money.

Future Scenario

Some of the IT solutions that are essential for the working of a modern insurance company are given below. This will help build brand, strengthen loyalty from customers and business partners (agents mostly), and ensure a lean and mean company.

1. A good web site through which customers can actually transact business.

2. A good back office infrastructure which can deliver insurance products and documents. This would be connected with a rugged

computer network.

3. A study call centre fully integrated with all operations which will interact with the customer for all his requirements. The objective would be to ensure that all channels of business are fully integrated.

4. A rugged data warehouse which would provide the backbone for Customer Relationship Management(CRM), Data Mining, and channel integration.

5. Excellent storage management with failsafe disaster recovery infrastructure.

Global best practices are best possible only when the IT infrastructure uses best-of-class components. This will enable the company to work efficiently with the bare minimum staff strength and devote all its energies to customer care. The customer today is very demanding and will not do business if he feels that he is not getting excellent service. It is essential to provide him service levels even beyond his expectations if his loyalty to the insurance company is to be assured.

ANNEXURES

Annexure I
List of Important Insurance Products

Fire Insurance
1. Fire policy and its different variants such as loss and profit policy, Industrial All Risk Policy and Fire Reinstatement, Declaration and Floating policy

Marine (Cargo) Insurance
2. Inland transit policy - A,B,C
3. Import and Export Marine Policy
4. Special declaration Policy
5. Annual Open Policy
6. Special Storage Policy
7. Sellers Contingency Insurance

Marine (Hull) Insurance
8. Fishing vessels
9. Major fleets
10. Inland Vessels
11. Country Crafts/Motorised Boats
12. Builders Risk ship Body
13. Ship breakage risks
14. Major/Sundry hulls
15. Vessels under erection cover

Motor Insurance
16. Policy 'A' Act only insurance
17. Policy 'B' Comprehensive insurance

Aviation Insurance
18. Aircraft Comprehensive insurance
19. Legal liability for passengers

20. Legal liability for crews
21. Loss of licence
22. Flight Coupon (Personal Accident insurance)
23. Third Party Liability for Crews

Engineering Insurance
24. Machine-cum-Erection and Storage Policy
25. Machinery Breakdown
26. Contractors All Risks
27. Contractors Plant and Machinery
28. Advanced Loss of Profit
29. Electronic equipment insurance - Air conditioners etc.

Miscellaneous Insurance
30. Agricultural pumpsets
31. Householders Comprehensive Insurance
32. Shopkeeper's Comprehensive Insurance
33. Baggage insurance NTV
34. Coffee Plantation insurance
35. Neon Signs insurance
36. Personal Accident (Individual and Group)
37. School Children's Personal Accident Insurance
38. Fidelity Guarantee - Individual
39. Employees liability insurance
40. Medical Practitioners Professional Indemnity insurance
41. Burglary insurance (Business premises)
42. Cash insurance
43. Product Liability insurance
44. Bankers Blanket insurance
45. Personal Accident Social Scheme and Hut Insurance
46. Mediclaim - Individual and Group Insurance
47. Overseas Medical Claim
48. Boat and Shipbuilders' Insurance
49. Bhavishya Arogya

Annexure II
Major Recommendations of the Report of the Committee on Reforms in the Insurance Sector

The Government of India had set up a committee on Reforms in the Insurance sector in April, 1993 under the Chairmanship of Shri R. N. Malhotra. It comprised of 8 members. The Committee submitted its report in January, 1994. The major recommendations of the Report as pertaining to General Insurance Industry are given as under:

Insurance Intermediaries
1. There is a need to review marketing apparatus consisting of agents, development officers and insurance officials.
2. There is a need to promote and sustain professionalism among agents. To achieve it, there is an urgent need to upgrade the training and skills of the agency force. The commission structure for agents should be improved.
3. Direct agents should be encouraged.
4. System of brokers should be introduced.
5. The system of supervising agents may be developed for development of rural business.

Surveyors
6. The system of licensing of surveyors by the Controller of Insurance should be given up. Insurance companies should be free to empanel in their discretion, surveyor possessing the qualifications laid down in law. It is necessary to set up an institution of professional surveyors, loss assessors and adjusters with wide participation from survey professionals. It should be mandatory for a prospective surveyor to pass an examination to be conducted by the institution.
7. The minimum limit of Rs. 20,000 above which claim is required to be surveyed by professional surveyors should be raised.

Product Pricing
8. The area under tariffs should progressively be reduced with the objective of limiting it to only a few classes such as marine hull, aviation hull, loss of profit insurance, fire and engineering insurance etc. Personal lives of covers should be taken out of tariff regime at the earliest.
9. Market agreements which have the effect of informal tariffs should be discontinued forthwith.

10. TAC should be delivered from GIC and should function as a separate statutory body under the supervision of the Insurance regulatory authority.

11. TAC needs immediate restructuring. It should be chaired by the Head of the regulatory body or by any other officer of that body. Its membership should be broad-based.

12. Regulatory authority should have the power to advice the insurers to modify non-tariff rates, where necessary.

13. Steps such as controlling claims costs, reducing management expenses should be taken up for more equitable product pricing.

14. Motor premium rates should be raised in light of persistently growing adverse motor claims experience.

Investment

15. The investment of general insurance industry should be as under: (a) Not less than 20% in Central Government securities; (b) not less than 35% in central and state government securities, and (c) in approved investments inclusive of (b) above being of not less than 75%. To reach these levels, it would be necessary to reduce, in the first instance, the mandated investments of the general insurance companies inn appropriate stages till their investments conform to the aforesaid recommendations.

16. Sections 27A and 27B of the Insurance Act contain many provisions setting out the eligibility of various types of investments as approved investments. These are in the nature of prudential norms which should be taken out of the Act. The insurance regulatory authority may reformulate them and modify them from time to time as may be necessary, in the light of the evolving financial markets.

17. No insurer shall invest or keep involved in the equity shares, debentures or other debt instruments of any one company more than 10% of the subscribed share capital, debentures and other debt instruments of the company; provided that an insurer's investment in equity shares shall not exceed at any time 5% of the subscribed equity share capital of the company.

Rural Insurance

18. There is need for more intensive work in rural areas for spreading non-traditional insurance business. For this purpose, help may be taken from panchayats, co-operatives and NGOs.

19. The new entrants may be required to undertake a specified proportion of their business as rural non-traditional business.

20. Request from the co-operative institutions to transact general insurance business may be considered favourably.

21. Welfare oriented schemes such as Pass and Hut should be transferred to concerned government authorities.

Reinsurance

22. GIC should cease to be the holding company for its present subsidiaries in India and it should not write any direct insurance business. In that event, the exclusive function of GIC would be that of reinsurer. It should remain as Indian reinsurer. There should be statutory cession of 20% of all direct insurance business written in India, in favour of notified Indian reinsurer.

Regulation of Insurance Business

23. There is an urgent need to activate the insurance regulatory apparatus even under present set up of nationalised insurance sector. The this purpose office of the Controller of Insurance should be restored.

24. Legislation and government notification through which LIC and General Insurance companies were exempted from several provisions of Insurance Act should be withdrawn.

25. Strong and effective insurance regulatory body should be set up.

Information Technology

26. LIC and general insurance companies should improve their technical efficiency by upgrading their information support and by developing strong R&D Departments in their respective organisations.

27. Management of LIC and GIC should accept meaningful computerisation as a total managerial responsibility and adapt appropriate strategies for its implementation.

28. Information technology should be used as a tool to increase the companies competitiveness and its prosperity.

Restructuring of the Industry

29. GIC should cease to be holding company of the four subsidiary companies and they should, therefore, function as independent companies on their own. GIC should, in future, function exclusively as a reinsurance company and as the Indian reinsurer under the Insurance Act.

30. The net worth of GIC should be raised to Rs. 200 crore, 50% of which should be held by the government, the remainder being held by the public at large including employees of GIC.

31. The holdings of subsidiary companies should be withdrawn from GIC and be held by the government. The capital of each company should be raised to Rs. 100 crore, with government holding 50% thereof; the remainder being held by the public at large including employees of the respective companies.

32. The organisation of the head offices of the four companies and that of their regional offices needs to be reviewed in order to reduce excessive staff and the number of levels within their hierarchies. The four subsidiary companies are over-staffed and need to reorganise their work in order to use the available manpower in an optimal manner.

Liberalisation

33. The private sector should be allowed to enter insurance business. No single company should be allowed to conduct both life and general business.

34. The minimum paid up capital for a new entrant should be Rs. 100 crore.

35. The promoter's holding of a private insurance company should not exceed 40% of the total. However, if the promoters wish to start with a higher holding, they should be permitted to do so provided their holding is brought down to 40% within a specified period of time through public offering. No person other than the promoters should be allowed to hold more than 1% of the equity.

36. If and when entry of foreign insurance companies is permitted, it should be done on a selective basis.

37. The nationalised companies should quickly upgrade their technology, reorganise themselves on more efficient lines and should operate as head-run enterprises.

Annexure III
General Insurance Industry: Public Sector Companies
Gross Direct and Net Premium (in India and Abroad)(Rs. crore)

Year	Gross direct premium	Net premium	Net premium as % of gross direct premium
1973	184	170	92
1974	220	187	85
1975	254	217	85
1976	287	244	85
1977	306	253	83
1978	343	288	84
1979	388	323	83
1980	469	385	82
1981	585	489	84
1982	723	599	83
1983	857	731	85
1984	991	850	86
1985	1158	983	85
1986	1361	1142	84
1987	1565	1320	84
1988-89	2248	1971	88
1989-90	2174	1909	88
1990-91	2796	2419	87
1991-92	3287	2945	90
1992-93	3792	3284	87
1993-94	4766	4427	93
1994-95	5271	4879	93
1995-96	6377	5956	93
1996-97	7348	6734	92
1997-98	8086	7360	91
1998-99	9158	8402	92
1999-00	9982	9364	94

Sources: 1. Report on the Committee on Reforms in the Insurance Sector, Government of India, 1994; 2. Annual Reports of GIC.

Annexure IV
General Insurance Industry : Class-wise Financial Results

	1973	1995-96	1996-97	1997-98	1998-99	1999-2000
I. Fire:						
a. Gross Premium Income as % to total premium income	33	25	24	25	24	24
b. Net Premium Income as % Net Premium Income	40	27	26	26	24	26
c. Net Incurred Claim Ratio	34	52	44	40	42	41
II Miscellaneous:						
a. Gross Premium Income as % to total premiuim income	44	60	62	62	65	66
b. Net Premium Income as % to Net premium income	39	58	62	63	66	65
c. Net Incurred Claim Ratio	56	90	91	105	93	99
III Marine:						
a. Gross Premium Income as % to total premiuim income	23	15	14	13	11	10
b. Net Premium Income as % to Net premium income	21	15	12	11	10	9
c. Net Incurred Claim Ratio	65	55	69	61	66	70

Source: Annual Reports of GIC (*various years*).

Annexure V
Insurance Regulatory and Development Authority Act, 1999

After the decision of the government to liberalise the insurance sector, an interim body known as Insurance Regulatory Authority (IRA) was set up at Delhi. The opening of the sector took place as result of passing up of 'Insurance Regulatory and Development Authority Act", (IRDA), 1999. The Act also provided for establishment of Insurance Regulatory and Development Authority (IRDA). As mentioned in the Act. "IRDA is an Act to provide for the establishment of an authority to protect the interests of holders of insurance policies, to regulate, promote, and ensure orderly growth of insurance industry or for matters connected therewith or incidental thereto and further to amend the Insurance Act, 1938, the Life insurance Act 1956 and the General Insurance Provisions (Nationalisation), 1972". The main provisions of the Act or those flowing after the amendments to Insurance Act, 1938 and the General Insurance Business (Nationalisation) Act, 1972 are as under:

1. The IRDA shall consist of (a) Chairperson, (b) not more than five whole time members, and (c) not more than four part-time members.

2. There shall be 'Insurance Advisory Committee" (IAC) to be appointed by the Authority consisting of not more than 25 members. In addition, it will also have ex-officio members representing the interests of commerce, industry, agriculture, consumer fora, surveyors, agents, intermediaries etc. The objects of the IAC will be to advise the Authority on matters relating to making of regulations under section 26 and also on matters as prescribed and laid down.

3. The provisions of this Act shall be in addition to and not in derogation of the provisions of any other law for the time being in force.

4. The powers and functions of the Authority shall include -

   a. issue to the applicant a certificate of registration, renew, modify, withdraw, suspend or cancel such registration;

   b. protection of the interests of the policy holders in matters concerning assigning of policy, nomination by policy holders, insurable interest, settlement of insurance claim, surrender value of policy and other terms and conditions of contracts of insurance;

   c. specifying requisite qualifications, code of conduct and practical training for intermediary or insurance intermediaries and agents;

   d. specifying the code of conduct for surveyors and loss assessors;

   e. promoting efficiency in the conduct of insurance business;

   f. promoting and regulating professional organisations connected with the insurance and re-insurance business;

g. levying fees and other charges for carrying out the purposes of this Act;

h. calling for information from, undertaking inspection of, conducting enquiries and investigations including audit of the insurers, intermediaries, insurance intermediaries and other organisations connected with the insurance business;

i. control and regulation of the rates, advantages, terms and conditions that may be offered by insurers in respect of general insurance business not so controlled and regulated by the Tariff Advisory Committee under section 64U of the Insurance Act, 1938 (4 of 1938);

j. specifying the form and manner in which books of account shall be maintained and statement of accounts shall be rendered by insurers and other insurance intermediaries;

k. regulating investment of funds by insurance companies;

l. regulating maintenance of margin of solvency;

m. adjudication of disputes between insurers and intermediaries or insurance intermediaries;

n. supervising the functioning of the Tariff Advisory Committee;

o. specifying the percentage of premium income of the insurer to finance schemes for promoting and regulating professional organisations referred to in clause (f);

p. specifying the percentage of life insurance business and general insurance business to be undertaken by the insurer in the rural or social sector; and

q. exercising such other powers as may be prescribed.

5. IRDA has already notified IRDA (Actual Report and Abstract) Regulations, 2000; IRDA (obligations of insurers to rural or social sectors) Regulations, 2000; IRDA (licensing of Insurance Agents) Regulations, 2000, IRDA (General Insurance Reinsurance) Regulations, 2000; IRDA (Assets, liabilities and solvency margins of Insurers) Regulations, 2000; IRDA (Meetings) Regulations, 2000; Insurance Advisory Committee (Meetings) Regulation, 2000.

SELECT BIBLIOGRAPHY

A Comparison of Social and Private Insurance in Ten Countries, 1970-1985, Sigma Swiss Reinsurance Co., Zurich.

Ahuja, R. (1998), *Bundling Savings and Insurance : Reasons and Implications*; IGIDR Discussion Paper No. 99/154.

Ashan, M.A., *Agriculture Insurance: A New Policy for Developing Countries*; Gower Publishing Co. UK, 1985.

Asia's Insurance Industry on the Rise: Into the Next Millennium with Robust Growth; Sigma Swiss Reinsurance Co., Zurich, No. 6/1996.

Austin, Derek: *What's IT All About?*, Insurance Technology, April/May 2000, p. 42.

Ayyar, Sesha: *New Insurance Products in the Next Century*; Fair Review, March 2000, 115, pp. 35-39.

Bannister, J.E. and P.A. Bowcutt, *Practical Risk Management*, Witherby and Co. Ltd., London, 1981.

Barrese, James, Gardner, Lisa, Trower, Ellen: *Changing Attitude About Insurance Through Education*; CPCU Journal, Fall 1998, 51(3), pp. 144-159.

Browne, Daniel, Gammill, Linda, Nielson, Norma, Seville, Mary: *Information and Ethics in Insurance*; CPCU Journal, Winter 1998, 51(4), pp. 227-237.

Capoor, Jagdish: *Deposit Insurance Reforms in India*; RBI Bulletin, November 2000, pp. 1269-1272.

Carter, R.L. and G.M. Dickinson (1992), *Obstacles to the Liberalisation of Trade in Insurance*, New York: Harvester Wheatsheaf.

Creedon, Seamus: *E-Insurance-Problem or Opportunity for Brokers*; The Actuary, June 2000, pp. 24-25.

Crop Insurance Compendium 1991, FAO, Rome, 1992.

Crop Insurance in Asia; Asian Productivity Organisation, Tokyo 1987 and 1991.

Cummins, J.D. and M. Weiss (1993), *Measuring Cost Efficiencies in the Property-Liability Insurance Industry*, Journal of Banking and Finance, 17, pp. 463-81.

Doman, Andrew, Duchen, Theodore, Markus, Martin: *Brokers vs. Insurers*; Canadian Insurance, October 1999, 10(11), pp. 52-58.

Economies of Scale in the Insurance Industry, Sigma Swiss Reinsurance Co.

Economic Survey - 1999-2000, 2000-2001, Government of India, Ministry of Finance.

Emerging Markets: The Insurance Industry in the Face of Globalisation; Sigma Swiss Reinsurance Co., Zurich, 4/2000.

FICCI, *Indian Insurance*, 1999.

Gardner, L. and M.F. Grace (1993), *X Efficiency in the US Life Insurance Industry*, Journal of Banking and Finance, 17, pp. 497-510.

General Insurance Corporation of India, *Annual Reports (various years)*.

Giarini, Orio: *Insurance Within the Financial System*, Asia Insurance Review, August 2000, 10(8), p. 60.

Grace, M.F. and M.M. Barth (1993); *The Regulation and Structure of Non-life Insurance Income in the United States*, WPS. 1155, The World Bank, Washington D.C., USA.

Harris, S. and J. Katz (1991), *Organisational Performance and Information Technology - Investment Intensity in the Insurance Industry*, Organisation Science, 2, pp. 263-95.

Hazell, Peter et. al (eds.), *Crop Insurance for Agricultural Development*; John Hopkins University Press, 1986.

Hohman, Peter: *Return on Investment*; Canadian Insurance, June 2000, 105(7), pp. 18-19.

Horrigan, W., *Risk Management and Insurance*, Withdear Publications, Hove, 1969.

Hsee, Christopher, Kunreuther, Howard: *The Affection Effect in Insurance Decisions*, Journal of Risk and Uncertainty, March 2000, 20(2), pp. 141-159.

Humphreys, David: *E-commerce in Insurance-Current Uses and Future Business Models*, Asia Insurance Review, May 2000, 10(5), pp. 69-70.

IMF, *World Economic Outlook*, 1995.

Institute of Company Secretaries of India; *Chartered Secretary-Insurance Special*, December 1998.

International Conference on Insurance: Vision 2000; CII, 1996.

IRDA; *Regulations Framed Under Insurance Regulatory and Development Authority*; 2000.

Jeleva, Meglena: *Background Risk, Demand for Insurance, and Choquet Expected Utility Preferences*, The Geneva Papers on Risk and Insurance Theory, September 2000, 25(1), pp. 7-28.

Job, Sallyamma: *Insurance Sector Reforms for the 21st Century-Salient Features*; Insurance Times, November 2000, V. XX(ii), pp. 22-23.

Jodd, Jerry D. : *Nature and Characteristics of Insurance Agent Fraud*; CPCU Journal, Fall 2000, 53(3), pp. 152-167.

King, R.G. and R. Levine (1993), (i) *Finance and Growth: Schumpeter Might be Right*, Quarterly Journal of Economics, August 108(3), pp. 717-37.

Lok, Russel: *Strategies for Corporate Transformation and Cost Reduction for Insurers*; Asia Insurance Review, February 2000, 10(2), pp. 66-67.

Phillips, Richard D. in Harold D. Skipper, Jr. ed. *International Risk and Insurance: An Environmental and Managerial Approach*, Chicago, Ill., Richard D. Irwin.

Ray, P.K. (i) *A Practical Guide to Multi-Risk Crop Insurance for Developing Countries*; Oxford and IBH Co., 1991 (ii) *Agriculture Insurance: Theory and Practice and Application to Developing Countries*; Pergamon Press, Oxford, 1981.

Reinhardt, E. (1993), *The German Health System: Providing Equitable, Universal Access to Health Care and Controlling its Costs*, July 29-31.

Report of the Committee on Reforms in the Insurance Sector, Government of India, Ministry of Finance, January 1994.

Ripoll, J. (1996); *Domestic Insurance in Developing Countries: Is There Any Life After GATS?*; UNCTAD Discussion Paper, Geneva.

Saibaba, M.S., K.S. Gopalkrishnan: *Insurance and Information Technology*; Insurance Times, March 2000, 20(3), pp. 16-17.

Sanbaraiah, K.: *How to Reduce Time Lag in Settlement of Claims*; Insurance Times, June 1999, 19(6), pp. 5-6, 14.

Satia J., Mavalankar D., Bhat R. (1999); *Progress and Challenges of Health Sector: A Balance Sheet*; IIM, Ahmedabad, October Working Paper 99-10-08.

Schanz, Kai-uwe, Hu, Wanhong: *Asian Insurance Markets Facing a New Era of Competition*; Asia Insurance Review, January 2000,

10(1), pp. 22-24.

SCL: *RBI's Draft Guidelines for Entry of NBFCs into Insurance*; SEBI and Corporate Laws, May 2000.

Shegwalbar, P.C.: *Education in Insurance Marketing*; Insurance Times, November 2000, V. XX(ii), pp. 5-6.

Shenbagaraman, K.: *Total Quality in Service Sector-Insurance Industry*, Insurance Times, 20(10), pp. 18-20.

Skipper, Harold D., Jr. (1987), (i) *Protectionism in the Provision of International Insurance Services*, The Journal of Risk and Insurance, LIV (1), pp. 55-85, (ii) *Foreign Insurers in Emerging Markets: Issues and Concerns*, IIF Occasional Paper I, 1997, (iii) *Insurance Regulation in the Public Interest: The Path Towards Solvent, Competitive Markets*; Geneva Paper on Risk and Insurance, October 2000, 25(4), pp. 482-504.

South Africa Insurers: Unbundled; The Economist, September 1997.

Srivastava, D.C. (1999); *Details of Various Medical Insurance Schemes Being Marketed by the Insurance Industry in India*, New Delhi; Presented at the seminar on Health Insurance Development, Berlin, November 9-19, 1999.

Stears, Gary: (i) *Regulatory Reform*, Insurance Trends, January 2001, Issue No. 28, pp. 1-6., (ii) *Liberalisation of Insurance Markets*, Insurance Trends, January 2001, Issue No. 28, pp. 17-23.

The Global Reinsurance Market in the Midst of Consolidation; Sigma Swiss Reinsurance Co., Zurich, No. 1/1999.

UNCTAD, *Agriculture Insurance in Developing Countries*; UNCTAD/SDD/1, November 1992.

UNCTAD (1993), (i) *Insurance in Developing Countries: Privatisation of Insurance Enterprises and Liberalisation of Insurance Markets*, Geneva: UNCTAD Doc. No. UNCTAD/SDD/INS/3.

Vittas, Dimitri and Michael Skully (1991), *Overview of Contractual Savings Institutions*, Working Paper No. 605, World Bank, Washington, D.C.

World Development Report-1999-2000, 1998-1999; The World Bank, Washington, D.C., USA.

World Insurance in 1997: Booming Life Business, But Stagnating Non-life Business; Sigma Swiss Reinsurance Co., Zurich, No. 3/1999.

INDEX

A
Actuary, 45, 58
Adam Smith, 4, 143
Agency business, 239, 249
Agriculture productivity, 207
Alternate Risk Transfer, 298, 307, 309

B
Banacassurance, 241
Basket approach, 102
Boardroom design, 119
Brokers, 240, 251
Business risk, 285

C
Capital-output ratio, 7
Cat models, 319
Claim ratio, 226
Coinsurance, 268
Comprehensive crop insurance scheme, 227
Congruent coverage, 160
Copycat mentality, 119
Crop insurance, 215

D
Datawarehousing, 315
Direct marketing, 245
Diversification of spread, 159

E
ESIS, 191
E-insurance, 246, 248, 320, 321

F
Facultative reinsurance, 270, 278
File and use system, 123
Financial intermediaries, 19
Future creep, 119

G
Gross domestic product, 4, 55
GIBNA, 66

H
Harold D. Skipper, 17
Health insurance, 187
Hedging, 291

I
Indemnity, 68, 217
Indian Reinsurance Corporation, 65
Insurance Act, 1938, 56
Insurance density, 24, 55, 76, 79, 83
Insurance interest, 68
Insurance penetration, 24, 76, 81
Intermediaries, 59, 138, 238
IRDA (1999), 56, 57, 345

J
JM. McCandish, 143

L
Lloyd, 64, 65
Liquidity, 159

M
Morris David, 5
Mediclaim scheme, 190
Moral hazards, 213
Malhotra Committee, 168, 169, 261, 317, 339

N
National Agriculture Insurance Scheme, 230
National reinsurer, 279
Net-retained account, 276
Non-proportional treaty, 272

P
Piggy-riding products, 103
Proportional treaty, 271
Proximate cause, 68, 69

R
Reinsurance, 59, 226, 268, 330
Reinsurance treaty, 270
Risk financing, 293
Risk management, 215, 283
Risk pooling, 20
Risk pricing, 19
Risk transfer, 288

S
Safety of investment, 158
Segmentation, targeting and positioning, 108
Self retention, 267, 291, 294
SEWA health insurance scheme, 195
Software, 313
Solvency margin, 44, 58

Standardisation, 262
Subsidies, 222

T
Tariff Advisory Committee, 57, 66, 257
Threshold yield, 228
Transparent disclosure, 139
Triton Insurance Co., 65

U
UNCTAD, 219
Utmost good faith, 68, 69

Y
Yield of assets, 158